SKYSCRAPER
PUBLICATIONS

Published by Skyscraper Publications Limited
20 Crab Tree Close, Bloxham, Oxon OX15 4SE
www.skyscraperpublications.com

First published 2019

A CIP catalogue record for this book is available from the British Library.

ISBN-13: 978-1-911072-25-6

Typesetting by
Chandler Book Design

Printed in the EU on behalf of
One World Books Ltd UK

MY TALISMAN

SELECTED VERSE AND A BIOGRAPHY OF ALEXANDER PUSHKIN

Translated, with a biography of the poet
by

JULIAN HENRY LOWENFELD

*

INCLUDING PUSHKIN'S DRAWINGS

2019

Разскажетъ повѣсть дальнихъ странъ

Мстислава древній поединокъ

И гибель Россіянъ

На лонѣ мстительныхъ Грузинокъ

И воспою тотъ славный часъ

Когда, почуя бой кровавый,

На негодующій Кавказъ

Поднялся нашъ орелъ двуглавый.

Когда на Терекѣ

Впервые битвы грянулъ громъ

И грохотъ русскихъ барабановъ,

И въ сѣчѣ съ дерзостнымъ челомъ

Явился пылкій Цицiановъ:

Тебя я воспою, Герой

О Котляревскій, бичъ Кавказа!

Куда ни мчался ты грозой

Твой ходъ какъ черная зараза,

Губилъ, ничтожилъ племена....

Но ты днесь ... саблю мести!

DEDICATION

Before all else thanks are due. If we don't remember to be thankful for our blessings, we have already lost them. As Pushkin wrote to the poet Zhukovsky, "I would rather seem flippant than ungrateful".

This book would simply not be in your hands without my beloved teacher Nadyezhda Semyonovna Braginskaya. Her devoted encouragement, rigorous scholarship and impeccable standards, her heartfelt approach to life itself, her constant care and kindness to me, her sense of humour – and of wonder, her tremendous, infectious love for Pushkin, her patience, understanding, inspiration, and amazing faith in me were all that made this book possible. I dedicate this book to her blessed memory with all my love.

My heartfelt thanks as well to Alexander Korobko, Vsevolod Bagno and the staff of the Institute of Russian Literature (Pushkin House) of the Russian Academy of Sciences in St. Petersburg, Yevgeny Bogatyrev and the staff of the State Pushkin Museum in Moscow, Valentin Nepomnyashchy, Yury and Yevgeny Kurneshov, Jerry Kelly, Anna Nemaltsina, Anna Labunskaya, Natalya Dymova, Vyacheslav Udovenko, and Maria Kovtun.

TABLE OF CONTENTS

(Individual poems are indicated by titles where Pushkin gave them, otherwise by first lines.)

NOTE ON THE TEXT

A fruitless quest for arid exactitude is the bane of most scholastic prose, as is the insatiable academic mania for footnotes. The two brothers who devised the main rival systems of Cyrillic transliteration into English, Sergey Yakobzon and Roman Jakobson, couldn't even agree how to spell the family name! Heedless of "system" and the bitter, ongoing academic fratricide, I care not who was right; it is better far to err on the side of readability and liveliness. So what if the names "Tchaikovsky" and "Chaadayev" in Russian both begin with the Cyrillic letter "Ч" and yet I spell them differently? Fiddledeedee!

Pushkin would surely have agreed with Ralph Waldo Emerson that "a foolish consistency is the hobgoblin of small minds." Speaking of inconsistencies, there are, as with Shakespeare, various slightly different editions of the Pushkin canon. This book follows the ten volume official edition of Pushkin's complete works published in Moscow in 1962 by the USSR Academy of Sciences' Institute of Russian Literature (Pushkin House).

I have also tried to avoid confusing English-language readers by omitting Russian patronymics, even referring to Pushkin's wife, Natalya Nikolayevna Goncharova, in the English version of the book simply as "Natalya." In the 19th century, naming another man's wife without the patronymic would have been unforgivable familiarity – grounds, perhaps, even for a duel. But this book is meant to cross the language barrier in the 21st century. Especially for foreigners whose languages lack them, patronymics can spur confusion. I refer offended purists to Pushkin's joking rebuke to Gogol, in a letter dated August 25, 1831: "Your Nadyezhda Nikolayevna, that is, my Natalya Nikolayevna, thanks you heartily for remembering her."

The winsome drawings in this book are all by Pushkin himself (unless otherwise indicated).

JULIAN HENRY LOWENFELD *London 2019*

A BLESSING

Russian literature is an acknowledged spiritual treasure trove of global culture. The whole world knows the great Russian geniuses of prose: Dostoyevsky, Tolstoy, Chekhov... But alas, our greatest treasure, Pushkin – "our all" – has remained a mystery wrapped within an enigma, trapped behind the precious veil of our language, impermeable to many seeking communion with our great Russian culture.

"Pushkin is untranslatable" has long been an axiom with which no one argues. After all, for nearly 200 years, though many (even such luminaries as Nabokov) have tried to translate him into any foreign language – no miracle yet has occurred. Pushkin has remained a mystery.

I do not take the word "miracle" lightly, but in this book you now hold in your hand, a miracle has indeed taken place. Finally a soul capable of feeling, understanding, and living alongside our great poet has appeared to transfer his incomparable majesty and depth into the language spoken by nearly half the planet. His name is Julian Henry Lowenfeld, and he has grasped Russia with all his soul, and believes in her. Though a born and bred American, he has become truly Russian at heart. And this is why he truly understands and feels "our all" just as we feel him, why he so successfully transports our spirit into the English language.

In Julian's inspired translations, finally we hear "the spark of God, and inspiration, and life, and tears at last, and love" of our Pushkin. We can recognize and hear his grandeur, and depth, and warmth, his Christian compassion and capacity for love, which mark him as the foremost Russian genius. And reading the insightful and entertaining biography of the poet Pushkin, written with heartfelt understanding and love by a fellow poet, we understand in a new way "the universal sympathy of the Russian soul" so uniquely personified by Pushkin.

God grant that this book will be read throughout the entire world. It is very important indeed in these troubled times, when Russia and its history and culture are all too often deliberately demonized by some. All the more reason to rejoice that suddenly a wise and caring soul has appeared, who loves and understands "our all!"

With all my heart, I bless both this book and its author's spiritual mission.

METROPOLITAN (ARCHBISHOP) TIKHON *Pskov (2019)*

PUSHKIN SET FREE

Will Pushkin always be "a captive of the Russian language?" It seems there is no other great writer in world literature who is valued so strikingly differently in his own country and beyond its borders. If we speak of the emblem of a national culture, then without doubt, both natives and educated foreigners, remembering Italy, will speak of Dante; remembering England, of Shakespeare, Germany, of Goethe, and Spain, of Cervantes. But if we speak of Russia, Russians will name Pushkin, while foreigners will name either Dostoyevsky or Tolstoy. Foreigners know Pushkin poorly because the translations they have of Pushkin are poor. Virginia Woolf remarked: "the great Russian writers are like men deprived by some earthquake or railway accident of all their clothes... what remains is a crude, abased and humiliated hint of the initial meaning." The great French Slavicist Georges Nivat agrees: "Pushkin has suffered from this mistreatment more than anyone. All extant translations of his poetry are simply frightful, both dry and replete with the crudest mistakes. The brilliant pupil of Arina Rodionovna and Benjamin Constant above all stuns us with his paradoxical simplicity and natural ease, which hitherto nobody has ever managed to convey into a foreign culture. And so, Pushkin remains unknown."

This leads us to expect of any translator of our national poet not just the obvious professional minimum of scrupulous exactitude and complete scientific approach, but no less than an embodied miracle. We expect the kind of Pushkin we know ourselves, in which the brilliance of the poetry shines out for all, and not just for a small group of academics, so that anyone whose soul is filled with yearning could feel in Pushkin what Nabokov called "that particular Pushkinian state in which you feel yourself somewhere, somehow, anyhow, locked in union with a higher, deeper, power, someplace where art, curiosity, tenderness, grace, and joy are the norm."

This norm is finally found in the inspired work of the American poet and translator Julian Henry Lowenfeld. His translations keep the original's music, rhythms, rhymes, without ever losing their freedom. The amazing depth, clarity, sparkling intelligence, and warmth of Pushkin's verse are faithfully preserved in Lowenfeld's brilliant translations. And it is not just that the rhythms, rhymes, and shades of meaning completely match the original, and not even that the exact number of syllables and their stresses strong and weak are kept with effortless exactitude, which is, I might add, totally characteristic of all other English translations. No, the entire voice and music of Pushkin's voice is preserved with uncanny aptitude and love.

"We will be hollering to each other with Pushkin's name," prophesied the poet Khodasevich. And now we will be able to holler all over the world. For Lowenfeld has translated Pushkin not just into the English language, but into the English language of Keats and Byron. It is because of this that the significance of this translation is difficult to overestimate.

Marina Tsvetaeva wrote to Paul Valéry in 1936: "They say Pushkin is untranslatable...How can something be untranslatable when it has already been translated into words once already? Is not verse above all the expression in human language of the inexpressible, an embassy in human speech of the divine, the ineffable? Ah, yes, but the translator of this translator must first of all be a poet himself."

In this book, at last a poet has translated a poet, an American poet has grasped our Russian bard, and as a poet, has he heard and conveyed in his own native tongue what Pushkin what once heard and gave to us in ours.

VSEVOLOD BAGNO

Director, Institute of Russian Literature,
Pushkin House, Russian Academy of Sciences
St. Petersburg

A NOTE TO BRITISH READERS

My interest in Russia actually first began before I even knew a word of Russian, when I was young and studying in Britain. It was a very happy time in my life that I remember vividly and fondly, and it left me with a lifelong affection for your great country.

Educated Britons have long been fascinated by Russian literature, particularly the novels of Tolstoy and Dostoyevsky and the plays and short stories of Chekhov. And yet, even many highly educated Britons remain relatively unacquainted with Russia's own most favourite writer, its national bard, Alexander Pushkin. And truly this is a pity, for Pushkin is the poet of the Russian soul, justly famed for his uncanny sense of harmony, for his majestic simplicity and sense of serendipity, for extolling the joys of life and the beauties of nature, which in turn inspired him above all to love.

With profound affection and friendship for the United Kingdom, I hope this book may return some of the good feeling, warmth, and inspiration your country has always given me. In these troubled times, when discord and political divisions around the globe are fraying the bonds of friendship between the nations, may "the sunshine of Russian poetry" yet bring closer that day which Pushkin himself believed in against all odds, that day:

> ...When all the peoples of this world, their quarrels forgot,
> In one great family will be united.

With warmest best wishes,

Julian Henry Lowenfeld, London, 2019

Ilya Repin and Ivan Aivazovsky
Pushkin by the Sea. "Farewell, farewell, free force of nature!"

A MEDITATION ON PUSHKIN

What good is poetry?
What good are songs when madmen capture power in the asylum? –
When books burn, and soon their readers?
With so much suffering in the world
How can melancholy dreamy spirits
Fight with an inferno? What is one man against an army,
One freak of kindness in a sea of hatred?

Too often the unthinkable is common,
Too casually the unspeakable slips from our lips;
Long for no "good old days;" – the histories of this world
Prove over and again what Shakespeare knew too well:
"Humanity must perforce prey upon itself,
Like monsters of the deep."

The more I cease to disbelieve that such things happen,
The more that cruelty seems commonplace,
The more I'm numbed; there's no more left in me to feel or sleep,
The sun itself seems dark as it begins to rise,
The moon seems counterfeit,
Whatever stars gleamed through the anguished fog fade faster away,
Leaving neither day nor night,
Just an empty, senseless blight.

And yet, in my despair, I always turn to you,
"My very first and priceless friend"
(Whom I've never met, yet have carried so close to my heart
These many years of folly and self-doubting),
My high priest and my heretic,
My seer, my sage, my fool – my talisman:
I seek your portrait hung above my desk,
And look into your keen, warm, dancing eyes, and ask:
"What can a poem do against machine guns?
What verses about flowers hinder murders?
What right have we, the children of the few spared,
To steal joy from our grief
And treasure even this pale gleam of morning
Denied to so many?"

You answer:
One poet's longing brightens night's faint stars,
Provokes the nightingales to wake and sing.
One poet's longing,
One poet's gentle sobbing brings back spring!
One poet's listening deep within,
And singing into a blizzard, even a bit off key,
Sets off cathedral bells, cures numbness and soul-blindness,
Thaws mighty harbours, frees great rivers' flow,
Cracks the thickest ice in the coldest heart...

What, warmest heart, was in your overpowering lightness,
So crystal clear yet deep as an enormous Lake Baikal of the soul,
Washing away the meaningless from the serene,
Leaving me keen and crying?
...Sometimes, like you, I've walked alone by the sea,
Felt its endless urging and churning crashing within me,
Wild wind in my hair, champagne-cold hissing foam chilling
And bracing, tugging sand from beneath numbed toes,
And odd tears came from some temple of the sublime
And melancholy where you abided always...

I too have longed to flee from everyone who cannot hear
That sound of that sea, those waves of love, as you did!
And, taking comfort in my own oceanic language,
I've tried to help your bright sun at long last
Shine forth in another climate.
Where I've failed, the fault's all mine:
"...But here's
A partial, feeble rendering,
A pallid print of a live picture..."

Yet if, sometimes, just slightly, here and there,
Your warmth beams through the dark windows of a foreign tongue –
Springs like a small white flower, improbable and alone,
I saw once, stubborn in the crack of the concrete
On a pedestal of a forgotten monument to you,
In a wistful meadow, by an autumn wood,
By a lake in the blissful, misty middle of nowhere,
If ever once this book helps someone smile,

Moves the disconsolate to stop and listen
To the true heart's silence,
That drinks in poetry like waters healing,
If ever once this book reveals your joy,
Then this "sacred sacrifice" of hours to you devoted,
Filched from vain pursuits, in search
Of an echo of your spark ineffable,
Will be but the first faintest, slightest token
Of what you've meant to me.

JULIAN HENRY LOWENFELD

MY TALISMAN

Deliver me, my talisman.
Deliver me from fear and fleeing,
Days of remorse and worry healing:
On a sad day you clasped my hand.

When rising by the ocean strand
The waves around me crash in pounding,
And when with lightning clouds are sounding,
Deliver me, my talisman.

Lost in seclusion, in strange lands,
In boredom's lull my bosom taming,
In the alarm of battle flaming,
Deliver me, my talisman.

You are my soul's own magic lamp,
You sweet and sacred trickery,
When you drop down, are flickering!
Deliver me, my talisman.

Wounds of the heart help me withstand
Forever; bad memories burn with fire!
Farewell, fond Hope; and sleep, Desire;
Deliver me, my talisman.

Alexander Pushkin. Self-portrait

INTRODUCTION

Under Stalin's Terror, as millions died in prisons and camps, the Soviet secret police often made its daily quota of arrests at three in the morning, grabbing victims when they were surest to be groggy and unable to resist. Imagine for a moment being "back in the USSR" at this cruel time: the dread knock on the door, rude men crudely taking you away, without pity, without explanations. You'll probably never see home and family again...You've got just a few seconds before being swept into the merciless whirlwind of history...What do you do? The great Russian poetess Anna Akhmatova recorded how the last free act of countless Russians upon arrest was to clutch at a pocket book of Pushkin's poetry for solace on their fateful journeys.

Pushkin's poetry for many Russians is literally their talisman of hope. A dear friend of mine (now in England), during the height of the Cold War, risked his life fleeing through the bare strip of no man's land from East to West Berlin – taking with him nothing but a small book of Pushkin's verse in his pocket. In World War II, countless such books were found on battlefields from the Arctic to the Black Sea, from the Volga to the Elbe, sometimes bloodstained, or pierced with bullet holes, or scarred by shrapnel. So literally close to their hearts – and so very deep in the depths of the celebrated "Russian soul" is Pushkin!

Of heaven's realm on Earth a witness,
With all within my soul on fire,
I sang before the throne of goodness
That warmth and beauty did inspire.
And love and secret inner freedom
Taught my heart hymns and honest tales.
My voice, which never was for sale,
Expressed the Russian people's yearning.

Pushkin's "love and secret inner freedom," that soul-freedom, which no worldly power can take away, have been the Russian soul's beacon of light in the darkness, its sacred talisman for all life's fateful journeys. Now (here and there – in Moscow, at least) some statues of Lenin have been torn down, as the statues of the Tsars were before them. It's not clear what new statues – if any – will ever take their place on the empty pedestals of now-bankrupt ideals. But on more than 500 monuments to Pushkin throughout Russia, even on the bitterest, coldest days of winter, you will always find fresh flowers.

For Russians "Pushkin is our all." He is the very lodestar of the Russian culture and the creator of the Russian literary language. Gogol, Tolstoy, Dostoyevsky, Chekhov (the Russian writers best known in the West) all acknowledged themselves Pushkin's heirs and literary debtors. To Gogol, "Pushkin is an extraordinary phenomenon, perhaps the only true expression of the essential Russian spirit;" to Dostoyevsky, Pushkin was "the height of artistic perfection." Tolstoy wrote that he gained mastery of his craft by intense study of Pushkin's *Tales of Belkin*, and, wishing to praise Chekhov's genius, called him "Pushkin in prose." Truly, from Pushkin Chekhov inherited many of the qualities we now consider innately Chekhovian (deep, passionate emotions subdued with ironic intensity into a few words of unadorned, almost simple, stylistic grace, an absence of any overt preaching, just sympathy and understanding). For Russian poets from Lermontov and Tyutchev to Bely, Blok, Mandelstam, Mayakovsky, Akhmatova, Tsvetayeva, and Yesenin, a passionate devotion to Pushkin was something akin to religion.

Pushkin is the "Prophet" of Russian literature, the giver of its law, of its breadth, depth, richness of expression. In Russia, to this day, the poems of Pushkin still "burn people's hearts up with his word." Yet, while Russians revere Pushkin as English-speakers do Shakespeare, the West knows Pushkin far less well than it knows his literary heirs. The incomparable mastery of Pushkin's art has eluded translation, leaving even educated people in the West sometimes wondering vaguely whether perhaps Pushkin was Tchaikovsky's librettist. That would be like calling Shakespeare the "librettist" for various Verdi operas!

It is hard to describe Pushkin's magic to non-Russians. His genius in its sublimity compares with Mozart's: miraculous, prodigious feats of creativity, wrought with seemingly effortless, seamless grace, evocative power, warmth, wit, passion, sheer musicality, inventive rhythmic swing, and rhyming playfulness – and all imbued with a certain divine purity, a wisdom born of innocence, a childlike, sweet, direct, natural, vigorous, limpid, language – which is, alas, all the more mysteriously difficult to translate for its simplicity and clarity.

If only everyone so felt the power
Of harmony! But no! For then indeed
The world could not exist. No one would think
To bother for the lowly needs of living;

> We'd all just lose ourselves in free creation.
> So we're but few, we chosen happy idlers,
> Who, of mere use neglectful and disdainful,
> Are high priests of the One, the Beautiful.

These words, from Mozart's last speech in Pushkin's *Mozart and Salieri*, speak not only of Pushkin's own uniqueness but of the lonely relationship between a creative genius and the world around him. But how can English-speaking readers grasp something of the power of Pushkin's harmony? Nabokov's foreword to his own celebrated translation of *Eugene Onegin* voiced the just fears of many scholars:

> Can Pushkin's poem [*Eugene Onegin*], or any other poem with a definite rhyme scheme really be translated?...The answer, of course, is no. To reproduce the rhymes and yet translate the entire poem is mathematically impossible. But in losing the rhyme, the poem loses its bloom, which neither marginal description nor the alchemy of a scholium can replace.

Nabokov therefore chose to bequeath us as literal a translation as possible – apologizing in advance that "to my ideal of literalism I sacrificed everything (elegance, euphony, clarity, good taste, modern usage, and even grammar)..." Yet, with all due reverence for an incomparable stylist and scholar, such an entirely literal translation of Pushkin results in a lifeless specimen – neatly pinned, perhaps, to a label in a glass case by the master lepidopterist – but with none of the ineffable grace and beauty of a butterfly in flight.

To grasp Pushkin one must hear his musicality. Not just Tchaikovsky, but virtually all the great Russian composers – Mussorgsky, Rimsky-Korsakov, Prokofiev, Rachmaninoff, Glinka, and Glazunov – felt compelled to set his verse to music. The music is already there: it swirls in his sounds:

> Snowstorm, gloom-filled, heavens drowning,
> Wild the snowy whirlwind flies,
> Sometimes, like a beast, it's howling,
> Sometimes, like a child, it cries.

Pushkin was indeed one of the highest priests of the Pythagorean idea of the One, the Beautiful. The Pythagoreans, it is said, used to cure the sick with poetry, believing in the unique healing virtues of certain verses of the *Odyssey* and *Iliad* when read aloud in the proper way. Like Homer, Pushkin derives indescribable power as much from the sound – as from the sense – of his words, from their lilt, their swing, their magical incantation: their spell.

Yet the subtly inflected Russian language is infinitely richer in natural rhymes than English. Too many translators have veered from the Charybdis of "literality" to the Scylla of sacrificing Pushkin's natural unaffected language into impossibly stilted poses, just to fit into a given rhyme scheme. Various eminent scholars (Arndt, Johnston, Deutsch, Falen, and Mitchell, to name but a few) attempted strict rhyming translations. Yet Pushkin's majestic lightness was not thereby conveyed. Too often Pushkin's Russian verses, so easy and magnificent in the original, came out with an incongruously comic effect derived from the forcing of the rhyme, like some Tin Pan Alley jingle, or at best W. S. Gilbert – but nothing like Pushkin. Translation must never seem like torture and betray the sweat in the brow. Rather than scrimping for absurdities, just to keep a "perfect" rhyme. I have used approximate rhyme (like Yeats or Dylan Thomas). The inner ear gets the assonance it craves, while staying natural, keeping the freshness of the original. But another problem arises in the frequent disparity in the number of syllables between Russian and English synonyms. For example, let us – or at least those of us who read Russian – look at the first quatrain of what is probably the most famous love poem in the Russian language. Literally, it says:

Я помню чудное мгновенье:	I remember a wonderful moment:
Передо мной явилась ты,	You appeared before me
Как мимолетное виденье,	Like a fleeting vision,
Как гений чистой красоты.	Like a genius of pure beauty.

No literal translation captures the magic of this famous moment. Flaubert, given its literal translation by his friend Turgenev, is said to have remarked: "Il est plat, votre poète." ["He's flat, your poet."] Magic requires "poetic license." It is better to add or omit a few words with loving caution, to keep the "swing," the Pythagorean talismanic power, the spell woven into the rhythm. Very slight liberties with the exact truth are justified when they reveal the higher truth:

A wondrous moment I remember:
Before me once you did appear;
A fleeting vision you resembled,
Of beauty's genius pure and clear.

Pushkin himself revelled in "poetic license" when translating. Most of the foreign verse he rendered into Russian "loses something in the original." Even Goethe, Ariosto, Shakespeare, and Chenier he treated not as codices to be reproduced word for word, but as themes to be played with as musicians improvise on given tunes. For example, look how Pushkin "translated" a poem by the obscure English country poet Brian Waller Procter, (1787–1874), known as Barry Cornwall.

Cornwall	"Translation" Translated
Inesilla! I am here!	I'm here, Inesilla,
Thy own cavalier	Your window beneath.
Is now beneath thy lattice playing;	While all of Sevilla
Why art thou delaying?	Embraces gloom's sleep.
He hath ridden many a mile	With valourous heart, here,
But to see thy smile.	In broad cloak I'm sheathed,
The young light on the	With sword and guitar, here,
Flowers is shining, but he is repining.	Your window beneath.

Pushkin cuts the "verbiage" and adds music; transformed into Don Juan, the reader is transported to the Spain of Pushkin's dreams, where "Night's soft breeze/ blows easeful; clear/ and flowing/ foams / Guadalquivir." Another of Pushkin's lifelong dreams was to visit Italy, "sacred to Apollo's grandsons." His works have over ninety quotations from Dante, Petrarch, Ariosto, and Tasso – in the original Italian. His love for Italian culture seems to have imbibed the spirit of the Renaissance, the humanist artistic philosophy expressed in Baldassare Castiglione's *Book of The Courtier*.

> But having considered often how grace is acquired (aside from those who have it from the stars), I find it a rule most universal which seems to me valid in practically all things human which are said or done... and that is to avoid, like the sharpest and most dangerous of shoals, affectation, and – to coin a new phrase perhaps – to use in all things a certain *sprezzatura* [nonchalance, lightness, disdain, detachment], which hides its own art, and shows all that is done and said to be effortless, almost without even thinking about it. From this I believe much grace is derived, because everyone knows the difficulty of performing things rare and difficult, such that ease therein engenders the greatest wonder, whereas, on the contrary, laborious forcing of

> oneself, and, as it might be said, dragging oneself by the hairs of one's head, shows the highest want of grace, and causes us to little appreciate it, no matter how grand it be. But that art is true indeed which does not appear to be art.
>
> (*Il Libro del Cortegiano,* Book I, xxvi, my translation).

Pushkin's works sparkle with this effortlessness artlessness, this ineffable *sprezzatura.* His poems confide in you like a best friend, fill your soul with warmth like the "amber glow" of the room in which he wakes his love on *A Winter Morning.* There is something elusive about his transparency. Much stays veiled behind his glowing state of grace. Yet somehow, his verse seems to express that inexpressible, irrepressible, incomprehensible, so beloved and so loving "Russian soul" – and make it universal – what Dostoyevsky famously called "Pushkin's universal sympathy."

The Roman poet Terence wrote: "I will hold nothing human to be alien to me." Pushkin took this maxim to the max (as one might say in L.A.): "No one bores me – from a simple policeman all the way up to the Tsar." Fascinated by foreigners, he spoke 8 foreign languages, remaking the modern Russian tongue by sprinkling French, English, Italian, German, and Latin words into his works. He loved grand balls and the Frenchified finery of the court, yet adored peasant fairs, and folktales and proverbs. He was a prankster, once even taught a parrot to swear like a sailor – at an archbishop invited to tea. And yes, at times he had his doubts, but this made his turn towards faith all the more heartfelt: "*Our hermit fathers*" is perhaps the most sublime prayer in verse ever – and by a flibbertigibbet who used to scribble verses for stag parties!

Embracing all, rejecting none, he loved and wrote for both countesses and their maids. With Tsars and slaves alike, in palaces or jails, ballrooms or barracks, in the city, or in the country, in woods, fields, hills, mountains, ocean storms, and by tender little streams, by battlefields, graveyards, insane asylums, jails, and gambling dens... the reader of this book will observe Pushkin somehow everywhere at home, yet everywhere estranged, with the keen curiosity of the outsider.

He celebrated "experience, son of bitter errors, and genius, friend of paradox." Pushkin's characters are always three-dimensional, right at home in what Coleridge termed "willing suspension of disbelief": duality is everywhere in Pushkin's work. The great Russian critic Vissarion Belinsky rightly called *Eugene Onegin* "an encyclopedia of Russian life." Yet it is also a poetic heart-to-heart talk between Pushkin's warring selves, dressed up as different characters.

Pushkin's schoolmate, the poet Wilhelm Küchelbecker exclaimed: "Tatyana! – Why, she's Pushkin!" But another friend, the great Polish poet Adam Mickiewicz, taught in his lectures on Russian literature that in *Eugene Onegin* Pushkin had incarnated himself in Lensky and Onegin... Both bards were right; Pushkin was all his characters. Russian literature's grand tradition of compassionate objectivity, and of merciless detail suffused with warmth and soulfulness began, gloriously, with Pushkin.

In a letter whose perlustration by secret police earned "the sunshine of Russian poetry" exile and house arrest (for an offhand reference to "taking lessons in pure atheism"), Pushkin averred that he actually enjoyed reading the Bible. Or rather: "sometimes I need the Holy Spirit, though I prefer Shakespeare or Goethe." Pushkin, indeed, was so impressed by Goethe's *Faust* that he composed a new *Scene from Faust* while in exile. Later he was very proud to be honoured by Goethe with a present of a pen. Undoubtedly, in some ways the two poets were alike. Both essentially invented their respective languages' modern literary idiom. Both were Romantics; both were set to music by countless composers; both achieved what many consider the quintessential expression of their countries' souls. One might go so far as to say that each dramatized his county's virtues – and also flaws. Yet, while much admiring the "Muse of Weimar" (see illustration), Pushkin did not share Goethe's slightly didactic pragmatism, seen, for instance, in Goethe's *Wasser und Wein*:

Von Wasser allein wird man stumm.	From water alone speech is numb,
Das beweisen im Wasser die Fische.	Which is proved by the fish in the water.
Von Wein allein wird man dumm.	From wine alone one grows dumb
Das beweisen die Herren am Tische.	Which is proved by those gents' table chatter.
Und drum, um keines von beiden zu sein,	And – so that neither such state will be mine –
Trink ich mit wasser vermischt mein Wein.	With water diluted I drink my wine.

(My translation, J.H.L.)

Pushkin's Portrait of Goethe

The youthful Pushkin reacted with a very different *Water and Wine* indeed:

I love, when noontime's heat is blazing,
To suck the cool out from a stream.
And in a grove, secluded, shaded,
To watch the current dance and gleam.
When to the brim white wine is flowing
And foaming in our fateful bowls,
Who, friends, amongst you, aren't groaning,
Elated, eager in your souls?
But cursèd be that villain godless,
Who first should dare commit the crime,
Blinded, unbridled, and dishonoured,
Oh woe! To mix with water wine!
Curse him through every generation!
So drink no more then! Fine! So be it!
Or mix the glasses in their places
And call cheap swill Château Lafitte!

Pushkin was Russian: "if we're drinking, then let's drink!" And he was like Shakespeare, ever strong – even when wavering. And whether happy or grieving, he seems so sure of his masculinity, so in touch with both the god and the impish little boy within, so at-one indeed with his own manhood, that he freely celebrates the feminine in himself, even on occasion drawing himself as a woman. Perhaps his finest lines are about or for women. Another way of saying this is that Pushkin was always in love. And not just with women: also with nature, art, and life itself. Being in love was to him as natural as breathing:

My heart's again afire and loving, because – why?
It simply cannot not be loving.

Pushkin once joked in a note to a friend on the nature of first love, that his then-fiancée Natalya Goncharova was "in parenthesis my one hundred and thirteenth love." (In parenthesis, various scholars mistake this sarcasm for a statistic, and one could probably find 113 clueless tomes inspired just by this one flippant remark.) But there's no point losing sleep over everyone Pushkin might have slept with:

My friends! What does it really matter
Just where our idle heart gets rent?

In ballrooms bright, smart box-seat chatter,
Or in a nomad's wicker tent?

In truth Pushkin always loved not just the maid of the moment, but the divine energy she evoked in him. Any woman he exalted was his Muse, that spirit invoked by Goethe at the end of *Faust:* "*das Ewig-Weibliche*" (the "Ever-Feminine"). Pushkin's hymns to women attain a crystal purity that is somehow only deepened by his characteristically lighthearted and flippant attitude towards his own "light ease in suffering." His raging passions are no less intense or sublime for being self-deprecating, sly, airy, indeed, wryly aware of the possible silliness or capriciousness of his own caprice.

I do not dare to seek your love.
It may be I have sinned so much,
My angel, I am not worth loving.
But just pretend it! Your look sweet
Sublimely says all things demurely!
Oh dear! It isn't hard to fool me!
I'm glad myself to be deceived!

Could someone truly "deceived" ever pen such lines? Yet in the foolish giddiness of falling in love, in a "crush," like a glass too much of wine, in *umilenie,* deeply moved affection, Pushkin found wisdom and communion with all humanity. He preferred raw love poems to odes, once even gently chiding a friend for writing verses that were too grand because: "All poetry should be – God forgive me – kind of silly!" Pushkin's solace, in dark times, is that of a friend who does not hide behind his genius. He jokes and winks at us, joys in his own foibles, and is fascinated by ours. He knows that in the end, only accepting and embracing each other's flaws do we graduate from effortless being in love to Love itself, with its profound, mysterious contradictions. With exquisite intimacy, he even dares reveal the painful bliss of his own marital bedroom:

Oh, with what tortured joy for you alone I pine
When you, at last yielding to lengthy supplication,
Give yourself tenderly to me without elation,
Feeling ashamed and cold, my joyousness within
But scarcely answering, and not feeling a thing.
Till livening with time, you too start thrilling,
Till more and more at last my flame you share unwilling.

Self-portraits as a woman

Love – often openly erotic love – is the very fabric of Pushkin's *sprezzatura*. Yet being "all about love, and love, and love," Pushkin quite offended those who frankly wished he had been more political. Certain Soviet critics, notably the influential Vikenty Veresayev and his school, practically condemned Pushkin for anti-Soviet behavior. In the dead language of *Pravda* editorials, Veresayev complained: "In political, societal, and religious questions, Pushkin was unreliable and infirm, and in various years full of internal contradictions." (Like Whitman: "Do I contradict myself? Well then, I contradict myself! I am large. I contain multitudes.") Thus, *The Prophet*, *The Poison Tree*, and *A Message to Siberia*, fit neatly into the Soviet textbooks. More awkward, however, was his sympathy not only for the jailed Decembrists who rebelled against the Tsar, but for their jailors as well ("*God help you all, my dear, dear, friends*"), as was his concern not only for the Russian soldiers on "our side," but also for the soldiers of the enemy, as seen in *Delibash* (*The Turkish Captain*). The great Russian poet Alexander Blok extolled its light, almost casual touch, its bare detail so perfectly conveying the profound senselessness of war.

It is daring to be a moderate. Rejecting fanaticism was nearly capital treason in an age of cruel ideals. In Veresayev's time, "ten years with no rights to correspondence" [a Stalinist euphemism for execution] could easily have been the sentence for expressing these sentiments:

> I do not value much those rights hailed with such din
> From which so many people's heads just seem to spin.
> I don't complain and grouse about the gods' sharp practice,
> Denying me sweet rights to argue about taxes,
> Or make it hard for Tsars to war with Tsars.
> It little riles me if the press is free to charge
> And torment idiots, or tender censors' humours
> Offend themselves in every ragsheet's rumours.
>
> Oh! Can't you see that all this is just "words, words, words?"
> By other, better rights my soul gets stirred;
> Another, better sort of freedom I am seeking.
> Depend upon the Tsar? Depend upon the people?
> Isn't it all the same? Who cares?

Both Tsars and commissars, supposed tribunes of "the people" (today it would be conservatives and liberals) feared the poet's freedom.

Thus Veresayev, like the censor-spy Bulgarin 100 years before him, claimed to see "a striking difference between the live personality of the poet and its reflection in his works" – dismissing the inconvenient Pushkin by slandering him personally. Yet Pushkin's life and work are inseparable, and his "better sort of freedom," real freedom, the inner freedom of the soul, still preserves the Russians in true inner liberty.

His teaching lies in never preaching. Pushkin, like Oscar Wilde, claims to know nothing except that "life is too important to be taken seriously." Hermann in *The Queen of Spades,* eyes life with Napoleonic ruthlessness and "calculation." But Pushkin laughs at "German" materialism. Instead he embraces the mysterious, the flippant and quirky, the soulful, the feminine way of the moon:

Your melancholy's without reason.
You love with suffering and grieving;
But woman's heart loves laughingly.
Look up! See, in the inky vastness,
The moon so freely prances, preens,
On all of nature she, in passing,
Sheds equally capricious gleams.
Though any cloud she'll notice brightens,
And grows majestic with her hue –
Just then on other clouds she lightens –
And doesn't visit there long too.
Who'll dare to bound her heavenly dancing?
Who bids her stop, cuts off her range?
Who'll give a maiden's heart commandments:
"Love only one, and never change?"

Like love itself, the moon can be capricious and demanding. In Pushkin's poems the moon's dreaminess usually is paired with that lovely melancholy which Brazilians call "*saudade*" and Russians call "*toskà*." But to Pushkin, dreamy moonlit starlight was ever so much more precious than his place under the sun. Only the subtle gleam of the moon evokes that essence which the light of some Sun-King might obscure. Only in soft starlight can the poet find his inner bliss:

> Near lands where sovereignty of golden Venice rules,
> A lone nocturnal gondolier his way plies through the pools.
> By evenstar's soft light, he – singing – turns his oars
> Of Reynald, Godfred, and Erminia – by their shores.
> He loves singing his song, for pleasure sings his story,
> Lacking all further plans, he sings heedless of glory,
> Of fears heedless, of hopes... Filled by the silent Muse,
> Above the waves' abyss with bliss his wake he hews:
> So, in this sea of life, where cruelly the tempest
> In darkening gloom to my lone sail grants no rest,
> Not minding what men say, I sing and I rejoice,
> Dreaming up secret poems with my secret voice.

But sometimes his songs do not "rejoice" – especially in his last eight years, trapped in "this piggish Petersburg." (And yet – "I love you, town of Peter's making"). The "chosen, happy idler" (whose friends nicknamed him "the Cricket" in his youth) soon chirped less, and mourned more, merged with a darker man, grieving (*Remembrance*), fearing madness (*May God forbid I go insane*), and morbidly obsessed by death (*When past the city gates in wistful thought I roam*). Actually, that dark man was always present. *I will fall silent soon* and *I have outlived my aspirations* were written in cheerful days when he was still teaching parrots to swear at bishops, or chasing comely gypsy girls, or racing to fresh oysters ("*And so I lived then in Odessa*").

Some blame his increasing gloom of later years on disillusionment with his wife, on jealousy over her flirtation with a handsome French officer, Georges D'Anthès, who later killed him in a duel. Others blame the poet's growing frustration at the pompous, meretricious, stifling atmosphere of the imperial court, expressed in the last of his 78 letters to his wife: "Here, just being a decent human being is enough to earn one a scolding by the police...Why did the Devil let me be born in Russia – and with a soul and talent to boot?"

A poet understands a poet, and Aleksandr Blok concluded: "Pushkin was killed not so much by D'Anthès' bullet, as by lack of air" for his free soul to breathe in. He hated dragging along with his wife and her sisters to fancy balls, dressed as an imperial chamberpage, a flunkey of a court so cold, so focused on empty glitter that it could not see its own most brilliant jewel. He watched and brooded as his wife flirted with men who were handsomer, richer, and more attuned to what amused her. To love her, and yet feel unloved by her, must have become ever more unbearable. Two years before his death he wrote:

> It's time, my friend, it's time! For peace the heart is calling.
> Day flies by after day, and every hour is tolling
> A bit of being away: together you and I
> Suppose that we will live – but see! but then – we die!
> There is no joy on earth, but there is peace and freedom:
> Long time of enviable fate I have been dreaming,
> Long time, I, tired slave, have dreamed of secret flight
> Unto a distant shrine of toil and pure delight.

Yet who but the very freest of spirits truly dares call himself a "tired slave"? To joy in grief and mourn in happiness requires "genius, friend of paradox." Keats wrote "in the very temple of Delight/Veil'd Melancholy has her sovran shrine." For Pushkin, "my melancholy's bright": his fundamentally playful, attitude to life extended, in its way, even to playfulness with death. For example, in one duel (later recounted in his short story *The Shot*) Pushkin let his opponent shoot at him from 12 paces as he stood calmly, "plucking wild cherries out of his cap, and spitting out the pits." In another duel (caused by a quarrel with a drunken officer over whether a cafe orchestra should play a mazurka instead of a quadrille), Pushkin's foe missed at sixteen paces, as a wild snowstorm was swirling. The poet offered his foe another shot at just twelve paces. Another miss, and the storm grew so wild that the foes reconciled. The officer was deeply moved and said: "You stand up to bullets as well as you write!" Pushkin then threw his arms around him. Yet another example: Pushkin's schoolmate Küchelbecker challenged him for a verse describing a hangover as feeling "Küchelbeckerish and bleary." Pushkin refused to shoot, and, when his friend missed, extended his hand and said: "Enough clowning around, my dear, let's go have tea."

In *Delibash,* Pushkin advised: "Cossack, hey! Race not to battle." Yet in the only battle he himself ever took part in, he had to be dragged off the field, "after seizing a lance from a slain Cossack and charging headlong against the enemy horsemen." (Regards to Whitman!)

Pushkin was mortally wounded in the final duel of the more than 20 in his life. One wonders: did Pushkin note the many parallels between his final duel and the duel that killed his poet Lensky in Book VI of *Eugene Onegin*? A silly spat, provoked by the poet's jealousy over a frivolous society beauty who seems briefly attracted to a rake... both duels took place at nearly the same date and time, with the same wintry scenery... It becomes uncanny: in both duels the poet used the same Lepage pistols, and died when the rake shot first. Did Pushkin, before his duel, reflect on Lensky's tragic end? Why did Pushkin, so superstitious that he would turn his carriage around and ride home if a hare crossed his path, proceed, despite bad omens and a prophecy, to his fatal duel? Did he want to die?

> But, oh my friends, I do not want to die;
> I want to live, to think, suffer, and pine.

Why then did he leave for his duel without a turquoise ring he usually wore for protection against violent death? Did he just forget? Was he tired of suffering and longing for release? Or is that story itself just a legend? We cannot unlock that secret now. We can only share his courageous readiness, his melancholy, lighthearted curiosity – even in the face of death itself:

> As I caress a child's head tender
> I think already: "Farewell" soon:
> To you my place I now surrender:
> For I must wither, you must bloom.
> Each day now, each year I'm amassing,
> I like to see off in my mind,
> Guessing the dates of my own passing,
> Trying the right one to divine.
> And where will fate send me my dying?
> In battle, wanderings, or waves?
> Or will the valley nearby lying
> Receive my ashes in its graves?

Certain Buddhists believe that the "higher self" chooses the time and manner of the soul's departure from the body. Musing and choosing how to die – did Pushkin's soul, if those Buddhists are right, not find it somehow entirely fitting to "meet his Maker" young and vigorous – because of love, and over a point of honour? It is quite the Pushkinian paradox: "my gift, like life, I frittered away heedless." He was so in love with life that he was willing to cast it away lightly, at the drop of a glove, to march, like his unnamed hero in *The Shot,* towards death's bitterness with the sweet taste of berries in his mouth. (Just before dying he asked: "give me some cloudberries").

Even at his bleakest, some other part of him, a "friend," wryly stands back observing all with a certain sardonic affection. Even at Onegin's deepest, most lovelorn depression, he manages to joke:

> A very poet he resembled
> Alone in his dark corner, there,
> Watching the hearth blaze up and blare
> And purring, murm'ring "*Benedetta*"
> Or "*Idol mio*," to the flames threw
> His paper – or sometimes his shoe!

Being able to laugh at himself, Pushkin was ultimately an optimist. Unlike his literary heirs, famed for "more skies of grey/than any Russian play can guarantee," Pushkin dared to write happy endings – heresy to radicals whose overpoliticized expectations demanded woe. Even his endings that aren't so happy easily could have been, as his beloved Tatyana laments, in her last rejection of Onegin:

> Yet happiness had been so close by,
> So possible.

Nabokov wondered about the ending of *Eugene Onegin*; he thought it doubtful even just how final its unhappy "finale" really is:

> At the risk of breaking the hearts of all admirers of "Princess Gremin" (as the two bright minds that concocted Tchaikovsky's libretto dubbed [Tatyana]), I deem it necessary to point out that her answer to Onegin does not at all ring with such dignified finality as commentators have supposed it to do. Mark the intonations...the heaving breast, the broken speech, the anguished, poignant, palpitating, enchanting, almost voluptuous, almost alluring enjambments, a veritable orgy of run-ons, culminating in a confession of love that must have made Eugene's experienced heart leap with joy. And after those sobbing 12 lines – what clinches them? The hollow perfunctory sound of a pat couplet... shrill virtue repeating its cue!

Here Nabokov goes too far. Pushkin was no Falstaff. To him, honour was no "mere escutcheon" – honour was dearer than life, for it was art and love and freedom, all in one, and in one all. Yet it is true that irony and ambiguity pervade Pushkin's moral universe. He never preached like Tolstoy or Dostoyevsky. He preferred to just show us choices and their consequences through forks in roads, corridors leading in different directions. (Hermann literally took a wrong turn, by following greed instead of love in *The Queen of Spades*.)

"Two fixed ideas cannot exist together in one moral space, just as two bodies cannot together occupy one and the same place in the physical world." So he wrote in the same story. Yet, with his usual ease, he does not force that law upon himself: simultaneously in Pushkin's world, Fate rules all, inexorably, and yet, man has free will, such that even the inevitable is transformable.

Perhaps, as Schopenhauer said, "man has free will, but not the will to use it." At any rate, Pushkin's stories feel like life itself: choice and chance, in dance together, weave a seamless harmony, and, as if effortlessly, arrive at a bittersweet perfection, an ironic state of grace, higher in his works than life's logic otherwise allows. And in the face of life's grand pageant: "I look through my bright tears and smile."

Alas, Pushkin himself never attained the choice he so dearly longed for, to "flee the rumour of the crowd" like the great Roman poet Horace, "for stillness pastoral"... "unto a distant shrine of toil and pure delight."

And yet the Tsar could only confine his movements; his heart stayed free. Even brooding on death, he found transcendence and higher wisdom. One of Pushkin's final poems is based on Horace's great ode: "*Exegi monumentum.*" In it, Horace took majestic pride in his enduring poetic legacy:

I've built a monument that outlasts bronze,
And looms up higher than the regal heaps of Pyramids,
That nor the devouring rainclouds, nor the North Wind
Blustering and impotent, nor row on row of years uncounted
Midst the flight of Time can possibly destroy.
Not all of me will die; much of me shall
Escape the Temple of the Dead, through and through
Growing in fresh praise, as long as the Pontiff shall
Climb up the Capitol, with silent Vestal beside him.
They'll say, where violent Aufidus roared its flood,
And where King Daunus reigned in a land of peoples
Bereft of water, that I, though sprung from lowness meek,
First brought Aeolian song forth to the measures of
Italian verse. Take then the lofty honours and rewards
You've strived for and won me, and freely, with Delphic Laurel,
Crown now, Melpomene, my hair.

Horace, Book III, Ode xxx (my translation).

Pushkin, more wisely than Horace, little prized the tinsel of temporal power. He knew grace was not bestowed by some pompous "*pontifex*," just as no empire could be depended upon to preserve the legacy of his soul. His crown came from the power of love, from the harmony between the godlike boy in him and the "eternal feminine."

Portrait of the poet Horace

Like love, grace comes from within, not on command of some Sun King. It lives, and gleams by itself – beneath the moon:

> No, I won't fully die: my soul, in sacred lyre,
> Will yet survive my dust, and, despite with'ring, thrive:
> I'll glorious be as long's in moonlit world entire
> One single bard is still alive.

In the end, all great poetry – especially Pushkin's – is always a monument to love, to that sacred weakness, the strongest force of all. Rome no longer rules the world, yet Horace is still here with us. Caesar's Vestal Virgins are long gone, but not the verses they inspired.

Just so, Pushkin's Tatiana (in her way too a vestal virgin, given away lovelessly to a fat crippled general) will ever be dear to the hearts of millions... She and her beloved Eugene are like that unknown youth Keats comforted in his *Ode on a Grecian Urn*:

Bold lover, never, never canst thou kiss,
Though winning near the goal – yet, do not grieve;
She cannot fade, though thou hast not thy bliss,
For ever wilt thou love, and she be fair!

For that single poet in the "moonlit world entire," for that poet inside of all of us, we need Pushkin, poet of poets, poet of the Russian soul. We need his inspiring call "to sacred sacrifice," we need his courage, accepting hardship and exile over any compromise in the flawless integrity of his art. We need his serenity, his ability to smile into the abyss with the taste of berries in his mouth, disdainful of all mere Delphic laurels.

We need his determined joy in the face of an unforgiving, uncomprehending world, his grace in turning mundane misery into divine grief, his ease and contentment, perhaps the greatest reward of all, in just being who he is, and just being who he is, and from others needing nothing:

And many years will I be favoured with the people
For waking up good feelings by my lyre's thrall,
Because in my cruel age I praised and gloried Freedom,
For mercy to the fallen called.

Unto the Lord's command, oh Muse, be ever heedful,
Fear not offense and shame, care not for glory's rule,
Take praise and calumny indifferently, not needful –
And never argue with a fool.

Pushkin's undiluted voice is long overdue in the English language. May this book help those not blessed with knowing Russian to hear it, perhaps, for the first time. And may those readers already blessed with Russian, perhaps raised on his voice from childhood, please forgive me every time they cannot hear his incomparable grace in my English renderings, which, I am the first to admit, can never really do justice to the divine original.

Yet I hope that even Russian-speakers may catch in this book a different glimmer from the brightest star in their linguistic firmament, as a light shined from a new angle, sometimes, reveals hidden facets in a brilliant jewel. Though "of mere use neglectful and disdainful," Pushkin's poetry, like all great art, has truly magical healing power – the deep mysterious potency of a talisman, protecting and comforting our own souls' fateful journeys.

JULIAN HENRY LOWENFELD

Coat of arms of the Pushkin family

A BIOGRAPHY OF THE POET

What is a poet? Someone who writes poems? Of course not. One is a poet not just because one writes poems, but one writes poems, harmonizing words and sounds – because one is a child of harmony – because one is a poet.

Alexander Blok. The Poet's Mission

Childhood. 1799–1811

Alexander Sergeyevich Pushkin was born in Moscow on June 6, 1799. (At least in the West. In Russia it was May 26, 1799, according to the Julian calendar used there till 1918; all further dates will be given as Pushkin himself experienced them, "in the old style.") The poet's father, Sergey Lvovich Pushkin, came from an illustrious, if impoverished, noble family. The poet's mother Nadyezhda Osipovna, née Gannibal, was called "*la belle créole.*" Her black grandfather, Ibrahim Gannibal, had been kidnapped in childhood from Central Africa, sold by slave traders to the Turks, and then bought and sent as a "gift" to Tsar Peter the Great. Peter baptized the boy Abraham, raised him fondly, and, seeing his aptitude, made him his personal assistant, then sent him to study military engineering in France. Abraham became Russia's chief fortress builder (he helped construct Kronshtadt and Revel), and wrote several textbooks in French on mathematics and the science of fortification. Proud of his African heritage, he chose his surname in honour of the great Carthaginian general Hannibal (Gannibal in Russian, which lacks a letter "h"). Twice decorated for valour, he retired *General en Chef* of the Imperial Russian Army. Empress Elizabeth, Peter's daughter, endowed him with estates, including Mikhailovskoye, in Pskov Province. And so a former slave became a Russian nobleman – himself the owner of 800 white slaves (serfs). Pushkin inherited many of his great-grandfather's African features: thick lips, curly, frizzy hair, and, as novelist Ilya Goncharov delicately recalled, a "tan" complexion. Pushkin later kept an inkwell on his desk with a statuette of a Negro slave unloading cotton bales, and he often joked about being a "Moor."

> Why does your pencil so divine
> Attempt to draw my Moorish profile?

Writers and poets frequented the Pushkin home, including Pushkin's uncle Vasily Lvovich ("You are my uncle even on Parnassus," his nephew later wrote). Pushkin's father was known for his wit, his mainly French language library, one of the best in Moscow, and for his literary salons, in which he read Molière aloud, with lively aplomb. Pushkin's mother was also fond of reading aloud to her children, and, in Pushkin's phrase: "Reading is the best teaching." If his family had not breathed with love for poetry, for the glories of European culture, and for Russian culture too, it is doubtful the boy's genius would have developed as it did.

Yet most biographers and memoirists are critical of Pushkin's parents. "Sergey Lvovich was a tender father, but all tenderness shrank at spending money; he was extremely miserly," recalled Pushkin's friend Prince Peter Vyazemsky. The chance breaking of a little glass costing 35 kopecks sufficed to put him in a great rage all day, and "he never gave the slightest help to his son Alexander, in his entire life sparing him barely 500 rubles in notes – though in his own way he was very proud of his son's successes," wrote biographer Mikhail Semevsky. His mother is depicted as charming but neglectful and moody. "She could sulk for days, months, even years," one grandson recalled. In fairness, eight surviving children (of whom Pushkin was the second; five others died in infancy) would be hard for anyone to handle, though for some reason she favoured the poet's younger brother Lev, and was noticeably unaffectionate with that *enfant terrible*, her restless, brilliant eldest son, Alexander. Some degree of connective warmth between the poet and his mother seems to have been attained only in their last few years of life. One senses in many of Pushkin's deepest love lyrics a grieving and yearning for the mother he missed in childhood. It does not seem coincidence that in a semi-autobiographic sketch, *A Russian Pelham*, the poet portrayed himself as motherless. And as to his father:

> My time under my father's roof has left nothing pleasant in my imagination. Father, of course, loved me, but didn't have the slightest interest in me, and left me to the care of various French tutors, who were constantly being hired and fired. My very first *gouverneur* was a drunkard, the second, though neither stupid nor uneducated, could fly into such rages that he once tried to murder me with a log for spilling a few drops of ink onto his waistcoat. The third, kept in our house for a whole year, was totally insane.

Is there a hint of Pushkin's childhood in his description of the young Tatyana? (*Eugene Onegin*, Chapter II, xxv)

> Unnatural, saddened, and withdrawn,
> As frightened as a forest fawn,
> She seemed in her own family
> A foundling, strange entirely.

Does this explain his irony towards his "near and dear ones?"

What does that mean, our near and dear ones?
Our near and dear ones are just these ones:
The ones we are obliged to kiss,
Caress, and love, and warmly miss,
Also, by custom and good cheer,
On Christmas we should pay them calls,
At least by mail should send them cards,
So all the rest of all the year
They'll never even think of us!
And so, God grant them health, I trust! (*E.O.* IV, xx)

Yet he wrote warm poems for his maternal grandmother Maria Alekseyevna and serf-nanny Arina Rodionovna, who once, out walking his pram in the park, got scolded by Tsar Paul I for not doffing to remove the boy's baby cap in the august presence of the Sovereign (an omen, perhaps, of problems to come). It was these strong women who taught him Russian (the first language of much of the Russian nobility back then was French). Childhood summers he spent in grandmother's country house in Zakharovo, near Moscow, by the ancestral lands of Tsar Boris Godunov. One senses the maternal warmth and affection given him by his nanny and grandmother merged in his perception with great storytelling and love into the sounds of the Russian language itself.

Of Mamushka could I not say a word,
Of nights mysterious made so bright by her
In her old night-cap, and her threadbare gown
Driving bad spirits off with prayers, frowns,
Devoted, crossing herself o'er my bed?
And then in whispers telling stories dread
Of bandits, ghosts, the great Bová, the dead
Who walked...Frozen in fear, with bated breath,
I'd listen, shudder, hug my quilt to death,
Could feel no more my toes, my feet, my head,
The icon's candle in a lamp of clay
Lit up her face and made its wrinkles play...

Even without dread tales, Pushkin seems to have had trouble sleeping at times. (See *I can't sleep; fire's out, no light* or *Remembrance.)* Insomnia may be one of poetry's occupational hazards. One day when he was nine, Grandmother found him up before dawn, wandering the house entranced, saying: "I am writing poems."

Youthful self-portraits

With his older sister Olga, he used to write and act various skits in verse. Pushkin's earliest surviving poem, in French, *bien sûr*, described the flop of his world première:

Dis-moi, pourquoi L'Escamoteur	Tell me, why was *The Kidnapper*
Est-il sifflé par le parterre?	So roundly booed by the parterre?
Hélas! c'est que le pauvre auteur	Alas! It seems its poor *auteur*
L'escamota de Molière.	Had kidnapped it from Molière.

Already – at the age of nine – we hear the first strains of Pushkin's voice: ironic detachment, self-deprecating wit, light, if mischievous, humour – masking, perhaps, a little sadness and inner loneliness...

He loved to read, to daydream, to lose himself freely for days in his father's vast library: Homer, Plutarch, Virgil, Ovid, Tacitus, Juvenal, Terence, Suetonius, Horace, Montaigne, Corneille, Racine, Molière, Beaumarchais, Laclos, St. Preux, Richardson, Sterne, Defoe, Diderot, Voltaire, Rousseau... Young Pushkin devoured them all, while lapping up *bons mots* at his father's literary soirées. A French family friend exclaimed: "What an amazing boy! How quickly he grasps things! May this boy live and live; you'll see what will become of him!"

Between the salon and library, Pushkin's French became so fluent that his schoolmates at the Lycée would nickname him "the Frenchman." Indeed, the heady brilliance of his parents' European salon, mixed with his grandmotherly singsong suckling in Russian folklore, uniquely endowed him to one day transform his own language, to employ it as Peter the Great used his grand new capital, Saint Petersburg, as a tool for Russia (in Pushkin's phrase) "to force a window free" to Europe. Pushkin's ability to straddle worlds, to feel effortlessly at home in two conflicting realities, was a gift even of his infancy, for it is paradoxically true that the "sunshine of Russian poetry" was a true child of the French Enlightenment.

The Lycée. 1811–1817

Originally his parents planned to send Pushkin to a French Jesuit school in St. Petersburg. But in 1811, Tsar Alexander I decided to found, in the pleasant suburb of Tsarskoye Selo, an elite academy (to which he donated his personal library) to be housed in the Summer Palace of the Tsars. Six years' continuous education (with no visits home or leaving school grounds allowed) were to be provided free of charge to young nobles destined for "highest office in the service of the state." Corporal punishment was forbidden, a rarity for that time. Verse-writing uncle Vasily Pushkin (that "man of rules, most honest") brought his nephew to St. Petersburg (splurging the boy's 100 rubles allowance ["for walnuts"] on... a mistress, and never returning them). Pushkin aced the entrance exam, and, together with 29 other boys was officially inducted into the Lycée, on October 19, 1811, a date he'd revere all his life, and commemorate in seven separate poems. No sooner was the imperial pomp of the inaugural ceremony over than all the boys ran out and got into a rousing snowball fight. From its founding, the Lycée and its close-knit students invoked in each other a spirit of boisterous boyish freedom, joy, deep friendship, competitive playfulness, joyous excess, and good humour, yet with an abiding reverence for a higher purpose in life, a devotion to love, art, and honour that came to be called "the spirit of the Lycée":

> My friends, how beautiful our union is!
> Eternal like the soul, it can't be broken.
> It withstands all, free, careless, and outspoken:
> Our links were formed by friendship and the Muse.
> Where'er we're cast by Fate, whate'er it's storing,
> Wherever happiness might let us roam,
> We're still the same: the whole world's strange and foreign,
> And Tsarskoye Selo is our true home.

Pushkin's friends from the Lycée, particularly the poets Anton Delvig and Wilhelm Küchelbecker, as well as Ivan Pushchin ("Jeannot"), the Decembrist, remained for him beloved soulmates, pined for and cherished literally until his final breaths.

The Lycée's curriculum was ambitious: "1. grammar: instruction in the Russian, Latin, French, and German languages; 2. moral sciences: introduction to religion, philosophy, ethics, and logic; 3. mathematics and physical sciences, algebra, physics, and trigonometry; 4. historical sciences: history of Russia and foreign countries, geography, and chronology; 5. foundations of literature: excerpts from the best authors, analysis, rules of rhetoric; 6. fine arts, gymnastics, calligraphy, drawing, dancing, fencing, horsemanship, and swimming..."

Pushkin as a child. Watercolour by Sergey Chirikov, 1810

We all did study (more or less so)
Something or other at some time...

Had Pushkin taken it all seriously, maybe he'd have become, like Prince Gorchakov, first Head Boy, then one day, Heaven forbid, Chancellor of the Russian Empire. Yet the poet was influenced by some of his more liberal teachers. Kunitsyn, his professor of moral sciences, lectured against serfdom and on behalf of "natural law" and the teachings of Adam Smith. The French master was the brother of the French revolutionary leader Marat. The schoolboys vividly experienced Napoleon's invasion of Russia in 1812, the battle of Borodino, and the burning of Moscow (at one point hurling away their French grammar books in protest).

Remember: row on row went marching by;
We said farewell then to our older bothers,
Returned to Learning's canopy and grumbled,
In envy of those lads who off to die
Went marching past...

In his *Notes on Pushkin*, Ivan Pushchin remembered his best friend in those days:

> We all saw Pushkin was way ahead of us, had read many things of which the rest of us had never even heard, and had remembered all he'd read. Yet the best thing about him was that he never showed off or acted important as gifted people often do at that age. On the contrary, he held all learning to be nonsense, and was only ever busy trying to prove that he was a swift sprinter, or could jump over piled up chairs, or hurl a ball...

Pushkin indeed became a master fencer and rider, an avid swimmer and walker, a gymnast, even one of Russia's first aficionados of what was then known as "French (i.e. lightweight) boxing."

His poetic talents also gained attention. His first publication, in 1814, came when his friends, as a prank, sent his manuscript of *To a Friend who Writes Poems* to the journal *Herald of Europe,* listing its author as "N.K.CH.P." (Pushkin backwards). In 1815, with his voice "ringing out youthfully," Pushkin declaimed his *Recollections of Tsarskoye Selo* at a Russian literature examination attended by Russia's most famous poet at the time, Gavriil Derzhavin. This got him so emotional that: "I don't remember how I finished reading; I don't remember where I ran away. Derzhavin was full of admiration, demanded to see me, wanted to embrace me...They looked for me, but couldn't find me."

He wasn't so thrilled about his other subjects. Even Professor Kunitsyn complained: "Pushkin expresses himself clearly, with wit and intelligence, but he's extremely lazy." With his mates Pushchin and Malinovsky, Pushkin was always getting up to some prank or other, such as brewing illicit hot egg creams laced with rum (for which they were denied meals and made to kneel in prayer for two days) or else leaving school grounds, or chasing girls *(see Mon Portrait)*. And "he wrote verse everywhere, especially in math class." The earliest manuscript of any Pushkin poem is already about love: *To Natalia*, written 1813, was about a young actress in Count Tolstoy's serf theatre. Pushkin wrote over 120 poems during his days in the Lycée, over twenty to Yekaterina Bakunina, a pretty maid in waiting at the palace (*The Bard, To Dorida*). It was then that he began his ironic epic *Ruslan and Lyudmila*.

In his last year, Pushkin sometimes cut class to carouse with various hussars quartered nearby. One of these new friends was Pyotr Chaadayev, a penetrating critic of serfdom and autocracy, who introduced the young poet to the English language, the philosophy of Hume and Locke and to the romantic, lyrical verse of Byron. In Tsarskoye Selo, he also met the famed Russian historian and sentimental novelist Nikolai Karamzin, and also Karamzin's wife Yekaterina, whom some scholars believe was Pushkin's "secret love."

On June 9, 1817, Pushkin graduated, scraping by 26th out of 29 in his class, with top marks only in Russian (no surprise), French, and fencing. Years later, when Pushkin became famous, one teacher grumbled: "What's all this fuss about Pushkin? He was a scamp – nothing more!" Engelhardt, the Lycée headmaster, took an even stronger dislike to his most famous pupil, and wrote in Pushkin's school report in 1816:

> Pushkin's only higher goal is to shine – in poetry, to be precise, though it is doubtful indeed he will ever succeed, because he shuns any serious scholarship, and his mind, utterly lacking in perspicacity or depth, is a completely superficial, frivolous French mind. And that is in fact the best thing that can be said about Pushkin. His heart is cold and empty: there is neither love nor religion in it. It is perhaps as empty as ever any youth's heart has ever been.

Curiously, in Buddhist meditation practice, "emptiness" can be great praise: an achievement of the highest order. Perhaps the very "emptiness" – or openness – of Pushkin's heart made it such a perfect vessel for sublime expressions of love. At any rate, his "emptiness" was to him a treasure, a gift he refused to clutter with mere skills for "the service of the state." Already in the Lycée he had decided:

> Farewell, farewell, cold sciences!
> I'm now from youthful games estranged!
> I am a poet now; I've changed.
> Within my soul both sounds and silence
> Pour into one another, live,
> In measures sweet both take and give.

St. Petersburg. 1817–1820

Upon graduation, Pushkin was made a lowly collegiate assessor, or bureaucrat tenth class, in the Russian Foreign Ministry. "Almost at once I took three months' leave to visit my mother's estate in Mikhailovskoye. I was enchanted by the country, the real Russian bathhouse, the abundant strawberries..." He also enjoyed meeting his black great-uncle and downing six shots with him of fiery home-made vodka. Back in St. Petersburg, he lived briefly in the home of Count Apraksin (now 174, Griboyedov Canal) then with his parents in cramped quarters by the Fontanka Canal. The floor above was rented by Pushkin's fellow Lycéen, Baron Modest Korf – whom Pushkin once challenged to a duel for striking the poet's beloved manservant Nikita Kozlov. Korf had been Engelhardt's favourite, and shared his headmaster's dislike for the poet and his family:

> All the Pushkins were oddballs. The father was a rather cheerful conversationalist in the old French school, full of jokes and puns, but was empty, muddleheaded, useless, and a particularly silent slave of his wife. She was not stupid, but was a sclfish, ill-tempered nag, incredibly absent-minded and particularly bad at running the home: it was always in some sort of chaos: in one room rich antique furniture, in another bare walls, without even chairs, lots of dishevelled, drunken servants, battered old carriages, tattered nags, gorgeous ladies' gowns and a constant lack of everything, from money on down to the last glass. Whenever two or three people visited them for dinner, they always needed us to lend them crockery!

This may well be spiteful exaggeration (as often elsewhere in Korf's memoirs). Yet doubtless after the heady freedom and cosiness of the Lycée, the poet's life with his parents again felt confining and deprived. In a letter to his younger brother Lev he recalled: "when I was sick in the autumn rains or bitter winter frosts, and hired a coachman to take me home from Anichkov Bridge, Father always scolded me about the 80 kopecks, which doubtless neither you nor I would even begrudge our servants." Paternal stinginess seems to have provoked in his oldest son a certain defiant, poetic carelessness about money. "One bright summer day," a friend recalled, "he was boating in company together with Sergey Lvovich [Pushkin's father]. It was calm and the water was so clear that you could see the bottom. Pushkin took out a few golden coins from his pocket and – to his father's horror – one by one deliberately dropped them into the canal, delighted by their clinking, plopping, marvelling at their bright gleam in the clear water."

He loathed his official duties, but loved the theatre – on which he wrote keen reviews – and naturally, pretty actresses, like Elena Sosnitskaya, "into whose net I nearly fell, but was lucky, and got off with just a poem" *(In Sosnitskaya's Album)*. Like most young Russian intellectuals, he was a liberal; unlike most, he was no radical. He joined the freedom-loving "Green Lamp" literary club; various friends (later known as "Decembrists") were by contrast seriously involved in revolutionary societies. His friends at the Arzamas Society of writers nicknamed him "the Cricket" for his approach to life that they felt resembled more the Grasshopper than the Ant.

One evening, at the home of Alexey Olenin, director of the Arts Academy and Public Library, he met the beautiful and coquettish Anna Petrovna Kern, married off against her will at the age of sixteen to a boorish, half-crippled general 35 years her senior. She recollected:

> A jovial banter began between us as to who is a sinner and who is not, and who'd go to heaven, and who to hell. Pushkin told my brother: "At least in hell there'd be lots of pretty girls, and we'd all be playing charades! Ask M-me Kern: wouldn't she like to go to hell?" I answered seriously and a bit curtly that I would not. "How about you, Pushkin?" asked my brother. "Well, now I've changed my mind," the poet answered, "I don't want to go to hell anymore – even if it does have lots of pretty girls!"

This incident would later be immortalized in the poem *A wondrous moment I remember* (p. 191).

In 1819 he was smitten by Eudoxia Golitsyna, known as "Princesse Nocturne" for her midnight soirées:

Where is a woman's fairness not like ice,
But captivating, fiery, and alive?
Whose conversation's easy and unfrightened,
With brilliant wit that's happy and enlightened?
With whom are we not cool, empty, and bland?
My Fatherland I almost hated, really...
But then I saw Golitsyna last evening...
And – now – I'm fine with my dear Fatherland.

That same year he visited the famed German fortune-teller Mme. Alexandra Kirchof (who, supposedly, had helped Tsar Alexander I stand firm against Napoleon in 1812). Mme. Kirchof foretold great fame for Pushkin, two terms of exile, and a long happy life, if only at the age of 37 he avoided "trouble over a white horse, white (i.e. blond) head, or white man." Pushkin believed in all her predictions – and, it must be said, in the end they all came true.

Gossip went all over town about this wild young flibbertigibbet, heedless of warnings against wine, women, and song. Engelhardt, his Lycée headmaster, complained as usual: "how often have I sighed, if only that good-for-nothing Pushkin would be serious, he'd amount to something special in our literature!" His friend Alexander Turgenev despaired: "An idle laziness, dread slayer of all that's beautiful and talented, looms banefully over Pushkin... Mornings he tells Zhukovsky where he hasn't slept all evening, out with various sluts – or me, or Princess Golitsyna, or playing cards..." The poet Batyushkov wrote back: "We should lock our Cricket up in Göttingen for three years on a diet of milk soup and logic!" But Pushkin was quite happy partying:

I am fond of evening feasts
Where good cheer rules o'er our revel,
Where my idol, Freedom, sits,
Making law for all the table,
Where the cry is "drink" till dawn,
Drowning shouts and calls and singing,
Where the guests throng wide and far,
And the bottles crowd in, clinking.

Pushkin would rouse himself at dawn with ice-cold baths, then write for hours, lying in bed. He was finishing *Ruslan and Lyudmila*, an ironic Russian folktale in verse, which created an immediate sensation when it came out in 1820. The Russian public delighted in this new young bard's majestic exuberance and ebullient command of their language:

You rivals in the art of battle,
Allow no one of peace to prate,
Win gloomy glory, prove your mettle,
Drink jubilantly in your hate!
The world will watch you numbly, chilly,
With wonder at your dread display:
There's no one who your deaths will pity,
And no one who'll get in your way.
You rivals of a different station,
You knights of the Parnassian heights,
Don't make us laugh throughout our nation
At your immodest, noisy strife.
So scold – with caution though; keep stable.
But you, who rivals are in love,
Just get along as best you're able!
My friends, take it from me on trust:
When Fate unfailing, willy-nilly,
Decides who fair maid's heart shall win,
He will be loved though Heaven's reeling,
So anger's silly – and a sin.

The poet Vasily Zhukovsky, a translator of *The Odyssey* into stately Russian hexameter verse, reacted to *Ruslan and Lyudmila* by sending his portrait to Pushkin, inscribed "to the victorious pupil from his defeated teacher."

While, as noted, many of Pushkin's closest friends at this time were in secret revolutionary societies, the "Cricket" was too busy "chirping" to actually join any of these societies himself. Yet Pushkin did more for their cause than anyone, with his lyrics and biting epigrams against the government and its ministers (such as an *Epigram on Arakcheyev,* the universally loathed man who basically ran Tsar Alexander I's government). The young poet set an example in fearless self-expression. Ivan Pushchin recalled his friend once cheering when it was announced in a packed theatre that a bear cub had escaped its chains at the Summer Palace and nearly attacked the Tsar. Loudly, so all could hear, Pushkin yelled: "At last a man's been found in Russia – but he's only a bear!" (The poor bear was executed).

At a party in the Turgenev brothers' apartment (20, Fontanka Canal) overlooking the gloomy Mikhaylovskiy Palace of Tsar Paul I, Pushkin was asked to look out the window and improvise a poem. A few hours later he had penned a draft of his *Ode to Liberty* – banned in Russia until 1906.

It and other political works, such as *To Chaadayev*, and *The Country*, spread throughout the land, creating a sensation, inspiring dissidents and secret societies. Tsar Alexander I was particularly incensed by *An Ode to Liberty:* not only did it call for a constitutional monarchy, but it violated the gravest taboo by frankly mentioning the murder in 1801 of Alexander's father, Paul I, (in which Alexander was complicit). An agent tried to bribe Pushkin's loyal manservant Nikita Kozlov to betray forbidden manuscripts. Kozlov refused, and warned his master, who burned everything, and "I yearned for Siberia or the [Peter and Paul] Fortress to restore my honour." Soon Mikhail Miloradovich, military governor-general of St. Petersburg, summoned the poet to interrogation. Pushkin, in an act of true civic courage, wrote out from memory, word for word, his strongest verse against the government – into the now famous "Miloradovich Notebook." Warming to such bravery and talent, Miloradovich released Pushkin on his own recognizance.

But the Tsar was far less charmed, and planned to exile Pushkin to Siberia, or the frigid Solovki isles in the White Sea (later a site of one of the worst Soviet gulags). Last-minute lobbying by Miloradovich, Zhukovsky, and Karamzin helped make the place of exile far warmer: Russia's southwest frontier province, where he was ordered to serve under the command of General Ivan Nikitich Inzov. On May 6, 1820, Ascension Day, he left Petersburg for the South. In the epilogue to *Ruslan and Lyudmila*, Pushkin summed up his past 3 years:

I gloried with obedient lyre
Of olden days obscure the lore,
Sang, and forgot the wounded seething
Both of blind joy and bitter foes,
Of my Dorida, flippant, cheating,
While fools' and gossips' chorus rose.

Borne on the wings of my creation,
My spirit flew past earth and sea,
Not seeing nascent storm's formation,
Or gloomy cloud that swelled round me...
Soon I was doomed... Holy Protector
Of my first stormy days of old,

Tsar Alexander I

O Friendship, comforter so tender
Of my tormented ailing soul!
You calmed the ocean's gentle seething.
And gave my heart its peace anew,
And you preserved for me my freedom,
The idol of my bubbling youth!

Southern Exile. 1820–1824

After a bone-jarring, dusty, two-week trip on the famously appalling roads of the Russian Empire, Pushkin reported to General Inzov in Yekaterinoslav (now Dnepropetrovsk) – best known for its "Potemkin villages" – facades of non-existent settlements erected to deceive Empress Catherine the Great as she sailed past by riverboat. "After reaching Yekaterinoslav, I got bored, went rowing on the Dnepr river, bathed – and got a fever," he wrote his brother. Lying in bed unattended and delirious, he was met by General Nikolai Rayevsky, a hero of 1812, on his way with his two sons and four daughters to the Caucasus to take the waters. Rayevsky persuaded General Inzov to let Pushkin come along. Two months in the Caucasus mountains, hiking and drinking from healing mineral springs, completely restored his health and creative energies. He later recalled: "most of the springs were in primeval condition, bubbling, steaming, and flowing from the mountains in all directions, leaving red and white traces behind. We would draw up the boiling water with a pitcher, or in the bottom of a broken bottle... Nowadays the Caucasian waters are more comfortable, but I miss the way they were once, completely wild: those steep rocky paths, their bushes, their unguarded precipices, up which I used to clamber."

He got inspired to write a new long poem, *The Prisoner of the Caucasus*, about a Russian soldier, taken captive by Chechens, who falls in love with a Chechen girl. The poem marked Pushkin's ongoing growth as a poet, linking romantic passion with distinctive delight in descriptive detail:

It seemed the prisoner so hopeless
Got used to his new dreary life.
Grief of confinement, fire rebellious,
Deep in his heart unseen did hide.
He slouched up gloomy mountainsides
In the first hours of morning chill,
And fixed his ever-curious gaze
Towards distant, giant mountains, still,
Grey, rosy, blue peaks far away:
What views magnificent and sumptuous!

Great thrones eternal of white snows...
To distant eyes it seemed their summits
Were chains of clouds in unmoved rows:
Ringed giant, with twin-peaks dramatic,
Wreathed, sparkling, in a crown of ice,
Elbrus, enormous and majestic,
Whitened above the azure sky.
Then came a muffled roaring, rattling,
A storm-announcing thunderbolt,
Above the village sat the captive,
Not moving from his mountain top!
Clouds at his feet were smoking, writhing,
On plains below dust danced in rising,
And there amidst the cliffs so steep,
The frightened elks did shelter seek,
From precipices eagles flying
Met in the skies, were calling, crying:
The nomads' noises, lowing flocks,
Got drowned by lightning's voices striking...
Hail rained upon the valleys, dropped
From clouds, through thunderbolts came slicing
In rushing waves that steeply carved
And brushed aside the ancient boulders;
The rain in torrents plunged and smouldered,
The captive, from his mountain top,
Alone, beyond the clouds that thundered,
Awaited the bright sun's return,
Untouched by storms beneath him brewing;
He heard the lightning's feeble fury,
And somehow joy within him burned.

Nikolai Gogol (whom Pushkin later befriended) considered this youthful trip a watershed in the young poet's life:

> The gigantic Caucasus range, with its peaks perpetually snowbound, and its lush, sultry valleys amazed him. You might say it called forth all his soul, and broke the last few chains which had held back the utter freedom of his thoughts. He was captivated by the poetic life of the bold mountain tribes, their battles, their quick, unanswerable raids...From that time his brushstroke acquired that amazing breadth, that quickness and daring, which so amazed and enchanted a Russia only just beginning to learn to read. If he described the skirmish of a Cossack with a Chechen, his words flashed lightning, gleamed like the glint of sabre, flying faster than the battle itself. He alone is the true bard of the Caucasus.

Crossing the Black Sea from the Caucasus to the Crimea aboard the brig *Mingrelia*, "I couldn't sleep all night; there was no moon, and the stars shimmered brightly; the southern mountains beckoned to me in the mist." That night Pushkin composed his lovely, somewhat Byronic elegy *The day's last gleam is disappearing*. He wrote to his brother:

> Our ship sailed past mountains covered with poplars, vineyards, laurels and cypresses, and little Tatar villages scattered here and there, and stopped in sight of Gurzuf. I spent three weeks there. My friend, the happiest minutes of my life were spent with the family of the admirable Rayevsky... Besides the war hero, the glory of the Russian army, I loved in him the man with a clear mind and simple, open heart, the forgiving, respectful friend... a witness of Catherine's time, a monument of 1812, yet a man without prejudices, forceful, though sensitive... All his daughters are enchanting, and the oldest is a remarkable woman. Judge for yourself how happy I was: a free, unworried life in the bosom of a warm family, a life I love and never have before enjoyed: this happy southern sky, this lovely, gorgeous land, this nature made for my imagination: mountains, ocean, gardens!

In a draft of a letter to his friend, the poet Delvig, Pushkin wrote:

> I bathed in the sea, and gorged myself on grapes, and felt at once so at home in this Southern sunshine that I wallowed in it with all the carefree languor of a rascally Neapolitan lazybones. I loved waking at night to the sound of the sea, which I could hear and hear for hours. A young cypress grew near the house; I used to visit it every morning, and by the end I felt we two had developed something resembling friendship...

General Rayevsky's son Nikolai took him to tour the former palace of the Khans of the Crimean Tatars in Bakhchisarai. He recalled:

> I arrived sick... I had heard of that strange monument of the lovelorn Khan. **** had poetically described it to me, calling it *la fontaine des larmes* (the fountain of tears). When I went in the palace, I saw a ruined fountain, with water trickling in droplets from its rusted iron pipe. I walked round the whole palace, indignant at the disrepair in which it had been left to decay, at the crude pseudo-European attempts to fix up a few of the rooms. NN practically forced me down a rickety staircase to see the ruins of the harem and the Khan's cemetery. But it wasn't this.
>
> That set my heart back then a-heaving:
>
> I was wracked by fever. Explain to me now why that southern shore and Bakchisarai have for me such inexpressible charm? Why now do I long so violently to go back and visit those places

> which I left with such indifference? Is memory indeed the strongest force in our souls? And does it charm all it touches?

Pushkin revisited that rusted "fountain of love, fountain alive" only in a new romantic meditation, which he called *The Fountain of Bakhchisarai:*

> I visited Bakhchisarai,
> Its palace now forgot, abandoned.
> Amidst its quiet halls medieval
> I wandered where that scourge of peoples,
> The Tatar fierce, once held his feasts,
> And, after raids of dread and horror,
> Did laze in splendid languor sweet.
> That bliss still breathes and is remembered
> In restful garden groves, it seems:
> The waters' playing, roses' blushing,
> The vineyard grapes so thick and luscious,
> And on the walls the gold still gleams.
> There's still wrought iron tracery:
> Cages, behind which, in their spring,
> Clasping an amber rosary,
> Young silenced wives would sigh, not sing.
> I saw the great Khans' burial place,
> Great rulers' final residence.
> I saw the columns o'er the graves
> With marble turbans crowned, but fraying,
> It seemed to me the will of Fate
> Was speaking loud and clear, and praying.
> Where are the Khans and harem now?
> Around all's still and drear, hope-killing,
> Yes, all has changed. Yet that's not how
> I thought back then, with my heart brimming:
> ...The roses' breath, the fountains' purl
> Against my will made me oblivious,
> Unwillingly my thoughts did whirl,
> Myself not sure why I was nervous;
> A shade did flit about the palace,
> A maiden flashed before my eyes...
> Whose shade, my friends, was it I saw?
> Tell me, whose was the form so tender
> Who haunted me there for so long,
> Indelible, with me forever?

Was it Yekaterina Rayevskaya? To that "remarkable woman" Pushkin wrote *The flying wisps of clouds are thinning, scattering far.* Or perhaps was it her sister Maria? Some scholars believe Maria was the "one love of my soul" to whom Pushkin dedicated the narrative poem *Poltava.* She herself (a faithful "Decembrist wife" who joined her husband, Sergey Volkonsky, willingly in Siberian exile for 30 years) demurred, saying only: "as a poet, Pushkin felt obliged to be in love with every pretty woman and fine young girl...In truth he adored only his Muse, and poeticized all he saw."

Perhaps all these "secret love" theories merit a digression (Pushkin was quite fond of digressions himself, especially on this very topic).

> Let's speak now of the strangenesses of love
> (I can't imagine other conversation).

Pushkin was above all a poet of love. No other writer in Russia before him or after ever expressed so much love in so many ways. Love for him was not so much a choice as an unstoppable universal force, of which he was but a blessèd conductor. Love, protean and unpredictable, is in almost everything he wrote. And all he wrote, in the end, is really about love in one way or other. Love at first sight, or at long last, by chance or by arrangement, erotic or platonic, sexual or spiritual, jealous or calm, ironic or accepting, ruefully bitter, or reconciled and uncomplaining, bitter and murderous or soft, faithful and accepting: all kinds of love were his theme, love in which every happiness seemed to lead to grief, yet every grief seemed to lead to happiness. Pushkin captured that mysterious quality of love, which defies definition precisely because it can only be felt. Yet though we cannot define it, love is the mystery that defines us, and in Pushkin's words "there is no truth where there is no love."

Certain Soviet or postmodern Pushkinists (Freudian Marxists, or vice-versa) obsess (perhaps enviously?) over every name on Pushkin's jokingly compiled so-called "Don Juan list." (Its very existence is hardly "politically correct"). But hindsight can be uncomprehending, and often misses the wood for the trees. All Pushkin's "experience, sired of errors grievous," blessed us with a transcendent wealth of lyrical love poetry. We should all re-read a letter Pushkin once wrote, rebuking his friend Prince Vyazemsky's interest in gossipy memoirs of some of the stormier details of Byron's intimate life:

> Leave curiosity to the mob, and be at one with genius. We know all we need to know about Byron. We saw him enthroned in his glory, and in his torments, as a great soul, and then we saw him buried in a Greece reborn. Who needs to see him on his potty? The mob greedily reads confessions and memoirs because, in its baseness, it gloats at the humiliations of the great and the weaknesses of the mighty. At the discovery of any filth, the mob cheers: "he was base, like us; he was filthy, like us!" Lying scoundrels! He was base and filthy, but not like you at all – he was different!

Even Pushkin's earlier, earthier love poems had a unique economy and sense of balance he'd imbibed from childhood mastery of the classics. Even his teenaged half-drunken and half-joking odes to easy women were light and graceful, eschewing vulgarity, which, for Pushkin, was one of the ultimate sins. Yet whether it was the Caucasus, as Gogol supposed, that released the last chains on the freedom of his thoughts, or a new inner harmony that sprang forth from communion at dawn with a cypress tree, the Pushkin that emerged from Southern wanderings became – till death – a far more spiritual, meditative, inward-looking, and fundamentally mysterious poet.

Mystery is indeed essential to all great poetry. Pushkin's favourite author, Shakespeare, shrouded himself in his works with such anonymous mystery that, as Mark Twain once quipped, "Shakespeare must be the most famous man who never lived." Whoever indeed was the genius of our English language, one senses his fondness for anonymity, his joy in strolling through humanity incognito, like his Henry V on the eve of the battle of Agincourt, or like his pensive "fantastical duke of dark corners" in *Measure for Measure.* Even "the Bard's" most personal works, the sonnets, don't reveal much about him: the focus is on the object of his love, on her qualities:

My mistress' eyes are nothing like the sun;
Coral is far more red than her lips red;
If snow be white, why then, her breasts are dun;
If hair be wires, black wires grow on her head.
I have seen roses damasked, red and white
But no such roses see I in her cheeks;
And in some perfumes there is more delight
Than in the breath that from my mistress reeks.
I love to hear her speak, yet well I know
That music hath a far more pleasing sound;
I grant I never saw a goddess go;
My mistress, when she walks, walks on the ground:
And yet, by heaven I think my love as rare
As any she belied with false compare. *(Sonnet CXXX).*

With Pushkin, the mystery is less *her qualities* than *his own feelings.* We learn not how she looks but how she makes him feel: otherwise, – deliberately no clues – none of our business! (In an age where marriage was all too often imposed without love, love all too often arose without the bonds of marriage. Many of Pushkin's *amours* were unhappily married; their reputations needed guarding.) He often struck whole lines and stanzas which he felt might identify who had inspired them (See "*A drizzly day fizzed out, a drizzly night's dull haze*").

When *The flying wisps of clouds are thinning, scattering far* was published, Pushkin was furious; its last lines' mention of his beloved's astronomical interests, compromised, he feared, the stargazing Yekaterina Rayevskaya. But in truth secrecy and mysteriousness were more than just practical. They were part of the very sadness of love itself:

What is there is my name for you?
It will die out, like sad waves sounding
Their last, on distant shorelines pounding,
As in deaf woods night's sounds ring through.

Within your album it will leave
A deadened trail, like in description
To tracings on a grave's description
In a strange language you can't read.

His poems are more sublime for being utterly independent of whom they're for, or how she looks, or acts, or what she does or says... She just is. That is enough. Details and reasons would be superfluous (and nothing is superfluous in Pushkin). As the Talmud says, "the love that has a reason lasts only as long as the reason; but the love that has no reason lasts until the end of time." Here Pushkin is like Shakespeare: his words express feeling through sound as well as sense.

If his focus turns from subjective feelings to identifiable qualities of the object of his love, this, paradoxically, is a clue his feelings aren't too serious (e. g. *Confession, To a Kalmyk Girl, Round Izhora I was riding*). Even in these more jocular poems, less is more. He gives just enough detail to frame the outpouring of his own heart... And so Pushkin with unparalleled intensity conveys the feeling, the experience of being in love. He takes us ever more deeply into his own revelations, fears, hopes, elations – even brings us along with him as he wakes his love, as it seems that with Love itself:

Our whole room with an amber sparkling
Gleams in the dawn...

True, Pushkin dedicated certain love poems by name, or wrote others into his beloved's albums. Yet mostly he liked to keep his love in a kind of blissful Rembrandt twilight. To guess (with prurient diligence) just whom any given masterpiece is for is to singe that lovely murk with searchlights... why need we seek in vain for Pushkin's "secret love"? Why must we pry into whom it was that the poet loved "with such unsated endless passion"?

Alone she'd understand, decipher
My blur of verse, confused, unclear;
Alone within my heart she'd fire
The lamp of love that's pure, austere!
Alas, in vain such aspirations!
My prayers, all my invocations,
My heart's grief – all – she would not heed!
Of cries of earthly joys and passions,
Of the divine, she had no need!

Cherchez la femme! Pushkin's "secret love" may have been the most famous woman who never lived (at least to Russians). But you won't find her in the archives... She is eternal... She is Woman.

Alas, Pushkin's idyll by Southern seas and mountains was not eternal, but ended abruptly, like the above digression. In September 1820 he was summoned for duty to the desolate flatlands and muddy lanes of Kishinev, Moldavia, whence General Inzov had moved headquarters. There wasn't much to do, and Pushkin found little to like about the place at first, except its dubious honour as the supposed site of exile of the great Roman poet Ovid. In November 1820 Pushkin begged leave to visit Kamenka, the Ukrainian estate of General Rayevsky's relatives, the Davydov family. Granted two weeks, he stayed six months. General Inzov extended his leave and, like a good-natured father, wrote the Davydovs: "I've been so worried about Mr. Pushkin. I feared that in spite of cruel frosts, biting winds, and blizzards he might try to come back, and something bad might happen on those awful roads in the steppes. But after your letter, I am calm and hope your Excellency won't permit him to travel till he regains his health." On December 4, 1820, Pushkin wrote to his publisher and friend Gnedich (the *Iliad's* translator into Russian): "Eight months already, my dear Nikolai Ivanovich, I've been leading the life of a nomad. First the Caucasus, then the Crimea, then Moldavia, and now I'm in Kiev Province, at the estate of the Davydovs', very dear, intelligent brothers of General Rayevsky. My time is spent twixt aristocratic dinners and democratic arguments... a colourful mix of the most original and famous minds in Russia are here. There are few women, but much champagne, much ardent wit, many books, and just a few poems." Most of those "original and famous minds" at the estate were in secret revolutionary societies; one of those "few women," the Polish beauty Karolina Sobanskaya (yet another candidate for "Pushkin's" "secret love"), was a secret police spy, snooping on "conspiracies twixt Château Lafitte and Veuve Clicquot." While everyone was toasting to uprisings in Spain and Portugal, the Americas, Naples, and Greece, the Cricket was busy writing *The Prisoner of the Caucasus* and then *The Fountain of Bakchisarai.*

Not that the elder Davydov brother needed much excuse for tippling... Pushkin described him as: "a second Falstaff: lecherous, gluttonous, cowardly, boastful, shrewd, amusing, unscrupulous, whiny, and fat. Yet he had one distinctive feature which gave him still more charm: he was married. Shakespeare never got around to marrying off his bachelor; Falstaff died without learning the joys of becoming a cuckold and a father." Pushkin may have had a brief affair with Davydov's wife Aglaia (whose famously easy virtue prompted sharp epigrams from him in Russian and French). He also wrote this sweet little trifle for the Davydovs' daughter Adèle:

> Play on, Adèle,
> And know no sadness.
> The Graces dwell
> With you in gladness.
> Your cradle bells
> They gently rattled.
> Your springtime youth
> Is calm, clear, smooth.
> For sweet sensations
> You're born for sure.
> So catch elation
> On the run!
> Your youth so boisterous
> Give up to love,
> In this world's noises,
> Still love, Adèle,
> My pipe's soft swell.

By March 1821 Pushkin was back in Kishinev. General Inzov, angry that the government had not paid the exiled poet's salary, took him into his own house, full of exotic plants and an aviary. Pushkin was fond of "good old Ivan Nikitich," who admired his talent (even for such forbidden songs to freedom as *To a Bird* and *The Captive*) and looked the other way at Pushkin's pranks and eccentricities. Kishinev was a frontier town, peopled by many ethnic groups. Pushkin, who had himself been teased for being "African," was not only free of any prejudice towards other peoples, but fascinated and sympathetic. Sketchpad in hand, he'd stroll round town in a Moldavian cassock, or a fez hat and Turkish robes, or in Hasidic garb... Pushkin had various Jewish girlfriends; his sympathy for the plight of a poor Jewish family is plain from his fragment *The lantern in the Jewish hovel.* He thrilled, too, in the Greek struggle for independence and had an affair with a Greek lady rumoured to have been Byron's mistress (*To a Greek Woman*). Entranced by a gypsy girl, he ran off to join her troupe for a while. His memories from this adventure set the scene for his tale *The Gypsies...*

The gypsies in a noisy throng
Through Bessarabia are wandering.
This night their tattered tents along
A riverbank are pitched, meandering.
Like freedom, happy is their rest,
Peaceful their sleep beneath the heavens.
Between the wagon wheels are decked
The rugs that they hang up like curtains.
Gathered around a fire's blaze,
A family cooks; in empty fields
Beyond their tent their horses graze,
Their trained bear's sprawled out at his ease.
All's full of life among the steppes:
The tranquil cares of roving clans
Readied to move off in the morning,
Wives sing, kids shriek; throughout the band
Their travelling anvil pounds its clonking...
But soon upon the nomad's troupe
A sleepy silence shrinks and falls,
And in the stillness nothing moves:
A few dogs bark, some horses snort...

General Inzov
"*The good Ivan Nikitich*"

His amorous adventures, biting wit, and keenly felt sense of personal honour involved him in about twenty duels during this period – all bloodless, some even jocular.

Yet his friend Colonel Liprandi recalled: "When face to face with death, when a man fully discovers himself, Pushkin was possessed of the highest degree of inner calm, in spite of his emotionality. When the time came to take his paces, he seemed cold as ice." In one duel, while his opponent was aiming and firing at him, Pushkin calmly ate ripe cherries, then cast away his gun. In another duel, fought in a wild snowstorm at sixteen paces, he deliberately missed, then, when his opponent shot and missed, he offered his opponent a chance to hit him from twelve paces. The duel ended with his opponent saying: "you stand up to bullets as well as you write" – and Pushkin embracing him. Periodically, Inzov would try to keep his protégé out of trouble by putting him under house arrest and dragging him off to church. Pushkin, ever a prankster, taught Inzov's beloved parrot obscenities in two languages – quite startling an Archbishop who had been invited for tea. Pushkin wrote an ironic note in verse to Davydov:

> Now I've grown smart, started pretending,
> And fast, and pray, with faith heart-rending
> That God forgives my acts perverse
> Just as the Tsar forgives my verse.
> As Inzov fasts, my soul he's saving:
> For him I've quit Parnassian raving,
> My lyre, my sinful gift from Fate,
> For books of hours and midday prayers,
> Dried mushrooms on my Lenten plate.

While in Kishinev, perhaps rebelling against the pieties being imposed on him, as a prank, he wrote the *Gabrieliad*, a sparkling "spot of mischief," spoofing the story of the Immaculate Conception. This irreverent way of killing time would nearly kill him on charges of blasphemy and atheism. Only on Tsar Nicholas I's personal command would charges later be dropped. Its last lines read cruelly in light of the poet's final days.

> But fleet the days, and slowly greying time
> With silent silver will anoint my head,
> And solemn marriage with a lovely wife
> Will cause me to an altar to be led.
> O Joseph's dear and beautiful consoler!
> I beg you now, and sink on bended knee:
> Protector and defender of all cuckolds,
> I beg you then cast blessings over me.
> Bequeath me carefree joy and resignation,
> Bequeath me patience, time and time enough,
> And restful sleep, trusting my wife's devotion,
> And peace at home, and for my neighbour love.

Fate would deny him these things, yet back then the Cricket was happy as a lark. In May 1823 he began work on his great novel in verse *Eugene Onegin*. He soon reported to his friend, the poet Delvig: "I'm writing a new long poem, a novel in verse, in which I babble freely on whatever I please, beyond all limits... Publication is quite unthinkable; the censor would cry if he saw it... Lord only knows when we'll be able to read it together... I write with rapture, and cannot stop." During his southern exile Pushkin wrote several chapters of the novel, concluding with *Tatyana's Letter to Onegin*.

In July 1823, Pushkin was transferred to serve under the Governor-General of Southern Russia, Count Mikhail Vorontsov, headquartered in the port of Odessa, which was then "a half-Italian *porto franco*" – all signs were in Italian as well as Russian. Pushkin frolicked at the beach, in the opera, in cafés and restaurants, befriended a former Moorish corsair named Ali, and, pining by the sea, considered fleeing Russia forever.

But leaving General Inzov's tender care, "a new sadness pangs my breast: I miss the chains I've left behind." And, with more distractions, life in Odessa was much more expensive. His salary was paid sporadically, and he had only gotten 500 rubles for his manuscript of the *Prisoner of the Caucasus.* (There was no copyright law in Russia until 1828, and even that first weak statute was so weakly enforced that Pushkin was helpless all his life to prevent pirates from robbing him of thousands by copying his works without his consent). However, as modern Russia's first professional writer, ("I see a poem as a cobbler would a pair of boots, as a finished good, which I intend to sell for a profit"), he negotiated a great deal for his manuscript of *The Fountain of Bakhchisarai:* three thousand rubles – more than four years pay – soon spent with abandon. Pushkin later poignantly described his memories of life in Odessa in a poetic fragment omitted from *Eugene Onegin* ("*And so, I lived then in Odessa*"). Again and again, Pushkin dreamed of escaping Russia for Italy, immersed himself in Italian culture (having begun to learn "the tongue of golden Italy" in Kishinev). And he fell in love with Amalia Riznich, a Venetian Jewish beauty who had come to Odessa from Trieste with a dullish husband, a Serbian trader. Amalia is thought to have inspired such poems as *Will you forgive my jealous reverie, Into your bower, my friend so tender, Bound for your distant country's shoreline, Beneath the blue skies of your native land,* and *Invocation* (though the latter is more likely an improvisation on a theme by Barry Cornwall). But she did not stay in Odessa long, and Pushkin was soon (briefly) head over heels in love again with Karolina Sobanskaya, paramour of Witte, head of the secret police in the South (and perhaps the subject of his passionate *Night*).

During Pushkin's last months in Odessa, it is widely supposed that his love was yet another Polish beauty, Countess Elizaveta Vorontsova, wife of the almighty Governor-General of Southern Russia. She is yet another candidate for the role of "Pushkin's secret love" – more than 30 drawings of her are in Pushkin's manuscripts. Their strolls by the sea may be immortalized in *Eugene Onegin's "Pedal Digression,"* Chapter I, xxix-xxxiv, though Nabokov argued that only one of those "sweet feet, sweet feet that I treasured" was Vorontsova's, while the other foot was Maria Rayevskaya's. Many say it is Vorontsova who gave Pushkin the ring with the Hebrew inscription ("Joy"), which he treasured all his life. (He bequeathed it on his deathbed to the poet Zhukovsky, from whom it passed to the novelist Turgenev. In 1917 the ring disappeared). Supposedly that ring was his *Talisman.*

Pushkin's sister Olga claimed Vorontsova wrote to Pushkin when he was sent to further exile; some think this is the context for his thrilling *The Burned Letter.* Did she dare risk correspondence with the disgraced poet, knowing all too well his mail was perlustrated? Or is *The Burned Letter* just a riff on an elegy by Clément Marot that Pushkin had learned in the Lycée? Another work written in Odessa, *The Demon,* was, according to Pushkin himself, about the paralyzing effects of doubt, cynicism, and negative emotions. Yet many suppose its subject to be General Rayevsky's oldest son, Alexander, the open, practically official, paramour of Countess Vorontsova, and thus a false friend to the poet.

Pushkin's rocky relations with her husband, Count Vorontsov were marred by far more than mere jealousy (Vorontsov, notorious for his own philandering, is said to have been indifferent to his wife's dalliances). Formal and stiff, Vorontsov modeled himself on the English lords with whom he'd been schooled in Cambridge. Yet fine English manners could not conceal his ruthlessness in cowing the uneasy new southern provinces of the empire. Though not above dabbling in trade, and using his official position to profit from his own commercial activities, Vorontsov railed against Pushkin's habit of writing poems instead of reports while on duty. He tried to force Pushkin to do bureaucratic work, and ordered him to compose an official report about a plague of locusts attacking the Kherson Peninsula. Pushkin defiantly replied:

> To write a memorandum is completely foreign to my nature. For seven years I've ignored such duties, never wrote a single legal report, never tried to curry favour with any bosses...But I do not consider these years lost. Writing poems is my profession. ...Just because I'm paid 700 rubles a year doesn't mean I am obliged to serve. I accept these 700 rubles a year not as a bureaucrat's salary, but as compensation for my involuntary exile... If the Count wishes me to retire, I am ready.

"The Cricket" was officially forced to report on the locusts. But his "memorandum" was naught but this little verse (oft taught to students struggling to master the eccentricities of Russian perfective and imperfective verbs):

> The locust host was flying, was flying,
> Alighting,
> Sat dining, sat dining – all-smiting,
> Then went back to flying.

Vorontsov's deputy recalled the Count asking: "You seem to like Pushkin. Can't you control him, and get him to do anything useful?" "Excuse me, sir, but people like him can only be great poets." "Well then," said the Count, "what use are they at all?"

Naturally, Pushkin resented being sneered at. "Vorontsov is a vandal, a Court boor, and petty egotist. All he saw in me was a tenth-class collegiate assessor, and, I must say, I see myself a bit differently." Pushkin wrote several epigrams about Count Vorontsov:

> Half a milord, half merchant, he:
> Half a savant, half ignoramus,
> Just half a knave, but hopes inflame us
> That soon at last he'll be complete!

Vorontsov denounced the poet to St. Petersburg as a radical, urging his removal. An excuse came when police read his letter to his friend Küchelbecker: "Want to know what I'm up to? Writing romantic poems, and taking lessons in pure atheism. There's an Englishman here, a deaf philosopher, who has scribbled some 1000 pages just to prove there could not possibly exist any intelligent Being, Creator and Regulator, while demolishing weak proofs of the immortality of the soul. Not as comforting as you'd think, though, alas, he's probably right..."

Doubt under the Tsars was nearly as grave a crime as faith would one day be under the commissars. By order of Tsar Alexander I, Pushkin was stripped of all rank and duties, and put under house arrest at his parents' estate in Pskov Province, "under the supervision of local authorities." His carriage was commanded "to travel exactly following the itinerary given him by the governor of Odessa – straight to the city of Pskov; he may not rest anyplace along the way, but immediately upon arrival in Pskov must report to the Governor."

A day before leaving, Pushkin wrote his poetic farewell: *To the Sea.* He set off northwards on July 31, 1824. Waiting for fresh post-horses in the town of Mogilev, he recognized a fellow Lycéen. Midst bearhugs and tears, he was dragged off to a grand impromptu Russian midnight feast and poetry reading: at four in the morning, the carousers tried dunking their beloved bard in a champagne bath... He was sent on to his family home, which he reached on August 9, 1824. The second exile foretold by Madame Kirchof had come to pass.

"Half a milord, half merchant, he..." Count Vorontsov at billiards with a mask

Exile in Mikhailovskoye. 1824–1826

Almost a week's hard riding from Moscow or St. Petersburg, "in this abandoned hole/ This shrine of desolation, frost, and snowstorms," Mikhailovskoye was a modest manor house, with a park and garden and a few cottages for the surrounding serfs. The whole family was in the living room when he arrived (his father was playing French songs on the guitar). But "being with my family has only added to my griefs and sorrows. The government was brazen enough to request that my father act as its agent in persecuting me... Father was craven enough to accept this 'proposal', which makes him play utterly false with me. As a result every moment I'm not in bed I spend either on horseback or in the fields. Anything that reminds me of the sea grieves me. A fountain's murmur makes me truly ill, and I think a clear blue sky would make me weep with rage – though here, thank God, our sky is grey, and our moon is exactly a turnip." (See *A drizzly day's fizzed out.*) Pushkin's father soon gave up, (or refused – versions differ) informing against his own son, and left. The whole family was gone by November 1824, leaving the poet blissfully alone with a few household serfs and Arina Rodionovna, his doting nanny. He had always adored her – and she him. Her constant care, good-natured affection, and singsong speech, full of proverbs and phrases from fairy tales, made her truly beloved. He called her "mama, mamushka," and, after the ruinously expensive oysters and French wines of Odessa's restaurants, he revelled in her homegrown buckwheat kasha, baked potatoes, pickled vegetables, hard-boiled eggs and stewed apples, her home-made berry jams – and firewater. Pushkin wrote a friend in Odessa:

> I'm stuck in the utter boondocks, bored, with nothing to do. There's no sea here, or southern sky, or Italian opera – though at least there's no locusts, nor Milords Worontsov. My solitude is utter – magnificent idleness! In the evenings I hear fairy tales told by my nanny, the original nanny of my Tatyana. She is my only friend, and only when with her am I not bored.

Arina Rodionovna's is one love that was not secret. Her caring and spiritual warmth in bleak times are remembered in *A Winter Evening* and *To my Nanny*, as well as *Eugene Onegin* and *I went back again*. Pushkin recorded dozens of songs she taught him, as well as seven fairy tales, which he would transform into verse while keeping the folktale elements and embellishments passed to him by oral tradition. One of those folktale flourishes became the immortal first line of a prologue he added to *Ruslan and Lyudmila*'s second edition. Those who don't know *Ruslan and Lyudmila* may yet recognize the line which sister Masha in Chekhov's *The Three Sisters* repeats as if entranced:

> A green oak grows by a cove curving...

Other consolations from "magnificent idelness" were his neighbours in Trigorsk, the estate of the family of Praskovya Aleksandrovna Osipova-Wulf. Pushkin liked making his entrance leaping into her dining room through the open French windows. He befriended her young son Aleksey Wulf, and courted all of Aleksey's pretty sisters:

> Oh, the hermit's life's a marvel!
> In Trigorsk we play till dusk,
> Here at home till dawn we dodder....
> Days to love are given up,
> Nights are ruled by our good tankards,
> And we're either deadly drunkards,
> Or we're smitten dead by love.

In Trigorsk, Pushkin wrote his light-hearted *Confession* for Praskovya's stepdaughter Alina Osipova, while in the album of Praskovya's daughter Evpraksinya Vulf ("Zizi, the crystal of my soul"), he wrote *If perchance life should deceive you.* In June 1825, the sisters were visited by their beautiful cousin, Anna Petrovna Kern, whom the poet had met six years ago in St. Petersburg. The night before Kern left for home, Pushkin gave her a manuscript of Chapter II of *Eugene Onegin*. Stuck within its pages was the poem *To **** (*A wondrous moment I remember*) – the most famous love lyric, perhaps, in the Russian language, set to music by Pushkin's friend Glinka, as well as many other composers (p. 261).

He rather shocked the sleepy local priest in Trigorsk by requesting a memorial mass for "the Boyar Georgiy" – Lord Byron. Despite his light-hearted scepticism on matters of faith, Pushkin often visited the local Svyatogorsky Monastery, and its chief monk, Father Ioann. He enjoyed the monastic library, with its old texts and chronicles, as well as the monastery's fairs, at which he would wander amongst the crowds, hearing the tales of beggars, pilgrims, and "holy fools." It was all grist for his blank verse tragedy, *Boris Godunov*. He would wake before dawn, write by candlelight, and sometimes not leave his little room for days. Verse was pouring out of him. He wrote Nikolai Rayevsky: "My soul has reached full strength: I can create!"

On November 7, 1825, he wrote Prince Vyazemsky: "I have finished my tragedy. I read it aloud to myself, then clapped till my palms hurt, cheering: "Hooray, Pushkin! Hooray! You son-of-a-bitch!" (That was nearly the only applause for this play Pushkin would ever hear. Its public performance was forbidden until 1866.) The beautiful, sonorous verse of *Boris Godunov,* and its profound meditation on the nature of power, ethics, and the individual have never really crossed the language barrier; it is known in the West as the plot for the great opera by Mussorgsky. As Pushkin himself wrote: "what is the play about? The fate of a man is the fate of a people." Some consider it the Russian language's finest drama. Russia's most eminent critic, Vissarion Belinsky judged: "Like a giant among pygmies, Pushkin's *Boris Godunov* looms above the host of quasi-Russian tragedies, in splendid sober solitude, in its exalted, unimaginable purity of style, its noble, classical perfection."

On November 19, 1825 Tsar Alexander I died childless; Pushkin reacted: "As a loyal subject, I ought to be sad at the Tsar's death, but as a poet, I look forward in joyful anticipation..." Alexander's oldest brother Constantine was expected to assume the throne, but due to his morganatic marriage to a Polish Catholic in 1823, had renounced his claim in favour of his brother Nicholas. Yet few knew this; many soldiers and officers, considering Constantine the true heir, refused to swear allegiance to Nicholas. On December 14, 1825, in what would be called the Decembrist Uprising, officers and soldiers led by nobles from secret revolutionary societies, gathered in Senate Square in St. Petersburg (where the Bronze Horseman stands) demanding: "Constantine and a Constitution." The crowd refused to leave; shooting began: St. Petersburg's governor Miloradovich (who'd been so kind to Pushkin) was killed. Nicholas had the crowd dispersed with grapeshot, and "in the square the snow ran red with blood."

Police dumped the wounded with the corpses of those shot dead into the frozen Nevá. Following a six-month police inquest, five Decembrists were hanged, and 120 were exiled to Siberia.

Pushkin had planned to escape to Petersburg upon hearing of Alexander I's death, and even forged himself a fake internal travel passport. It describes one "Aleksey Khokhlov, height, two arshins, four vershky [about 5'3"], dark red hair, blue eyes, clean-shaven, age 29." But hardly had Pushkin set out for the capital, when a hare crossed his path; then he met an Orthodox priest. At such portents of bad luck, Pushkin, ever superstitious, if not ever religious, turned back. Seeking solace in Shakespeare, and perhaps sensing (though unaware of) the bloody events taking place in Petersburg, he pondered the curious quirks of accidents, and the role of individual fate in history:

> Rereading *The Rape of Lucrece*, one of Shakespeare's weaker poems, I thought to myself: what if it had just occurred to Lucrece to give Tarquin a good slap in the face? What if, perhaps, that would have cooled his ardour, and he'd have had to retreat in shame? Lucrece would not have stabbed herself, Collatine would not have been enraged, Brutus would not have banished the Kings, and the world and history would be utterly different. And so it seems we owe the Republic, the consuls, the dictators, the censors, and the Caesars all to one overwrought scene of seduction a bit like something that happened the other day to our neighbours in the Novorzhevsky district. The thought of parodying both this story and Shakespeare at once occurred to me, and, being unable to withstand such double temptation, I wrote this little tale in two mornings. It is my habit to date my writings... *Count Nulin* was written December 13–14, 1825. There are strange coincidences in life. (*Note on Count Nulin*, 1830.)

In *Count Nulin*, Pushkin pokes fun at his "Lucrece," yet empathizes:

> There by the windowsill she sits,
> And Volume Four on her lap flits
> Of a most sentimental novel:
> *The Love of Elise and Armand, or*
> *Letters Twixt Two Families.*
> A classic tale of morals strong,
> Amazingly long, long, long, long,
> Most proper, teaching right and wrong,
> Without romantic fantasies.
> At first Natalia Pavlovna was
> Reading, raptured, serious,

But somehow soon she drifted off,
Then out the window came a quarrel
Between a goat and courtyard mongrel:
She was transfixed in watching this.
All round a bunch of boys were laughing.
Beneath her windows, though, there mourned
A gaggle of wild geese, their cackling
Inspired by rain-drenched rooster's dawn.
Three ducks were splashing in a puddle;
Across the yard an old hag went
To hang old linen on the fence;
The weather seemed to presage trouble:
It seemed snow wished to tumble down...
And then a little bell did sound.
Whoever's lived in backwoods gloomy,
My friends, knows, surely all too well,
How distant tinkling bells can truly
At times just make our heartbeats swell.
Is it an old friend out there, lagging,
A bosom pal of our youth dashing?

A year ago, as dawn was breaking on January 11, 1825, Pushkin's beloved "Jeannot," Ivan Pushchin, had arrived; Pushkin, hearing the sleigh bells, rushed in his nightshirt barefoot into the snow to hug him. Soon nanny Arina, with no idea who had come, was hugging both of them. Pushchin, in a secret revolutionary society, could only stay one day. Soon Jeannot would be one of hundreds of Decembrists exiled to Siberia as "criminals against the state."* Yet that one embrace with his best friend in a snowy courtyard has lasted longer than his 30 long years of exile; it is remembered in *My very first and priceless friend.*

* Pushchin's *Notes on Pushkin* brim with the humanitarian warmth and boyish ideals known as "the spirit of the Lycée." However, there are those who ignore all that the good "Jeannot" had to say except two sentences about a little room in Pushkin's home where some serf girls were sewing. "There I saw one figure sharply different from the others...He read my mischievous thought and smiled significantly." The "figure" was Olga Kalashnikova, winsome daughter of the manager of the Pushkin family estate at Boldino. Soviet poet Mikhail Dudin called their fling, which, despite her serfdom, was open and mutual, "the true wonder of 'the wondrous moment'." To*** (*A wondrous moment I remember*) was actually for Anna Kern, though the national poet's passion for a simple peasant girl was splendid for Soviet propaganda. In 1826, Olga, pregnant by Pushkin, left to give birth at her parents' side in Boldino. Pushkin, exiled and under strict surveillance, could do no more than ensure that his friends looked after their child. But little Pavel died shortly after birth. On receiving title to a portion of Boldino in 1830, Pushkin immediately gave Olga her freedom. She then married a petty nobleman, and became owner of a few serfs herself. Pushkin later stood godfather to her son by her new husband.

After Pushchin's sentence, Pushkin risked a possible new term of exile or worse to send that poem to his friend along with his now-famous (and long forbidden) *Message to Siberia.*

As always, friendship and poetry were linked in his imagination, and "it was Poetry that saved me, Poetry, like a consoling angel, and my soul was reborn." Another close friend, the poet Anton Delvig, risked a visit in the spring of 1825, and helped Pushkin compile his first book of poems. Pushkin thanked his friends in an elegy commemorating the Lycée's anniversary, *October 19th,* a cherished part of every Russian poetry anthology. *October 19th* combines the melancholy splendours of the fall with the warm sensation of the poet's lonely glass of wine to heighten his nostalgia as an exile, his hopes – and pining – for his Lycéen friends.

Blaze up, o hearth, in my bare room, my prison.
And you, dear wine, friend of the fall's sharp frost,
Pour joyous tipsiness into my bosom,
Oblivion brief, make bitter cares seem lost.

For I am sad, and without any friend
To drink with, healing woes of separation,
Whose hand I'd clasp in heartfelt admiration
And wish good cheer for many years on end.

The poet, though unforgiven by the Tsar, nonetheless lightheartedly shows compassion for the human being who had banished him:

He's but a man, and slave to time's illusions,
Of rumours, doubts, and passions but a slave,
So let's forgive his unfair persecution:
He captured Paris, founded our Lycée!

Shortly after the official coronation in the the Kremlin of Nicholas I, Pushkin was summoned to Moscow to meet with the new Tsar. It is thought that on his way to that fateful meeting, Pushkin composed his magnificent evocation of the poet's role as the conscience of his nation: *The Prophet.* With images from the Book of Isaiah, Chapter VI, it describes what might be called an operation by the Celestial Surgeon, in which the poet, who once was "babbling, idle, cunning, moody," transforms into an all-seeing, all-hearing vessel of the divine, sensitive and sympathetic to the voice of heaven and earth:

To Heaven's shuddering I hearkened,
And to the lofty angels' flight,
To slithering things in deep seas' night,
And valley grapes grown dull, cold, hardened.

The Prophet is the first of many poems Pushkin would devote to poetry itself, and to the poet's relationship to others (see *The Poet, The Echo, Autumn,* etc.). *The Prophet* rises above politics and sounds a clarion call for the poet to remember his divine mission in life:

> Arise, thou prophet, see, and hearken,
> By my will let your soul be stirred,
> And, wandering by lands and waters,
> Burn people's hearts up with my word.

Moscow and St. Petersburg. 1826–1831

> And so our maiden was enjoying
> The endless long dull road's delights:
> They rode for seven days and nights.
>
> But now they're near. Before them glistening
> Already white-stoned Moscow runs,
> Like fire, with golden crosses quivering,
> Its ancient domes gleam in the sun.
> Oh brothers! How my heart was happy
> To see the churches, bell-towers clanging,
> The gardens, courtyards, crescents' sweep
> Before me opened suddenly!
> How often in my exile grieving,
> Throughout my errant odyssey,
> Have I thought, Moscow, but of thee!
> Moscow! How Russian hearts are heaving
> At all that merges in that sound!
> How much in us it makes resound!

Pushkin arrived in Moscow on September 8, 1826, and was immediately brought to the Tsar in the Kremlin's Chudov Monastery, without so much as a chance to shave, wash, or dress for the occasion. Most of of the condemned Decembrists had been found with his poems in their possession. Many, naïve and idealistic, had little in the way of coherent plans or ideology but the sweet hopes his verse had stirred. Secret agent A.K. Boshnyak was dispatched to Mikhalovskoye to check whether Pushkin had been involved in seditious activity. Boshnyak reported that the poet was well liked by the peasants near his home for his good humour and generosity, despite his odd habit of jotting down their old wives' tales and folksongs. Oblivious to politics, he spent his days horseback riding, swimming, and strolling the countryside in a broad straw hat and colourful Russian peasant shirt. Very suspicious indeed! Worth further investigation!

Pushkin spoke with the Tsar for over three hours, and did not deny that many Decembrists were his dearest friends. He added that the harsh sentences meted out against them had not changed his feelings. Asked what he would have done if he had been in St. Petersburg on December 14th, he bravely replied that he would have joined his friends in Senate Square. The Tsar ordered him never again to write against the government, to submit all future writings personally to the Tsar for censorship, then announced that his exile was over. That evening the Tsar remarked: "Today I spoke with the smartest man in Russia." Yet despite the royal compliment, the Third Department, or imperial secret police, ordered Pushkin put under constant personal surveillance. (The poet liked to joke "The Tsar may love, but the master of his hounds loves not.") Why was the poet freed? Was it an attempt of an unpopular sovereign to improve his ratings? Pushkin was then the darling of the liberal intelligentsia of both capitals of Russia. When he gave a public reading of his *Boris Godunov* at the home of a friend in Moscow, it brought down the house:

Tsar Nicholas I

> He read his verse superbly. Unlike the usual style of declaiming verse in a singsong monotone, he spoke completely naturally, simply, clearly – yet so poetically, and with such animation! We all were beside ourselves: some flushed, some shivered; our hair stood on end, we laughed, we cried...when he was done, a hush fell on us all, then we mobbed him.

But one of those who "mobbed him" had been an informant for the secret police. Pushkin was reprimanded for not submitting his play to the Tsar before reading it aloud. Its performance was soon forbidden. Pushkin's drawings from this time depict gallows and hanged or exiled "friends, brothers, and comrades." Surrounded instead by "spies, whores, and drunkards," he pined again for the simplicity and peace of country life, for his nanny Arina Rodionovna – and she for him (*To my Nanny*). Old and new friends, including the great exiled Polish poet, Adam Mickiewicz, and even the boisterous company of gypsy dancers and singers did not much console the poet.

In January 1827 a police proceeding began against him for an ode which contained the following provocative lines:

> No more do ancient thrones cause awe;
> Our chains have fallen, and the Law,
> Propped up by freedom now, proclaims that all are equal.
> We cried out "bliss!" in great throngs cheerful!
> Oh misery! Mad dream gone wrong!
> Where's freedom? Where's the law? Unfettered
> Above us just the axe does reign.
> We've overthrown the Tsar, but killers and cruel henchmen
> Are our new chosen Tsars! Oh horror! Oh, what shame!

Pushkin was forced to testify and prove these lines came from a poem submitted to the censor well before December 1825, and thus had nothing to do with the brutal suppression of the Decembrists. Even though it was beyond question that the work was about the poet André Chénier, guillotined in 1794 during Robespierre's Reign of Terror, the matter was only closed in July 1828. (No one could foresee how accurately those lines would describe the Bolshevik Revolution).

For the next four years Pushkin lived several months each year in Moscow and St. Petersburg. The death and exile of his best friends had deepened his loneliness; ever more he longed for a wife, a home, a family. In May 1826 he proposed to Sofia Pushkina, a distant cousin, but nothing came of it. In May 1827, before leaving Moscow to see his parents in St. Petersburg, Pushkin wrote in the album of his new love Yekaterina Ushakova, *If they send me far from you*. Ushakova adored Pushkin and his poetry. Yet she was blonde, so they never married, for fear her "white head" might cause his death, as prophesied by M-me. Kirchof. They stayed friends; Ushakova's album has many (often whimsical) Pushkin drawings, and his famous so-called "Don Juan list."

In St. Petersburg, ever at work on *Eugene Onegin*, Pushkin renewed relations with Anna Kern, and was inseparable from his Lycée friend Delvig. On the anniversary of the hanging of his Decembrist friends, he wrote the poem *Arion*. He also began a historical novel about his great-grandfather, *The Blackamoor of Peter the Great*, written during a return visit to Mikhailovskoye. It was plotted to be something of a Russian *Othello* in prose. However Pushkin set the novel aside after six chapters. Its crucial scene is sadly revealing of own insecurities and self-doubts in seeking a wife. The Moor Ibrahim speaks with Tsar Peter:

Alexander Pushkin. Portrait by Vasily Tropinin, 1827

> "If I were minded to marry, would the young girl's parents consent? After all, my looks..."
>
> "Your looks? What nonsense! Why aren't you just fine? A young girl should respect the will of her parents, and let's see what old Gavrila Rzhevsky will say if I myself am your matchmaker!" With these words the Tsar summoned his sleigh and left Ibrahim sunk in profoundest meditation.
>
> "To marry!" thought the African. "Why not? Am I really doomed to spend my life in loneliness, and never know the highest pleasures and responsibilities of a man just because I was born south of the Tropic of Cancer? I can't hope to be loved... So what?! What a childish objection... I won't demand that my wife love me; I'll be content if she is faithful, and will try at least to gain her friendship through constant tenderness, trust, and kindness."

In October 1827, while changing horses in the country station Zalazy, Pushkin was startled to see police manhandling his schoolfriend, the convicted Decembrist and poet, Wilhelm Küchelbecker. "We threw ourselves in each other's arms, but the guards rudely pulled the two of us apart." Days later, on October 19, 1827 a still-affected Pushkin commemorated the Lycée's anniversary: *God help you all, my dear, dear friends.*

Back in St. Petersburg (*Town resplendent, town of beggars*) during 1827–1828 Pushkin unrequitedly courted Annette Olenina (*Oh, blessed he picked with choice capricious*) as the secret police began yet another formal proceeding against him, this time accusing him of blasphemy for his authorship of the *Gabrieliad.* Annette's father was on the board of the commission. Things looked bleak for Pushkin (*Foreboding*) and the matter was only dismissed after the poet wrote a personal letter to Tsar Nicholas, which has not survived. In this time of renewed conflict with authority Pushkin wrote *The Poison Tree.* Characteristically, the poem never preaches; it just tells a story. Yet its powerful images, force, and passionate language lead the reader to ponder all the more deeply the problem of evil compounding itself, and the bitter price of blind subservience to unjust authority.

The almost existential grief and loneliness Pushkin experienced in 1828 can be felt in his sleepless meditation: *Remembrance*, as well as a poem – addressed to life itself – on the occasion of his own birthday: *Gift so futile, gift so random.* In this time Pushkin also wrote the lyric *I loved you once*, a light yet profoundly moving parting gift of love. Again, Pushkin does not singe the twilight of his feelings with glaring and unnecessary details. It does not really matter whom he loved; she is Woman, and his deep and abiding love is unrequited.

Those who know W. B. Yeats' *When you are old and grey* may find it evokes a similar mood. Somehow the very act of putting love into the past tense makes it everlasting; his overwhelming wistfulness, warmth, regret, grief, and true generosity of spirit simultaneously are crowned with a bittersweet irony, as what is lost is paradoxically preserved forever.

Despite his griefs, in 1827–1828, Pushkin kept working on *Eugene Onegin*, completing the work through Chapter VII. In 1828 Pushkin also wrote *Poltava*, a thrilling narrative poem (best known in the West as the basis for Tchaikovsky's opera *Mazeppa*). Maria, the heroine, is asked to choose between her father and the husband she eloped with, his mortal enemy – all against the backdrop of Peter the Great's defeat of the Swedish invasion of Russia in 1709. Pushkin continuously shifts focus to show the points of view of all the characters. On one side is his hero: Tsar Peter the Great, whose eccentric genius and indomitable will created a mighty modern nation, yet not without many innocent victims. On the other side is Peter's bitter foe, the Ukrainian rebel leader Mazeppa, struggling against fate and – at times – his own conscience:

Hushed the Ukrainian night,
And clear its sky; the stars are shining.
The very air, try as it might,
Can't shake off slumber. Only slightly
Some poplars quiver silvery leaves.
But gloomy, weird, unnatural dreams
Still haunt Mazeppa; constellations,
Like eyes that fill with accusations,
Look down at him in mockery.
Those crowded rows of poplar trees
All shake their heads now, silently,
Like judges' whispering secretly,
The summer night's warm murk is stale
And stifling, like a great black jail.

Yet "power corrupts" and Pushkin shows:

That there is nothing he holds cherished,
That all that's good in him has perished,
That there is nothing he does love,
That he would spill our blood like water,
That of all freedom he is scornful,
That there's no homeland in his heart.

Soon after finishing *Poltava*, Pushkin traveled to Moscow. There, in December 1828, at a friend's house, Pushkin saw a dancing master giving lessons; one of the girls in attendance was sixteen-year-old Natalya Nikolayevna Goncharova. "When I first saw her, her beauty was just barely beginning to be noticed in society; I loved her; she turned my head." Yet turned though his head was, it was still able to revolve in other directions. A few days later he left for St. Petersburg, stopping to visit friends in Malinniki, Tver Province, where he had something of a fling again with Annette Vulf, and wrote his wistful *The Little Flower*. Upon returning to St.Petersburg he wrote *When through the noisy streets I wander* (one of his most moving meditations).

Pushkin saw Natalya Goncharova again at a ball in Moscow in March 1830. A week later he had proposed. Natalya, or "Tasha" as she was called, was the youngest – and by far the prettiest of three sisters. Her mother, Natalya Ivanovna Zagryazhskaya, had been the mistress of a dashing Guards officer (who was also the lover of Empress Elizabeth, Tsar Alexander I's wife). After that officer was mysteriously nearly murdered, Natalya Ivanovna was hastily married off to Nikolai Afanasievich Goncharov, scion of a wealthy paper-making family in Kaluga Province. But Goncharov's father squandered the family wealth on extravagances, and Nikolay, Natalya's father, after a fall from a horse, went mad, and became a desperate alcoholic, prone to rages, fits, and profound depression. Natalya's mother saw in these traumas the hand of God, and became quite religious (which did not prevent her open affair with her estate manager). Although Natalya Ivanovna was, by all accounts, a harsh, domineering, and extraordinarily capricious mother, she made sure at least that her daughters spoke good French and danced perfectly – the only two skills society required. By marrying off the prettiest of her three daughters, her "Natalie," in Moscow, "the marketplace of brides," she hoped to fix the family finances.

Natalya Ivanovna was not in the least impressed by the fame and genius of the suitor for her daughter's hand. She disapproved of this "Moor" with scarce means, but ample troubles with the government, this swarthy, impudent imp whose romantic past was so chequered. Natalya Ivanovna would dictate cutting and haughty letters to Pushkin (which her daughter softened with tender post scripta). Imperiously requiring her daughter to feign cold indifference, in hopes Pushkin would go away, Natalya Ivanovna bluntly told Pushkin she hoped someone more "suitable" would come along. But no one else did, for the Goncharovs could provide their daughter no dowry. So Natalya Ivanovna (playing for time) rejected Pushkin's proposal of marriage as vaguely as possible. On May 1, 1829, the poet wrote back:

> On my knees with tears of gratitude I should write you now... your answer is not a refusal; you leave me hope. Yet if I murmur still, and if sadness and bitterness mix with my feelings of joy, do not tax me with ingratitude; I perceive a mother's prudence and tenderness! But forgive as well a heart that is sick at being deprived of happiness. I am leaving for now, but in the depths of my heart I bear the image of that celestial soul whom you have brought to the light of day.

Pushkin left for the Caucasus, where his friend Nikolai Rayevsky, the General's son, was fighting in the Russian army's almost perpetual war in the Caucasus – this time with Turkey. At one stop to change horses, he was invited by a family of nomads to join them for breakfast:

> A young Kalmyk girl, not at all bad looking, was sewing and smoking tobacco. I sat by her. "What's your name?" "***." "How old are you?" "Ten and eight." "What are you sewing?" "Trousers." "For whom?" "Myself." She passed me her pipe and began breakfast: salted tea with mutton fat. She gave me her ladle. I did not wish to offend by refusal and swallowed, trying not too obviously to take a deep breath. I doubt any national cuisine has ever produced anything more revolting. I asked if I could try something else. She gave me a bit of dried mare's meat. Even that was an improvement. But such Kalmyk flirtations alarmed me; I ran from her tent as quickly as possible and fled this Circe of the steppes. (From *A Journey to Arzurum.*)

As his carriage rolled south, Pushkin reflected on this encounter with warmth and humour in *To a Kalmyk Girl* (p. 253). He paused by Mount Mashuk to take the mineral waters where he had once found healing and inspiration. Returning to the mountains would spur several new poems, including *The Monastery on Mount Kazbek.* He proceeded south through Chechnya: "the Chechens hate us. We have driven them from their free pastures, ruined their villages, wiped out whole clans. No wonder hour by hour they slip away further into the mountains and from there carry out their raids against us. The friendship of so-called pacified Chechens is doubtful; they are always in the end willing to support their ungovernable compatriots." Yet he joined the army, and when the Turks made a surprise attack on the Cossack vanguard:

> "He ran from our quarters, leaped on his horse and rode to the front lines. Brave Major Semichev, ordered by General Pashkevich to keep Pushkin safe, had to drag him away by force from the firing line; Pushkin had grabbed a spear from a slain Cossack and charged headlong against the enemy horsemen."

This campaign was Pushkin's only experience of being "abroad." He filled his sketchbooks with drawings of Persian courtiers, minarets, and defiant Turkish prisoners. Coming home, and pining for Natalya, he wrote his sublime: *Upon the Georgian hills there lies the haze of night...* Once back in Moscow he threw himself at the feet of his beloved – again in vain. He later wrote his mother in law:

> What tortures awaited me on my return. Your silence, cold manner, and my indifferent and careless reception by M-lle N... I dared not express myself and left for Petersburg with death in my soul.

Pushkin consoled himself on his way north by staying again with his friends in Tver' Province, and wrote *Round Izhora I was riding* to Katya Velyasheva, with whom he vowed to "till November, fall in love." Snowbound on the Malinniki estate, he wrote his sardonic yet lyrical *It's winter. What's to do here in the country?* Its Byronic ennui and "spleen" are cured by the sudden arrival of sweet, pretty young girls. They make life worth living again: verses flow and the poet plunges light-heartedly into the pleasures of flirtation, dances, hints... then sensuous passion and joy, and "how warm – even in frost – the kiss she gives is, blazing." For a while, perhaps, it seems he ceased obsessing on "Kars" and "Mama Kars" – his nicknames for Natalya and Natalya Ivanovna (in honour of a Turkish fortress that had stubbornly withstood a lengthy Russian siege).

Back in Petersburg, he asked the Tsar's permission to travel "Unto the distant foot of the Great Wall of China,/To Paris bubbling" (*Let's leave! I'm ready now!*). As usual, he was refused; Count Benckendorf, head of the 3rd Department, or imperial secret police, was furious about Pushkin's trip to the Caucasus without his permission. Henceforth, until his death (even in transporting his coffin) the poet's every movement was restricted severely by the 3rd Department.

But foreign travel had been his fondest dream. Exiled in Kishinev, he had dreamed of joining Byron in fighting for Greek independence. In Book I of *Eugene Onegin* he dreamed in verse of fleeing to Italy. And from Odessa in January 1824, he had written his brother:

> I've twice begged for leave to be allowed at least a foreign vacation, and each time received a most august and merciful refusal. Only one thing remains: to write straight to So-and-So, address, Winter Palace, opposite Peter and Paul Fortress. Or else just grab my hat and cane and go check out Constantinople. Holy Mother Russia is getting to be quite unbearable!

From Mikhailovskoye Pushkin had begged for leave to go abroad for medical reasons; his mother wrote the Tsar about this personally. Again refused, he was directed to seek healing only in the provincial capital, Pskov. He replied:

> His Majesty's unexpected kindness greatly touched me, especially as the local governor had already given me leave to visit Pskov, yet I strictly obey our highest authority. Inquiring about getting cured in Pskov, I was referred to a certain Vsevolozhsky, a skilled veterinarian, quite well respected in the scientific community for his book on the treatment of horses.

In May 1826, he had written his friend Prince Vyazemsky:

> Of course I from head to toe despise my Fatherland. How can you, not chained up like me, remain in Russia? If the Tsar ever gives me freedom, I won't stay a month. It's a sad age we live in. When I imagine London, and railroads, and steamships, and free English journals, or Parisian theatres – or bordellos, then my desolate Mikhailovskoye just aggrieves and enrages me. In Chapter Four of *Onegin* I've described my life; one day you'll read it and ask with a sweet smile: "Where is my poet? He seemed talented." And you'll hear, my dear, the answer: "He's run off to Paris and will never – ever! – return to his accursed Russia! Hooray! Clever fellow!"

But it was not to be. The closest he ever got to England was the English Club in Moscow. (When teased that there was no worse contradiction in terms than the Moscow English Club, he replied: "How about the Imperial Humane Society?"). And so, the most completely European of Russian writers was denied even a glimpse of the Europe he so dreamed of. One can only wonder what would have happened had Pushkin been granted his wish to travel. The Russian painter Karl Bryullov recalled:

> In the fall [of 1836] Pushkin called one evening and asked me to dinner. I wasn't in the mood, and tried to refuse, but his stubbornness overcame mine, and he dragged me along. His

> kids were already tucked into bed when he showed them to me, cradling them gently in his arms one by one, and cooing affectionately. But something wasn't right. There was a feeling of sadness, as if he was trying to force upon himself this idyllic picture of family happiness. I couldn't take it anymore and asked him: "why the devil did you ever marry?" He answered: "I really wanted to travel abroad, but they didn't let me. Then I got in such a tizzy that I didn't know what to do. So I got married."

The winter of 1830 was particularly trying for Pushkin. In his popular journal *The Northern Bee* Tsarist propagandist (and spy) Faddey Bulgarin was writing vicious slanders and racial slurs against the poet and his "blackness." Pushkin shot back with *My Pedigree* and *An Epigram on Bulgarin*. As his chances to wed Natalya seemed dashed, he once more met his old flame, the secret agent Karolina Sobanskaya, in St. Petersburg. On February 2, 1830, in a fit of passion (or perhaps a game à l'amour?) he wrote (yet never sent) two notes to her (in French) that read a bit like prose drafts of *Onegin's Letter to Tatyana*. One says: "happiness is so little made for me, that I could not recognize it when it was right in front of me." In the other he wrote:

> Today is the 9th anniversary of the day I saw you for the first time. That day was decisive in my life. The more I think about it, the more I see that my existence is inseparable from yours: I was born to love you and follow you. All other cares on my part are either errors or folly. Apart from you I have nothing but remorse for a happiness I have been unable to attain. Sooner or later I will have to abandon everything and cast myself at your feet.

Why did Pushkin never send these letters? Perhaps he realized their futility? In Sobanskaya's album he wrote:

> What is there in my name for you?
> It will die out, like sad waves sounding
> Their last, on distant shorelines pounding,
> As in deaf woods night's sounds ring through...

By April 1830 Pushkin was back in Moscow wooing Natalya. Completely despondent, he proposed again to "Mama Kars":

> Only habit and long intimacy can help me win the affection of M-lle your daughter. Eventually I can hope to attach her to me, but I have nothing to please her. If she consents to give me her hand, I will see in this only proof of the tranquil indifference

> of her heart. Yet will this tranquillity of hers last when she is surrounded by admiration, tributes, and seductions? She will be told that mere bad luck prevented her from forming other attachments more fitting, more brilliant, more worthy of her... Maybe these offers will be sincere; doubtless she will think so. Will she not have regrets? Will she not regard me as a fraudulent ravisher? Will she take aversion to me? God is my witness; I am ready to die for her, but to have to die, and leave her a brilliant widow, free to choose a new husband the next day – this idea is hell.

What a melancholy proposal! How eerily it reads in light of what would follow! Why, besieged by pretty admirers, did "the most intelligent man in Russia," "the sunshine of Russian poetry," seek to marry someone who regarded him at best with "tranquil indifference"?

But two seasons had passed and Natalya's mother had received no better offers. Three weeks later Pushkin reflected archly, in a letter to Princess Vyazemskaya: "First love is always a matter of sentiment; the sillier it was, the sweeter its memories. Second love is a matter of voluptuous sensations...I could continue the parallel, but it would take too long. My marriage to Natalie (who is, in parenthesis my 113th love) has been decided." The engagement was announced May 6, 1830.

> My dream's come true. Our Lord Creator
> Sent you down to me, sent you, my own Madonna,
> Of purest grace the purest monument.

But his future mother-in-law somewhat marred his idylls. Ceaselessly she tried to break the engagement, while demanding ever more money from the poet, which he did not have. By August 31, 1830, he was writing his friend and publisher Pletnev:

> I'll tell you what I feel: grief, grief, grief. My future mother in law's finances are a mess, so our wedding gets postponed day by day. All the while my ardour dampens, as I think of the married man's cares and the charms of bachelorhood. To make things worse, all the gossip in Moscow reaches the ears of my fiancée and her mother, causing more tiffs, nasty remarks, uncertain reconciliations – in short, if I'm not unhappy, I'm at least not happy.

In September 1830 Pushkin went to Boldino, in Nizhny Novgorod Province, to mortgage part of a property his father had given him upon his engagement in order to pay Natalya's dowry instead of his future in-laws. No sooner had he arrived than cholera broke out in Russia. Quarantines and roadblocks were set up, cutting Pushkin off from return to Moscow. Holed up in the simple wooden house in Boldino, he wrote Pletnev: "*Cholera morbus* is all around. Do you know what sort of beast that is? Any moment it may hit Boldino and devour us all...You can't imagine how grand it is to give my fiancée the slip and just get down to writing." The famous Boldino Autumn had begun. 3 months later: "In Boldino I wrote as I have never written."

Indeed, what practically flew from his pen there is astounding. It includes 4 short plays or *Little Tragedies* in blank verse: *The Knight-Miser, Mozart and Salieri, The Stone Guest,* and *The Feast in Time of Plague.* Virtually unknown in the West, this work "represents the absolute pinnacle of brilliance in all Russian dramatic art" according to D.S. Mirsky's *History of Russian Literature* (published in 1925). Concise and full of action, they are the most "European" work in all Russian literature (the plays are set respectively in France, Austria, Spain, and England, with no "Russian" characters at all, none of the cumbersome patronymics, pauses, and other longueurs frequently associated with Russian drama). Many characterizations are gripping; Dostoyevsky called the Baron's monologue in *The Knight-Miser* the finest dramatic monologue ever written in any language, and called the *Little Tragedies* as a whole the most "universal" works of Russia's "most universal genius." They combine a Shakespearean grandeur with a more intimate, modern empathy, a Russian soulfulness and depth with a uniquely Pushkinian lightness.

In Boldino, Pushkin also wrote five brilliant short prose tales known as the *Tales of Belkin,* which are a watershed in Russian literature. Tolstoy judged them the finest prose ever written in Russian, and advised young authors: "read and re-read *The Tales of Belkin.* All writers should study every last word of them." At Boldino Pushkin also wrote over 30 poems, including *The Demons, Elegy, The Page, To the Poet, I can't sleep, fire's out, no light, Bound for your distant country's shoreline, When in the grasp of my embrace, Invocation.* There he also finished (except for *Onegin's Letter to Tatyana*) his masterpiece, *Eugene Onegin,* the crown jewel of Russian literature, after 7 years, 4 months and 17 days' labour of love.

Finally, now the time's come! I have finished my many years' labor.
Why, strange and secret, does sadness so trouble me now?
Is it, the deed being done, that I stand like a day-worker, useless,
Having been given my pay, foreign to all other toil?
Am I missing my work, my dear silent companion at nightimes,
Friend of my dawns swathed in gold, friend of my home's holy shrine?

Eugene Onegin is best known in the West by the Tchaikovsky opera, which lacks the novel's main character: Pushkin himself. While the music captures much of the novel's soulful magic it cannot replace the joyous heart that unfolds the unhappy plot. To some critics *Eugene Onegin* is a tale of a so-called "useless person," a microcosm of the disaffected Russian intellectual. Yet balancing its mutual unrequited love and missed opportunities, its friendship gone wrong and misunderstandings that lead to disaster is ever Pushkin himself, ever joying in life. Even tragedy itself is to him just a backdrop for his abiding happiness. And, by way of a seemingly aimless, but in fact precisely guided, loving, transcendant, poetic ramble, we arrive at "an encyclopedia of Russian life," in Belinsky's famous phrase. And that Russian encyclopedia becomes universal.

He returned to Moscow in December 1830, but quarrels with his future mother-in-law continued to delay the wedding, as did, in January 1831, the news of the death of Pushkin's dearest Lycéen friend, the poet Delvig. His profound gloom was not at all befitting an eager fiancé. Many noticed the poet's misgivings: one friend wrote: "Soon Pushkin is marrying Miss Goncharova, *entre nous*, a soulless beauty. It seems to me that by now he'd be glad to cancel the engagement." Just a week before his wedding, Pushkin wrote a friend:

> I'm married. Well – almost. I've already pondered all they might tell me in favour of bachelor life and against marriage. I've cold-bloodedly weighed my gains and losses in the estate I am choosing. My youth has passed noisily and fruitlessly. Hitherto I have not lived as most people do, and I was not happy. Happiness lies only on beaten paths. I'm over thirty. Most people usually marry at 30; I'm acting like most people, and probably won't have grounds to regret. I'm marrying without ecstasy or boyish enchantment; I see the future not all rosily, but in all its naked truth. Griefs will not surprise me; they are part of my domestic calculations. Any joys, though, will be completely unexpected.

Just two days before the wedding, he wrote his publisher: "I can afford to take a wife who has no money, but to plunge into debt just for the sake of her frilly clothes – that I can't afford. Yet I am stubborn and must insist on at least going through with this marriage. Well, there's no remedy. You'll just have to publish my short stories." Pushkin's gloom was not dispelled at his bachelor party; as gypsy maidens danced and sang, he burst into tears. The wedding day, February 18, 1831, began even worse: Natalya was ill, and a note came from Mme. Kars demanding a huge sum of money for a carriage, or else the wedding was off. In spite of everything, Pushkin and Natalya proceeded to marry in the Church of the Grand Ascension in Moscow (today marked by a monument opposite the TASS Building, near the Nikitsky Gates). During the ceremony, the bride dropped the ring meant for the groom, then a sudden draft blew a Bible and cross off the lectern, and snuffed out Pushkin's candle. Princess Dolgorukaya saw Pushkin turn pale and whisper: "*Tous les mauvais augures*!" ("All the bad omens!") But he composed himself, and carried on.

> My fate is decided. I am getting married... She whom I have loved for two whole years, whom my eyes ever yearn for first, with whom every meeting has seemed bliss... My God! She's mine... Awaiting the decisive moment was the most painful feeling in my life. The wait for the last card to be dealt, pangs of conscience, trying to sleep before a duel – all that is nothing in comparison... To marry! Easy enough to say! To most people marriage is about a fancy gown bought on credit, a new carriage, a silk rose nightgown. To others it's about a dowry and settling down. Others marry because everyone else does, because they're thirty... I'm marrying, in short, giving up my dear freedom, my carefree, happy-go-lucky, whimsical independence, luxurious habits, aimless wanderings, seclusion and inner calm, my inconstancy... to double a life which even now is far from full. I've never sought happiness; I never needed to. Now I seek enough for two. But where will I find it?

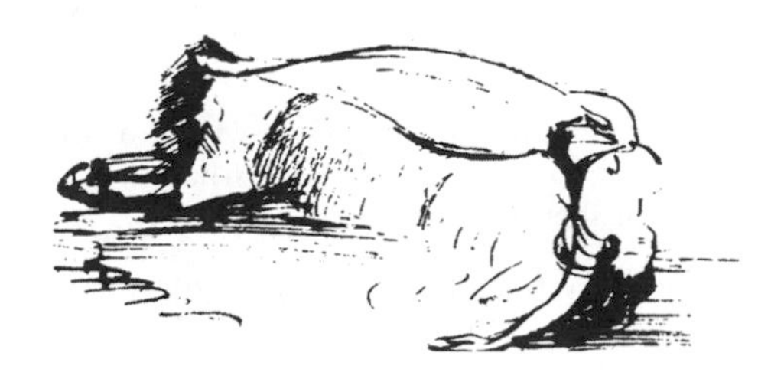

Married Life. St. Petersburg. 1831–1837

Biographers of Pushkin often discount any spiritual component to Pushkin's feelings for Natalya. The great poetess Marina Tsvetayeva opined (a bit jealously, perhaps?) "Natalya had only one good quality: beauty. Just beauty, simply beauty, without intelligence, wit, soul, heart, or talent. Naked beauty – sharp as a sword. And she pierced him through." Vladimir Sollogub (whose own excessive attentions to Natalya almost provoked a duel with the poet) remembered: "I have met many beautiful women, but none whose perfection seemed so complete, classical in both her features and her body... her presence made all other women fade away, even the most charming. Yet she seemed reserved to the point of coldness, and hardly ever spoke." By contrast, the poet Tumansky wrote: "don't imagine she's so extraordinary. She's pale, with pure naïve features, but her eyes are sly and flirty as any grisette's. She is gauche and stiff and reeks of the typical Moscow girl's vulgarity. That she's tasteless is clear by how she dresses, that she's lazy is clear by the mess she makes of her household: soiled napkins, tablecloths, jumbled furniture and crockery."

We do not have Natalya's letters to Pushkin, but 78 letters from Pushkin to Natalya have survived. It is obvious from their tender and deeply intimate tone that the poet, at least, found qualities in his wife beyond mere appearances. His letters evince devoted friendship, kindness, sympathy, caring, and indeed: "I love your soul much more than your face." Pushkin may have truly sympathized with his sweet young damsel in distress, and empathized with her childhood woes.

The newlyweds rented rooms in a charming house on Moscow's Arbat Street. It was there the poet Tumansky visited the new couple and was so singularly unimpressed by Natalya. Pushkin himself, in spite of everything, even bad omens, was truly blissful at first. Just a week after the nerve-wracking ceremony, Pushkin wrote his publisher:

> I'm married – and happy. I have but one wish: for nothing in my life to change. It will never get any better than this. This feeling is so new to me. It seems I am reborn.

Yet Pushkin's mother-in-law did not share his joy. She reproved her son-in-law's anti-clericalism, and commanded her daughter to keep lugubrious vigils, prayers, and fasts. Over and over she complained that her daughter had made a tragic mistake in marrying a good-for-nothing scribbler, a proven trouble-maker, a heretic, a libertine – all the while nagging that same detested "wastrel" for ever greater sums of money. Soon Pushkin could take no more, and left Moscow for good, writing his mother-in law in parting:

> I was forced to leave Moscow to avoid the unpleasantness you caused, which in the end would have robbed me of more than just my peace of mind. You have described me to my wife as an odious man, a greedy, vile bloodsucking usurer; you have told her she just was a fool, that she should not allow her husband even to...etc. You will admit that this is all preaching divorce. I have answered with both patience and mildness. Both, I see now, were quite in vain.

In May 1831, the newlyweds moved to a cozy little home by the park of the Summer Palace in Tsarskoye Selo, not far from Pushkin's beloved Lycée. Each morning he and Natalya would promenade around the lake. His sister Olga was happy that "they seem to adore each other." The poet Zhukovsky wrote: "Pushkin is my neighbour, and we see each other often. His wife seems a quite delightful creature, and he's so happy with her. I am gladder than ever for him that he is married. His soul and life and poetry all will gain from this." While honeymooning in Tsarskoye Selo, Pushkin added *Onegin's Letter to Tatyana* (and a few stanzas before and after) to the completed text of *Eugene Onegin*:

> ...every moment seeing you,
> And following where'er you go,
> Your lips that smile, your eyes that move,
> To catch with eyes in love, aglow.
> To hear and hear you, understand
> With all my soul your sweet perfection,
> In agonies before you stand,
> Turn pale and swoon! What bliss! What blessing!

The poet's wife

He expressed his new "tortured joy" in the poem *No, I do not hold dear that pleasure most rebellious*:

> Feeling ashamed and cold, my joyousness within
> But scarcely answering, not feeling a thing.
> Till livening with time, you too start thrilling –
> Till more and more at last my flame you share unwilling!

Yang conquers yin... During his honeymoon in Tsarskoye Selo, Pushkin wrote the happiest of all his fairy tales, *The Tale of Tsar Saltan*:

There's a princess, so they say,
From whom eyes can't look away.
During day than sun she's brighter,
Nights she makes the world shine lighter.
In her locks bright moonbeams are,
In her forehead gleams a star.
She herself, majestic, precious,
Like a peacock stately, paces,
When she speaks, her sweet speech seems
Like the murmuring rush of streams.

In 1831, Pushkin wrote *The Echo*, an allegory of a poet's obligation to sacrifice his own personality, to listen and reflect, to be "empty" as an echo (which lets Truth ring). Still missing his friend Delvig and other Lycée friends, he wrote a melancholy yet philosophical poem on October 19, 1831, the 20th anniversary of the Lycée's founding: *The more we do commemorate.*

That same year, while promenading in the park of the Summer Palace, Pushkin and his wife met the Tsar and Tsarina, who were very taken by Natalya. The Tsar remarked, "now that Pushkin is married yet not wealthy, he needs to put some kasha and cabbage soup in his bowl." And Pushkin was restored to his rank as a tenth class bureaucrat in the Russian civil service, and given access to the State Archives, and later Catherine the Great's celebrated Voltaire Library. He began work on a projected biography of Peter the Great (never finished) and a history of what might be called the first Russian civil war: the Pugachev Rebellion of 1773–1775. As part of his research, Pushkin received a gift from the Tsar of the laws (or rather, imperial edicts) of the Russian Empire. He marveled at Peter the Great's decrees: "some are written with a whip." Delving in the Archives, Pushkin began to see himself more and more as a historian as well as a poet, and to turn more and increasingly to prose. Uprisings in France, Poland, and peasant revolts in Russia returned his interest to themes of the individual against the state, and the contrasting excesses of power and rebellion, society and mutiny. His next novel, *Dubrovsky*, written in 1832–1833, incorporated many factual and historical materials, including a letter from his dear Arina Rodionovna, and, verbatim, the corrupt judgment from a court case in Murom Province, to create a romantic thriller about a ruined nobleman turned brigand who falls in love with the daughter of the man who ruined him. Yet he cast the work aside at its climax, leaving it, like many other of his works, beautifully unfinished, like a classical

Greek torso... Perhaps Pushkin had trouble reconciling within himself the conflict between romantic plot and historical study, between lyric poetry and prose, whose charm (in his view) should be always unadorned, unsentimental, plain, and clear as possible.

Speaking of prose, while in Tsarskoye Selo, Pushkin befriended one of its greatest masters, Nikolai Gogol, just arrived from the provinces, and woefully shy. Pushkin recognized Gogol's talent and even gave Gogol the plots for two of his most famous works: the comedy *The Inspector General*, and the novel *Dead Souls*. He also helped Gogol get a university professorship, edited and later published several of Gogol's *Petersburg Tales*, including *The Nose*, *The Carriage*, and *Nevsky Prospekt*, stood by Gogol despite his initial awful reviews, and helped convinced authorities to permit the staging of *The Inspector General* (for once, thankfully, they agreed).

Pushkin's first child Maria was born on May 19, 1832. As confirmed by his letters, Pushkin was a doting father. But life in the capital was ruinously expensive, especially in light of "Natalie's" taste for fancy clothes, carriages, hats, and gloves (though some outfits were gifts from her aunt Yekaterina Zagryazhskaya). While Pushkin took pride in his wife's success in Petersburg society, he could ill afford it, as he had foreseen before his marriage. And though coquettish, she herself was jealous. In the fall of 1832, Pushkin wrote to her from Moscow, where he was being honoured:

> I respond to your accusations point by point. 1) A Russian road traveller never changes clothes, but once he gets where he was going, piggish as a pig, goes straight to the bath-house, which is to us our second mother. Don't you know this, my dear heathen? 2) The Moscow post office accepts letters only till 12 and I only crossed Tverskaya Gate just after 11, so I put off writing till the next day. Can you see now that you're wrong? Wrong because (1) you've filled your head with all kinds of nonsense (2) out of pique you've sent Count Benckendorf's (probably important) packet for me off to Lord only knows where and (3) you flirt with the entire diplomatic corps – and to boot now you complain to me! ...As for me, I have nothing to write about. Without you I'm so bored, so bored, that I don't know what to do with myself... Goodbye, my angel, I kiss you and Masha.

Natalya bore Pushkin four children (a fact which her many critics often overlook). She was also grateful to her husband for bringing her into high society. But poetry, art, and the world of ideas little interested her. It seems she lacked even the slightest inkling of her husband's talent. She grew bored when he secluded himself to write, or read poetry with his friends. Alexandra Smirnova claimed she heard Natalya say at one reading: “Lord, Pushkin, I’m sick of you and your poems!” Lev Pavlishchev, Pushkin’s brother-in-law, recalled being present at another reading and hearing Natalya say: “Go ahead, read, I’m not listening.” One night Pushkin woke excited: verses had come to him in a dream. Natalya rebuked him: “nights are for sleeping.” As the great Pushkin scholar Valentin Nepomnyashchy notes, soon after marriage, Pushkin stopped writing love lyrics.

Was there a subconscious competitive aspect to their relationship (in Sollogub’s phrase “her dazzling beauty against his magic name”)? Why was her husband’s career less important to her than her own triumph in society? Why was her chief priority to have fancy gowns and hats and carriages, to be the “first beauty” of St. Petersburg? By 1833, Pushkin was writing his friend Nashchokin: “Life here in Petersburg is so-so. Money woes keep me from relaxing. I lack my old freedom, so necessary for writing. I spin about in society, where my wife’s a big hit. But that requires money; money comes from work, and my work requires seclusion.”

In 1833 Pushkin’s second child Alexander was born and the complete *Eugene Onegin* was finally published for the first time. Flushed from its success, Pushkin decided to write a historical novel about the Pugachev Rebellion. On July 30, 1833, he wrote to the acting head of the secret police seeking permission to do research in the places where the rebellion arose: “I have devoted the last two years to historical research alone, and have not written one line of pure literature. I need about two months of complete seclusion to finish research for a book I began long ago, which will bring me the funds I so need.” The request was granted; Pushkin made the laborious trip to Kazan, Simbirsk, Orenburg, and the Ural areas where the rebellion had begun. Stopping in Boldino to write his impressions, he was startled by a bad omen – a priest on the road. From his letter home one can guess what was on his mind:

> This isn’t just coincidence. Watch out, dear wife. Soon you may grow spoiled without me, forget me, and flirt too much. All hope lies in God and your Auntie. May they keep you from frivolous temptations. I’m proud to report for my part being pure before you as a newborn babe. All trip long I chased only 70 and 80 year old maids, and as for slutty young 60 year olds – I didn’t even spare them a glance. In a village where Pugachev spent 6 months I found a 75 year old Cossack woman who remembers those days just like you and I remember 1830...

Pushkin's second "Boldino Autumn" was again a phenomenal burst of creativity. He wrote his *History of the Pugachev Rebellion*, two verse fairy tales, *The Fisherman and the Little Goldfish* and *The Dead Princess and the Seven Knights*, and over fifteen poems, including *Autumn*, a sublime meditation on nature and its relationship to creativity, and also two long narrative poems. One, *Angelo*, which he later called "my finest work ever" was based on *Measure for Measure*, Pushkin's favourite Shakespeare play (scenes of which Pushkin also translated into Russian). A longer narrative poem, *The Bronze Horseman*, relates how a poor clerk in St. Petersburg loses his home and fiancée in the great flood of November 7, 1824, and comes, bereft and grieving, to the statue in Senate Square of "The Bronze Horseman," Peter the Great. Peter has killed his love and ruined his life by building his splendid capital by the shores of the restless sea, heedless of the cost in human suffering. The clerk threatens the statue: "just you wait!" At that, the Horseman leaves his pedestal to chase the clerk, a "little man," who flees and dies insane on a small island at the mouth of the Nevá.

The Bronze Horseman is at once both a paean to Peter and his great city, and a condemnation of the cruelty of Russian autocracy, personified by the Janus-like figure, ever larger than life, of the statue of Peter the Great. The theme of lost love again stirs ambivalent judgments on the nature of power and its relationship to individual freedom and fate. To me, *The Bronze Horseman* is like the *Iliad*: a meditation in sublimest poetic harmony upon the cruel disharmony of life.

Fate and freedom were themes of yet another masterpiece written in that Boldino Autumn of 1833. *The Queen of Spades* was a page-turner, a search for the no-risk risk, a gambling tale (and ghost story), a romantic intrigue, as well as a playful, almost satirical examination of the conflicts between the natural versus the supernatural, risk and certainty, free will and personal responsibility, of fate, mercy, and madness. Pushkin himself loved playing cards, yet in this story he transformed his own unhappy gambling experiences into something at once lighter and more profound. The fall of the cards becomes a powerful metaphor for the game of life itself, and for the self-destructiveness of ruthless ambition. (*The Queen of Spades* would greatly influence Dostoyevsky's *The Gambler* and *Crime and Punishment*). It is said that old Princess Golitsyna was Pushkin's model for the tyrannical Countess who possesses the fateful secret of the cards. Others see, in the Countess' caprices, portraits of Natalya's aunt – or mother. Or are there clues to Pushkin's sympathy for his wife in his depiction of the heroine Lizaveta Ivanovna, so bitterly oppressed by her relative?

> Countess *** was not, of course, evil-hearted. Yet she was capricious, like a woman spoiled by society, grown mean and stingy, sunk into a cold selfishness, like all old people who, having used up what store of love they had in the past, remain alien to the present. She took part in every frivolity of the *beau monde*, and dragged herself to balls, where she'd sit in a corner, powdered and rigged up à *l'ancien régime*, a hideous yet indispensable ornament of the ballroom. Arriving guests would bow low to her, in homage to an established rite; then no one bothered with her further. She received the entire town in her own home, where she practiced rigorous etiquette, since she could not recognize anyone at all. Her numerous retinue, grown fat and grey in her palace foyer and maid's quarters, did whatever they wanted, ever robbing their dying old lady every way they could. Lizaveta Ivanovna was the martyr of the house. If she poured tea, she was scolded for her excessive consumption of sugar. If she read aloud, she was blamed for all the faults of the author. When taking the Countess on her walks, she was held responsible for the weather and the state of the sidewalk. Her salary was hardly ever paid, and yet it was expected of her that she dress like "everyone," meaning like very few indeed. All knew her, but none saw her. At the balls she only got to dance when a pair could not be found. Ladies grabbed her arm and dragged her off into the toilet anytime they needed to adjust their gowns. Being proud, she keenly felt her humiliation, and looked round impatiently, awaiting her saviour. But young suitors, calculating in their flippant vanity, paid her no heed, even though she was a hundred times dearer than the brazen and cold brides round whom they fluttered. How often had she fled the soporific splendour of the ballroom to weep her eyes out in her shabby little room, with its painted wallpaper screen, commode, small mirror, painted bed, and cheap tallow candle sputtering darkly in its small brass candle-holder!

By the end of the story, Liza is herself a grande dame with a ward (only in Tchaikovsky's opera does she drown herself the icy Nevá in despair: either Tchaikovsky preferred the "*pathétique*" or ambiguous irony is an insufficiently operatic emotion).

And just as Pushkin's creative genius poured forth in Boldino, Natalya, shy and naive no longer, wrote, boasting how she had conquered all men's hearts – including the Tsar's. On October 11, 1833 Pushkin wrote back: "Don't scare me, stay healthy, look after the kids, and don't flirt with the Tsar." Three weeks later, he paused from *The Bronze Horseman* to write home:

> Yesterday, my friend, I got two letters from you. Thanks, but I want to scold you a bit...You appear to have been flirting way too much...You love it when men run after you like mutts after a bitch, with their tails in the air, sniffing her you-know-where! Is this something to joy in?... It's easy to train bachelor layabouts to chase you; just let them know you're that way inclined. That's the whole idea of flirting. Where there's a trough there are pigs. Why must you allow these men to court you? I kiss you, my angel, as though nothing were wrong, and am grateful to you for such honest, detailed descriptions of your life of decadence. Well, have fun, dear wife, but not too much, and don't forget me...Tell me how you look at these balls, now that the season, as you write, has started. But please, my angel, do not flirt. I am not jealous, and I know you would never get involved in anything serious. Yet you know how I can't stand anything that smacks of the typical Moscow girl, anything not *comme il faut*, anything *vulgar*... If I find when I come back that your dear, soft, simple, aristocratic manner has changed, I'll divorce you, by Christ, and go be a soldier from grief!

Pushkin came back to St. Petersburg in the wee hours of November 21, 1833; Natalia was out – at a ball. He found her parked carriage, hid in it, and sent a servant to find her, saying only that there was an emergency at home. When she did not come at once (being engaged for the mazurka) Pushkin fumed and fretted. At last, in a sumptuous pink dress, she got into her carriage and "I took her home as a hussar kidnaps a provincial missy from the mayor's wife's birthday party."

His spiritual equanimity, so restored by Boldino, was soon dashed again by two severe blows. At the beginning of 1834, Pushkin was appointed to the post of Imperial Chamber-Page "which is rather indecent to my age" [generally pages were teenagers], "but the Court wanted Natalya to dance at Anichkov Palace" [the Tsar's private residence]. This meant that Pushkin and his wife were now invited (i.e., obliged to attend) court functions – to his wife's delight, and to his own despair. Natalya's new gowns and popularity were ruinous to his pocket and peace of mind alike, and he loathed his page-boy uniform, Besides, he was a poet, who "grieves at this world's pastimes idle." Worse, the censors forbade publication of *The Bronze Horseman* (it was only printed posthumously). He began to gamble again, and run up gaming debts, (having abstained after marriage for three years, though he had once told the English traveller Thomas Raikes "I would rather die than not play cards")/ By March 1834 "my *Queen of Spades* is all the rage now; everyone bets on nothing but three, seven, and ace!"

Yet cards were no consolation for his ongoing humiliations. He so loathed his page-boy costume that he came once to a court ceremony in simple evening dress, for which he got an official scolding. This galled him further. In his diary more and more he fumed: "I am willing to be a subject, even a slave, but I will not be a flunkey or a fool even before the Tsar of Heaven!" ..."Our sovereign has in him a great deal of second lieutenant, and only just a tad of Peter the Great..." ... "All these balls and amusements will cost the state half a million. What of all our poor people dying of hunger?"

By 1834 Natalya was dancing in the Anichkov Palace twice a day, at noon and again at eight in the evening. Gogol fretted for his friend and mentor: "one only ever sees Pushkin at balls anymore. His whole life will be wasted this way, unless by good luck he can return to the country." Unable to leave his work in the Archives; but scared by the Tsar's attentions to his wife, Pushkin sent her and the children to summer in the Goncharov family estate in Kaluga Province*. The anguish he was feeling then and the desire to escape this "piggish Petersburg" can be clearly felt in the poem *It's time, my friend, it's time! For peace the heart is calling.* His relief at extracting his wife to the country may also be part of *In mournful storms I have become a man*, also written at this time.

The usual surveillance and perlustration of his letters intensified. One of his letters to his wife was opened and passed along to the Tsar to read. In it, the poet had written: "I've seen three Tsars. The first [Paul I] commanded me to remove my baby cap, and scolded my nanny about it. The second [Alexander I] didn't like me at all. The third at least made me a pageboy in my old age, but I've no wish to see a fourth. Leave well enough alone."

This letter provoked an official warning against lèse-majesté (disrespect for the Sovereign). As he wrote in his diary: "What a profound lack of any conscience or morals underpins our entire government! Police open a husband's private letters to his wife and bring them to the Tsar. And the Tsar (a well-brought up and honest man) has no shame in admitting it!"

* Did Natalya have an affair with the Tsar, as some have hinted? *Honi soit qui mal y pense.* There is no evidence of it. Could such a thing stay hidden all these years? The main source for this theory was A.P. Arapova, Natalya's daughter by her second marriage, whose memoirs hinted unsubtly that she was born of a liaison between her mother and the Tsar. But she was born long after Pushkin's death. Besides, Arapova's self-serving "social climbing" was transparent. Scholars do not take Arapova seriously. Yet Pushkin's fears about the Tsar's intentions at least, were not, perhaps, unjustified, for Nicholas I was indeed a notorious womanizer (Chapter XV of Tolstoy's *Khadji-Murat* depicts the Tsar trying to seduce a lady in a little ante-chamber of the Winter Palace kept just for this purpose).

But Pushkin was not intimidated. Clearly understanding that his letters would be read, he wrote frankly to his wife just what he thought of his tormentors. And, in spite of everything, again, as in *October 19th*, the unforgiven poet forgave the unforgiving Tsar:

> It's been so very long now you haven't written me, that, even though I don't like to worry myself about trifles, I worry... Are the kids in good health? And you? I've not written either: I was furious. Not at you, but at *the others.* One of my letters ended up in the police and so on... No one should know what goes on between us; no one should be allowed into our bedroom. Without privacy there is no family life... but swinishness in anyone has long since ceased to surprise me. Yet that swinishness has quite chilled my pen in writing you. The thought that we are being snooped on enrages me. I can live without political freedom, but without the inviolability of the family it is impossible. To be a convict labourer is far preferable. All of this is not addressed to you, my dear.
> To you: how are the mineral baths? Helping? Does Masha have new teeth?...Be healthy, clever, charming, don't ride any more wild horses, look after the kids, and make sure their nanny does too, and write me more often... My *Peter the Great* is coming along; by winter, Volume I may be done. As for *him* [the Tsar], I have stopped being angry, because, upon reflection, *he* is not really to blame for all the filth surrounding him. If you live in an outhouse, you get used to the shit, whether you like it or not; after a while it doesn't even stink anymore, never mind if you're a gentleman. Ah, but if only I could escape to the fresh air!

In the summer of 1834 Pushkin begged the Tsar relieve him of his official duties so he could retire with his family to the country. In vain; Natalya was dead set against it, and the Tsar took her side, threatening to revoke the poet's access to the State Archives, with his history of Peter the Great still unfinished. He was forced to retract his request. About then, according to my teacher N.S. Braginskaya, the poet visited an insane asylum, and wrote *May God forbid I go insane* (a meditation on the closeness of genius to madness).

Granted leave to visit Boldino briefly, he went again hoping for another miraculous autumn. But sadness so consumed him that he could not write. On September 25, 1834, he wrote Natalya: "I've been in the country for more than two weeks now, and there's still no letter from you. I'm bored, my angel. Poems no longer come into my head, and I can't re-write my novel. So I re-read Walter Scott and the Bible, and pine for you all the time. I don't think I'll stay long in Boldino this fall."

The "novel" he wasn't re-writing was *The Captain's Daughter*, which would take him until October 1836 to finish. In this last stay in Boldino, Pushkin wrote just the charming verse fairy tale *The Golden Cockerel*, based on *The Legend of the Arabian Astrologer* from Washington Irving's Tales of the Alhambra. *The Golden Cockerel* is an almost existential portrayal of the corrupting effects of power, greed, and lust, and yet its tale of a magic gift, which Man turns into a curse, is executed so light-heartedly that even the Tsar permitted publication, censoring as "lèse-majesté" only the Cockerel's refrain:

> "Kiri-ku-ku," the Cockerel cried,
> "Rule, while lying on your side!"

When the poet returned to Petersburg, Natalya, over her husband's objections, brought her two older sisters, Yekaterina and Alexandra, to live with her and be brought out in society. This forced Pushkin to move into a bigger, more expensive apartment. Now to that interminable round of balls, parties, and receptions which made up their lives in St. Petersburg, Pushkin was escorting not just one woman – but three. He griped: "I thought my expenses would triple because of this – but guess what? They've increased tenfold!"

He had hoped to recoup his finances on his *History of the Pugachev Rebellion*, which came out in December 1834. But the very politicized Russian readership was not ready for his objective historical perspective. Liberals disliked his unromantic portrait of rebel leader Pugachev as a bloodthirsty, power-mad brigand who committed atrocities. But the honest account of the government's cruelty, which had both sparked the rebellion, and made it so hard to supress, outraged conservatives, led by Sergey Uvarov, Minister of Education.

Pushkin's diary contains this note on Uvarov's meteoric career: "Began as pimp, rose to babysitter for the Finance Minister's kids... now suddenly he's President of the Academy of Sciences." Such quips created a powerful new enemy... and suddenly his travelogue *A Journey to Arzurum* was delayed in censorship, as was a second edition of the *Tales of Belkin*. Meanwhile, he had lost all peace in his home, now utterly consumed by the social whirl of his wife and her two sisters. In January 1835 Pushkin's ailing mother remarked sadly:

> Natalie's out dancing every single day. Yesterday we had a family reunion here with all the kids. She and her sisters talk but of feasts, balls, and spectacles. Little Masha is so used to seeing only luxuriously dressed people that when she saw me, she began to cry. We asked her why she didn't want to kiss Grandma, and she said: "her hat's old, and her dress is shabby."

In May 1835, a son, Grigory was born: the family kept growing. "But I earn my income from the 33 letters of the Russian alphabet, nothing else." And the increasingly arduous process of censorship was making it impossible for him to get published. Frustrated by the length of time it took other journals to get his works through the four separate layers of censorship required for publishing his works, he asked permission to start his own literary review; the request was denied. Four years of married life in the capital had plunged him over 60,000 rubles in debt. Desperately, he renewed his request to be allowed to move to the country for a few years, writing Count Benckendorf on June 1, 1835:

> I have no fortune; neither I nor my wife received any legacies. Till now I have lived by my works. My only constant income is the salary the Emperor has deigned to grant me. There's nothing humiliating to me about working for my daily bread. Yet, used as I am to independence, I am completely unable to write something just for money. The mere thought of this completely shuts me down. Life here in St. Petersburg is frightfully expensive. I am faced now by the need to do away with the expenses it entails, which drag me into debt and set up further worries and troubles – and perhaps poverty and despair. Yet three or four years of seclusion in the country would give me a chance to recover, and then return to Petersburg to resume the duties for which I am indebted to His Majesty.

But the Tsar wanted to keep the poet under surveillance. Pushkin was warned that if he moved, he would not just lose his salary, but all access for good to the State Archives. At last the Tsar consented to give Pushkin a loan of 30,000 rubles, paid for, however, by suspension of his salary for the next six years. The loan vanished at once on urgent old debts, and – even more urgent – new debts (each of Natalya's new hats cost about 250 rubles apiece). In the fall of 1835, the Tsar gave him leave to go back briefly to Mikhailovskoye to finish *The Captain's Daughter*. From there he wrote Natalya:

> You can't imagine how lively the imagination becomes here, sitting all alone, or walking in the woods, where no one stops you from thinking, thinking – thinking till one's head spins. But what am I thinking of? Here's what: how are we going to live? Father won't give me this estate, besides, he's squandered near half of it away already. Your family property is a hair's breadth from total ruin. The Tsar won't let me move to the country or be a journalist. To sell out and write what I'm told just for money – as God is my witness – I cannot do that. We haven't a penny of stable income left, with stable expenses of at least 30,000... What will come of all this, Lord only knows. For now, it's sad. But just kiss me, and maybe the grief will pass... If possible, could you please send me Montaigne's *Essays*? The four blue volumes on the long bookcase. Please find them...The weather is very cloudy... I walk a lot, and ride a lot as well, on some old nags who are very happy about this, because they get oats afterwards, which they weren't treated to before... I kiss you, my own dear soul, and all the kids, and bless you with all my heart.

Yet all that "thinking, thinking, thinking" was beginning to weigh on him, and a few days later he wrote home again:

> I've found everything in Mikhailovskoye the same as ever, except Nanny is here no more. And in my absence, next to my old friends the ancient pines, a new family of young evergreens has sprung up, saddening me like those dashing young guardsmen at all those balls where I no longer dance.

These observations form part of his haunting elegy *I came back again* written that day, walking around Mikhailovskoye:

> ...I came back again
> To that small plot of land, where once I spent
> Two years living in exile and unnoticed.

By now ten years have passed since then, and many
Have been the changes coming to my life.
I too, to universal law submissive,
Have changed myself, but, once more here,
All of my past embraces me with vigour,
And so it seems but yesterday I walked
In these groves, wand'ring.
...Here's the forlorn cottage,
Where with my poor old nanny I did live.
The dear old lady's gone – beyond the wall now
I cannot hear her footsteps heavy trooping,
Nor her devoted, always-caring snooping.
And here's the wooded hillock, on which often
I used to sit, not moving, and look down
Into the waves, remembering with sadness
The look of other waves, of other shorelines....

In this elegy (whose blank verse freedom marked a watershed in Russian poetry), Pushkin transcended his sadness and rose above thoughts of his own death, hailing, albeit wistfully, nature's eternal promise and life itself renewed through future generations:

But now a new young grove is growing up,
A family of green, its bushes thickening,
Sheltering beneath like children. Further off,
Their brooding gloomy friend is still there, standing
Like some old bachelor, and all around
Him still all is deserted... Greetings, youngsters!
So young, and so unknown to me. I won't
Be blessed to see your greening growth in fullness,
When you outgrow and pass my old companions
And hide their ancient heads with your new boughs
From sight to passersby. But one day may
My grandson hear your greetings whispered soft
When riding back from chatting at a friend's house,
Filled in his heart with happy, pleasant musings,
And, passing by your shade in gloom of nighttime,
Then think of me, remembering.

Back in St. Petersburg, one of those "dashing young guardsmen at balls where I no longer dance" was a tall, blond, handsome Frenchman named Georges D'Anthès. A partisan of King Charles X who fled France after the July Revolution of 1830, D'Anthès had been inducted into the Russian Imperial Horse Guards (earning, in his brief service to the Tsar, 44 separate reprimands for conduct unbecoming). D'Anthès was the live-in "toyboy" of Baron Heeckeren, Dutch ambassador to Russia, who formally "adopted" D'Anthès as his "son" when the "boy" turned 24 (the adoption was not recognized by the Dutch government). There is evidence of a secret homosexual relationship between D'Anthès and Heeckeren, including passionate correspondence. Yet D'Anthès was also a lady-killer, a flashy guardsman-playboy, a dandy fond of dancing, a foppish rake, a fashionable roué. His breezy charm, good looks, and the inestimable *cachet* of being a French nobleman in a society of Gallomanes, made him all the rage at court balls – in a way Pushkin could never hope to be. And besides being popular, D'Anthès was rolling in his "father's" money. In short, he was the antithesis of Pushkin, the *beau monde's* ideal *beau*, certainly the type "Madame Kars" (Natalya's mother) would have wanted for her daughter. Little wonder, then, that he quite turned Natalya's head (and the heads of her two sisters as well).

By late 1835 D'Anthès lusted for the ultimate society triumph: to seduce and conquer the first beauty in St. Petersburg: "Natalie." That she was the wife of the "sunshine of Russian poetry" concerned him not at all. He knew (and needed) no Russian – save a few drill commands and curses. Even his French was mediocre: he had read nothing, and the Muses were Greek to him.

Did Natalya in fact become D'Anthès' mistress? Many years later in Paris, this question was put to D'Anthès by Pushkin's friend Sobolevsky. D'Anthès replied: "Of course, it goes without saying." (Mere hussar boasting? Who knows?). D'Anthès claimed he had taken his Natalie's heart by storm, swearing that she was his soulmate... But, as Shakespeare warns (*Romeo and Juliet*, II, ii, 92–93): "At lover's perjuries they say Jove laughs..."

What matters is that Natalya believed him, or at least was flattered to see D'Anthès woo her, almost, one might say, with the passion of Onegin wooing Tatyana at the end of *Eugene Onegin*. By January 20, 1836, D'Anthès wrote Baron Heckeren to say that he loved Natalya, and "she loves me too, but we cannot see each other, for the husband is revoltingly jealous." The worst of this was that Natalya did not trouble to conceal from her husband – or pitiless gossip – her flirting with a handsome Guardsman.

She did this even as Pushkin's mother, Nadyezhda Osipovna Pushkina, was dying. Pushkin's old friend from Mikhalovskoye, Zizi remembered: "Pushkin was always extraordinarily attached to and fond of his mother, even though she plainly preferred her younger son to him. But in the last year of her life, the poet looked after her with such tender care and affection that she begged his forgiveness for not having been capable of appreciating him in his childhood." Anna Kern (who had remained a faithful friend of the family) remembered in her memoirs:

> I saw him one last time with his wife at his mother's house, not long before her death; she was too weak to get out of bed anymore, and was just lying on a cot moved to the middle of the room, facing the windows. They sat by her on a little couch, and Nadyezhda Osipovna just looked at them tenderly with love. Alexander Sergeyevich returned her gaze while holding in one hand the soft end of his wife's elegant fur boa, with which he gently stroked his mother, as if expressing, in that one gesture, all his love and tenderness at once for both his mother and his wife. All the while he could not speak a word. Natalya Nikolayevna's hair was in curlers. She was getting herself ready for a ball.

Pushkin's mother died on March 29, 1836. Riding all by himself through 250 miles of roads turned into quagmires by the spring thaw, he drove her coffin to the Gannibal family burial plot, by Mikhailovskoye, in Svyatogorsky Monastery. After burying her, he paid the monastery in advance for his own grave – right by hers. To Zizi he "lamented with exceptional distress how cruel Fate had been to him once again, giving him so little time to feel maternal tenderness which he had never in his life known before. And when he got back to St. Petersburg, the gossips were spreading malicious stories that he had laughed all through his mother's funeral."

Meanwhile, the Tsar had finally given Pushkin permission to publish his own quarterly journal, *The Contemporary* (albeit under four separate layers of censorship). In April 1836 the first issue came out featuring *A Journey to Arzurum* and several Pushkin poems, as well as the first publication of Gogol's *The Nose.* Unfortunately, circulation was poor, and reviews (by enemies, chiefly Bulgarin and Uvarov) were absurdly vicious.

The whole of 1836 was financially disastrous for Pushkin. As *The Contemporary* struggled to survive and gain circulation, virtually no income remained to support four children (a daughter was born May 27, 1836), his wife and her two sisters (in attendance at three balls per week), and his own younger brother. He was forced to fawn to pawnbrokers and to visit moneylenders; to borrow from Peter to pay Paul... Though handsome new publishing contracts for future years promised relief, in 1836 things got so bad that he very nearly had to give up buying books!

But perhaps biographers care more about the poet's bleak finances than he really did himself. We should remember that it was a fairly normal, even stylish, habit of the Russian aristocracy to live for years on debt, as described in *Eugene Onegin,* I, iii: "By serving honestly and nobly/His father lived, from debt to debt." And even though Pushkin could be quite unsentimental about money (he once quipped "I write for the same reason that the singer sings, the baker bakes, and the quack kills – for money"), there was always a part of him that had remained as carefree about finances as that youth who cast a gold coin in a canal just to admire its gleam underwater. He knew his work might well not get past the four separate layers of censorship to which it was subjected. He had written: "Poet! Care not for love through fame, now or hereafter!" To him beauty and artistic integrity were far, far more important than profit. He could always find happiness in himself as long as he was "filled with the silent Muse" (*By lands where sovereignty of golden Venice rules*).

What made 1836 the bitterest year of his life was unquestionably loneliness. Mourning the death of his mother and his increasing loss of freedom, he missed more than ever his true Lycéen friends, like Pushchin or Küchelbecker, exiled to Siberia – or Delvig ("no one was closer to me than Delvig: with him I could speak of what wracks the soul and pangs the heart"). Instead of this dear friend, he was surrounded by soundless, ubiquitous, and basically useless spies. "Spies are like our letter Ъ [eliminated by spelling reforms in 1918]: needed just in a few cases, and even then we could do without them, but no, they're used to butting into everything.".

While Pushkin was finding no one with whom to assuage the grief in his heart, D'Anthès was finding "Natalie" in every ballroom in town and, in the very finest hussar traditions, simultaneously wooing her, her own sister Yekaterina, Princess Baratinskaya – and not neglecting his "Daddy" either!

In the summer of 1836, after a post-natal illness, Natalya rented an expensive summer house in Kamenniy Ostrov, then a fashionable suburb of St. Petersburg (D'Anthès' regiment had been posted nearby).

Every day "Natalie" and D'Anthès (and sister "Catherine") went out horseback riding together. Pushkin, observing such cavalcades out of his window, wrote broodingly of death, sin, transience, and of his own poetic legacy. The so-called *Kamenniy Ostrov Cycle* (*Our hermit fathers and our nuns blessed and blameless, When past the city gates with wistful thoughts I roam, From Pindemonti,* and *Exegi Monumentum)* reaches, perhaps, the summit of Russian spiritual poetry. Pushkin also finished *The Captain's Daughter,* printed in the December 1836 issue of *The Contemporary*. Many critics consider it the finest novel ever written in the Russian language. Its gripping plot and themes of coming of age and tender love amidst rebellion, civil war, imprisonment, treachery, death, its mix of bitter conflict and compassion combined to make it an instant classic, selling out that issue of *The Contemporary* almost at once. In the novel, Pushkin warned prophetically: "God forbid there ever be an uprising in Russia. It will be pointless – and pitiless." The critic Belinsky called the novel "a miracle of artistic perfection," and no less a genius than Gogol wrote: "compared to *The Captain's Daughter* all our other novels and stories are like watery gruel. Its purity and poetic restraint attain such heights that reality itself seems an artificial caricature by comparison."

Yet, brooding, he was unable to finish yet another extraordinary work, which he had begun the previous year in Mikhaylovskoye. *Egyptian Nights* is an enchantingly intricate fabric of poetry and prose, mixing cynical Russian reality and Italian Renaissance ideals, and treating clearly autobiographical themes of a poet's struggle to keep his freedom amidst the enmity of authority and high society. The novel's poetic improvisations ("*The poet walks... his eyes are open*") link poetry with the nature of love itself, its utter self-sacrifice, its predatory, voluptuous sexuality, its inexplicable magic and power personified by the cruel, yet sublime, life-consuming and yet majestic figure of Egypt's fabled harlot queen, Cleopatra:

In passion's auction who'll start vying?
I sell my love, so speak, be free!
Which one of you dares to be buying –
Paid with your life – one night with me?

October 19, 1836, was the 25th anniversary of the founding of the Lycée. Pushkin, who saw himself as a a chronicler of the Lycée, had that morning begun a poem for the occasion, promising to read it at the traditional festive dinner party. He began to read:

There was a time our youthful holiday
Just shined, made noise, when roses crowned our hymning,
When goblets' clinking merged into our singing,
We sat together tight in warm affray.
Back then we all were carefree as a novice,
We all lived much more lightly, boldly, then,
We all did drink to hope, did lift our chalice
To youth itself, and all youth comprehends.
That's over now: we're tamed when we carouse.
With passing time, our feast no more is furious.
We've compromised, grown still, become more serious,
More hollow now our clinking healths do sound.
Our speech is much less playful now and daring:
With more space midst us, sadder now we sit,
Amidst our singing, laughter now is rarer;
We sigh more often, hushed in gloomy fit.

As he was reading, Pavel Annenkov relates, "tears welled up in his eyes and he began to sob. He put down his paper and withdrew quietly to a couch in the corner of the room. A friend picked up the paper and read the next six stanzas for him." Earlier that same day, he had just finished *The Captain's Daughter* and dated it "October 19, 1836." That very day, Pushkin had written to his old friend, Pyotr Chaadayev, whose "indictment of Russia," or *Philosophical Letter*, denounced Russia's autocracy, serfdom, corrupt servility before brute power, and lack of any civil society. Chaadayev blamed these ills on Russia's Orthodox faith and Byzantine heritage. For his frankness Chaadayev was promptly declared insane, and placed under strict house arrest. Pushkin therefore never sent his friend his reply:

> Thanks for the pamphlet you sent me. I read it with great pleasure, though I am amazed to see it translated and printed. I am far from agreeing with you entirely. Certainly the Schism of the Church separated us from the rest of Europe and we were left out of many of the grand events that followed. Yet we have had our own mission. It was Russia with its endless spaces that swallowed up the Mongol invaders; they were not able to pass our Western borders, leaving us dangerously in their rear. And so they withdrew to their desolate steppes; Western civilization was saved...We have been forced to develop a separate existence, which, even while we remained Christians, nonetheless made us strangers to the rest of Christendom. Still it was by our sufferings that Catholic Europe was able to develop energetically. You say that the source of our Christianity is impure, that Byzantium was contemptible. Excuse me, my friend! Who cares? Was not Jesus Christ himself a Jew?

> Is not Jerusalem the cradle of us all? The Russian clergy is indeed backward. Yet it has never stooped to some of the infamies of the Papist Inquisition, or provoked great wars of "reformation," just when mankind needed unity and brotherhood above all else. I flatly cannot agree with you that we have no history, and that our civilization is a nullity. Our history is a sad but magnificent painting... [From Kievan Rus through the Time of Troubles] is that not all history? And is Peter the Great not a universal history all by himself? What of Catherine II, who put us on the doorstep of Europe? And Tsar Alexander, who took you along with him to Paris? And put your hand on your heart: can you truly see nothing in the story of today's Russia which will one day be memorable to future historians? Although personally I am loyal in my heart to the Tsar, I am far from admiring all that I see around me. As a man of letters, I am harassed, embittered; as a man of principle, I am appalled. And yet I swear to you on my honour that I would not switch my country for any other, nor switch our history, even that of our forefathers, even that which God has given us...And yet, having just contradicted you, I must say, much of what you write in your Epistle is profoundly true. It cannot be denied that the state of our civil society is simply woeful. Our absence of free public opinion, our indifference to all concepts of honour and justice and truth, our cynical contempt for ideas, for the dignity of man, for all that is not mere personal necessity – this is indeed something truly grievous.

From this grief Pushkin still longed to escape, to move to the country. But he was trapped in a gilded cage. On October 20, 1836, he wrote his father: "I had wanted to go to Mikhailovskoye, but was not able to. This will set me back by another year at least. In the country I would have gotten a lot of work done. Here I do nothing but brood."

Uvarov and Bulgarin in his *Northern Bee*, which had panned even *Eugene Onegin*, renewed their onslaughts on the poet, and Zhukovsky noted "our journalistic liars scribbled that Pushkin was all washed up."

> No matter where I go, there I hear slander's buzz,
> And lying nonsense passing judgment,
> Hear envy's whisper, vanity and fuss
> Rebuking cheerfully with intent bloody.

The flirtation between Natalya and D'Anthès grew to a fever pitch, as did the mockery it aroused, and the rumours. On November 2, 1836, D'Anthès lured Natalya to an assignation and allegedly threatened to kill himself unless she became his mistress. She supposedly answered "you have my heart; why do you need my body?" (It seems a tawdry imitation in prose of Tatyana's rebuff to Onegin... What really took place at this tryst we will never know, but the rumors were merciless.)

On November 4, 1836, Pushkin and his friends received anonymous "diplomas" in French, "certifying" Pushkin as "coadjutor to the Grand Master of the Order of Cuckolds and Historiographer of the Order." The "diplomas" implied that Pushkin had been cuckolded not by D'Anthès, but by the Tsar. Pushkin subjected them to careful forensic analysis. "From the type of paper used, the vocabulary, and the style, I immediately verified for myself that the letter is from a foreigner, a member of high society, and a diplomat" – in other words, from Baron Heckeren. Anna Akhmatova argues Pushkin was right, and that he even proved his case to Count Benckendorf and the Tsar. Baron Heckeren genuinely hated Pushkin on behalf of his "son"; yet perhaps he was no less jealous than Pushkin of a relationship that was taking his "son" away from him. Akhmatova argues forcefully that the letters were Heckeren's "blind." Unable to challenge the Tsar to a duel, Pushkin would have to move away with his family, or at least send his wife away, thereby ending Natalya's relationship to D'Anthès, who would be left to be consoled by his "father." Other scholars believe that the "diplomas" were not from Heckeren, who could not, they argue, risk a scandal. (Others rejoin that this is precisely why the letters were anonymous.) Still others conclude the letters were just a prank. Yet whoever wrote them had taken a grave risk, impeaching the honour not just of Russia's national poet, but of two Sovereigns (the "diplomas" referred to L. D. Naryshkin, who had been cuckolded by Alexander I, again clearly implying that it was Nicholas I who had cuckolded Pushkin). Such risks could only be run either by someone with an extremely high rank in the government or with diplomatic immunity. Different "diplomas" were in different handwritings, so it may well have been a conspiracy. Years later, in a private dinner at the Winter Palace, Tsar Alexander II said that the diplomas were authored by the man who had once written the order for Pushkin's exile to Mikhailovskoye, Count Nesselrode, Russia's Foreign Minister – who was also Baron Heckeren's best friend in St. Petersburg.

That same evening, November 4, 1836, the poet showed his "diploma" to his wife. This seems to have prompted her to recount her version of her tryst of November 2nd, according to which she had behaved with exemplary modesty, while D'Anthès was little more than a stalker. Yet Pushkin found that she had various love notes and letters from D'Anthès... and as he read them, he realized she had accepted them... and kept them...

Enraged, the poet immediately challenged D'Anthès to a duel. The next morning, November 5th, Baron Heckeren promptly visited Pushkin, accepted the challenge on behalf of his "son," but requested a two-week extension due to surprising news. To the amazement of all in St. Petersburg society, D'Anthès announced his sudden engagement to Yekaterina Goncharova, Natalya's sister. Indeed, Yekaterina was pregnant by D'Anthès, a fact only recently proven by unearthed – and very earthy – correspondence between D'Anthès and Yekaterina). Under these circumstances, Pushkin reluctantly withdrew his challenge, on condition, however, that D'Anthès stay completely away from his home and from Natalya, and never expect either of them to socialize with the newlyweds. In vain: "my wife and her sisters do nothing but fuss over the dowry; it keeps them busy and completely engulfs them, but they enrage me, as they have turned my home into a fashionable dress shop." On January 10, 1837, D'Anthès and Yekaterina were married. At this, Pushkin quipped that he was curious what nationality his sister-in-law should by rights now claim: French, Dutch, or Russian?

Yet even though now married, D'Anthès carried on with Natalya more than ever, finding her at every ball in town, casting "longing looks" at her ostentatiously, as she in turned blushed, and cast her eyes down coyly... Even in Pushkin's presence, they danced together. Worse, in the poet's hearing, D'Anthès dropped sexual innuendoes about Natalya for all to hear. The rumor spread throughout St. Petersburg that D'Anthès had married Yekaterina solely in order to save Natalya's honour, while, in fact, D'Anthès was doing everything he could to stain it further. Pushkin could bear no more. On January 25, 1837, he wrote Baron Heckeren a letter which he knew would be certain to provoke a challenge:

> I have long known the conduct of your son and could not remain indifferent to it. I was content to play observer, ready to intervene when I judged it meet. An incident, which in all other cases would have been very disagreeable, happily rescued me from the affair. I received the anonymous letters. I saw that the time was right and I took advantage of it. You know the rest: I made your son play such a pitiable role that my wife, shocked by such cowardice and banality, could not help laughing, and the emotion that she had perhaps felt for this grand and sublime passion evaporated into the calmest contempt and most deserved disgust. I am obliged

> to admit, Baron, that your role has hardly been seemly. You, the representative of a sovereign crown, have been the paternal pimp for your own son. It seems his (by the way, quite inept) conduct has all been directed by you. It is you who probably dictated to him the sorry phrases and blather he tried to write. Like an obscene old woman, you've lain in wait for my wife to speak of the love of your bastard or self-styled "son" for her. While he in fact was laid up in your home with the clap, you'd tell her he was dying of love for her; you murmured: "Give me back my son!"
>
> You must grasp, Baron, that after all this I cannot permit my family to have the least relationship with yours. It was exactly on this condition that I consented not to follow through with this dirty affair, and not to dishonour you in the eyes of our court and yours, as I have the power and the intention to do. But I do not care for my wife to have to hear any more of your paternal exhortations. I cannot permit your "son," after his base behavior, to dare address a word to my wife, and still less will I let him subject her to barrack-room puns, and his overacted role of devoted, grand, unhappy passion when he is in fact no more than a coward and a scoundrelly rouè. I am therefore obliged to ask that you put an end to all this scheming, if you wish to avoid a new scandal, from which I will certainly not retreat.

There was no getting round such words. D'Anthès' challenge came on January 26, 1837; the duel took place on the afternoon of the next day, January 27, 1837. Getting dressed to go to the duel, Pushkin did not put on his lucky talisman against violent death, a present from his close friend and patron Nashchokin. Having left his home, he stopped, turned around, and went back to get his warm bearskin coat. As the ever-superstitious poet surely knew, in Russian tradition "to turn back is bad luck" – and yet... On his way to the duel, Pushkin's sleigh rode right past his wife's carriage (returning from an afternoon spent sledding). But she was near-sighted and he was looking the other way, so they missed each other – a potent last symbol, perhaps, of all the problems in their relationship that had led to such a fatal calamity.

The duel between Pushkin and D'Anthès on the snowy banks of the Black River near St. Petersburg bears an eerie resemblance to the duel between the poet Lensky and Onegin in *Eugene Onegin*. Both took place in January, on nearly the same day, both duels were provoked by an affront to a poet's honour by a rake; like Tatyana and Olga, Natalya and Yekaterina were sisters. Pushkin used Lepage pistols, as in *Eugene*

Onegin, VI, xxv (D'Anthès used a German Ulbrich model: three years later the French ambassador's son would duel with another great Russian poet, Mikhail Lermontov, using the very same fateful pistol once used by the Dutch ambassador's "son" against Pushkin). One wonders what thoughts raced through the poet's mind on that fateful day. Had he not taken Mme. Kirchof's prophecy so seriously that he had parted with Yekaterina Ushakova – just because she was blonde?

Why – precisely in his 37th year – was he getting into a duel with a blond man? According to his old friend Zizi, who saw him days before his duel, Pushkin had confided in her his desire to seek death, and his confidence that the Tsar would care for his wife and children. (He had certainly not shared such longings with the Tsar. In fact, after the first challenge in November, the Tsar had requested that Pushkin promise not to fight a duel.) Zizi's account may be belied – or maybe not? – by these lines he had also written, not long before:

> Oh no, I am not tired of living,
> I love to live, I want to live!
> Not all within my soul's gone chilly,
> Although from me my youth has slipped.

One senses an internal dialogue: was the cry "Oh no" responding perhaps, to some voice inside – saying "yes"? On the morning of his duel Pushkin seemed much happier than in a long time. All morning he was singing. Then he wrote a short letter connected to the upcoming issue of *The Contemporary*. He did not at all seem like a man planning to die (few of his friends even guessed what was going on). Yet at Pushkin's insistence the duel was fought at ten paces, nearly point-blank range ("the bloodier the better"), and he did not put on (forgot?) his turquoise ring, a "lucky talisman against violent death." D'Anthès fired first; his bullet landed where a button was missing on Pushkin's waistcoat, bursting through the abdominal cavity and shattering the sacrum. The wound was fatal. Bleeding in the snow, and unable to rise, in great pain, Pushkin nevertheless insisted on taking his shot. It glanced D'Anthès' right arm, and bounced off a button on D'Anthès' chest, knocking D'Anthès down, but no more. Thinking D'Anthès was dead, Pushkin remarked: "Strange; I thought I'd be pleased if I killed him, but now I feel I'm not."

The wounded poet was brought home and eight doctors were summoned, including Dr. Arendt, the Tsar's personal physician. All said nothing could be done to save him. Pushkin thanked them.

He then summoned a priest, as Zhukovsky recalled, and "confessed himself and heard rites of extreme unction with great passion." He summoned his second, Konstantin Danzas, and dictated a list of all his debts, including those not evidenced by any writing, and signed it. Dr. Arendt returned with a note from the Tsar, urging Pushkin to "die as a Christian. Don't worry about your wife and children; I will look after them." Pushkin asked Arendt to thank the Tsar and convey his request for clemency for Danzas (duelling, though quite common, was technically a serious crime in Russia). Despite agonizing pain, and great loss of blood, he lived on for forty-six hours after the duel. In his memoirs, Dr. Arendt wrote: "I've been in thirty battles, and have seen many deaths, but never saw anyone die with so much courage in the face of so much pain."

Pushkin blessed his children, then Natalya, and then told her, in French: "Move to the country and mourn me for two years. Then, if you like, remarry – but not to a good-for-nothing." Waving to his bookshelf, he whispered: "Farewell, my friends!" By his side were the poet Zhukovsky, and the dictionary compiler Dal, with whom the poet joked that for the first – and unfortunately the last – time in his life, he was permitting himself the liberty of addressing the learned doctor intimately, with the informal *ty*, instead of the formal *Vy*. Yet even as his apartment thronged with well-wishers, he was lonely, missing above all his old friends from the Lycée: "What a pity neither Pushchin nor Malinovsky are here! It would have been easier to die." In his final moments, he asked for cloudberries; Natalya spoon-fed him cloudberry jam... He died January 29, 1837. (Even the time of his death gives pause: the malevolent spirit of Countess in *The Queen of Spades* had fatefully appeared at 2:45 in the dead of night. Pushkin's benevolent spirit departed at 2:45 in the waning of the northern wintry afternoon.)

Sobbing and sobbing, Natalya hysterically cried out: "I killed my husband! I'm the reason he died!" Anna Akhmatova, with 100 years of hindsight behind her indignation, agreed: "She always did what she wanted and never cared about his feelings. She bankrupted him, denied him all peace of mind, didn't even let his dying mother into their home, yet brought her two sisters in, rented the most expensive villas and apartments, forgot his address whenever he traveled, ceaselessly related to him all her amatory victories, yet complained to D'Anthès about his jealousy. Then she made her own husband her confidant in the whole situation – and so precipitated the tragedy."

Yet Pushkin himself bore no grudges. On the contrary, he was tender and affectionate with his wife till his final breath. He told his friends "my wife is blameless in this affair," and refused to let them challenge Baron Heckeren and D'Anthès: "do not avenge me; I have forgiven everything." Had he simply resigned himself calmly to the fate once foretold to him? Or had death raised his consciousness to a higher level of sublime serenity? After stopping the clock, when everyone else left the room, the poet Zhukovsky stayed a while by his friend's side. He wrote Pushkin's father later:

> I sat down by him just looking at his face for a long time all alone. I never saw anything quite like his face in that first instant of death. His head was sunken slightly and his hands folded, as if resting after hard labours. Yet there was an odd expression on his face that I simply can't put into words, so new, yet so familiar; relaxed, yet neither sleeping nor resting. Not the usual wit and intelligence that always sparkled in him, nor some poetic pose. No! It was a sense of profound surprise, yet contemplation, of contentment, of some sort of all-encompassing divine, profound wisdom and light. As I kept looking at him, I wanted to ask: "What are you seeing, my friend?" What would he have said, could he only have been resurrected for an instant? I assure you that I never before saw in him such profound contentment, such majestic and triumphant joy. Of course joy had always danced before him and about him, but never was it revealed in such utter purity as in that moment when the hand of death lifted from him all earthly cares. That was the end of our Pushkin.

Profound shock gripped the capital at the news of Pushkin's death. Thousand gathered to mourn, thousands more bought his works, in a matter of days earning his estate far more than what it owed in debts. There was widespread outrage that a foreign favourite of the Court had murdered the national poet; many felt that the authorities who had so harassed the poet in life were responsible in some way for his death. Young Mikhail Lermontov expressed the public's fury in his *Death of a Poet* (which earned its author immediate exile):

> ...You crowd that throng our throne with greed relentless –
> Of freedom, genius, glory – killers true!
> You hide yourselves behind the law's protection,
> You hush the truth, and silence justice too.
> But there's a higher court, accomplices of evil!
> A dreaded court that waits –
> Whose judgment is quite deaf to clinking silver,
> And knows your thoughts and deeds every which way.

> Then you in vain will grasp at gossip's libel,
> No help to you from lies will come;
> Your black blood will not wash, for all your trying,
> The righteous noble poet's blood!

Gogol, more gently, wrote:

> All my joy and pleasure in life vanished with him. I never again wrote a single line without seeing him in my mind standing before me, and asking myself: what would he say of this? Would he like it? Would it make him laugh?

Thousands gathered by the poet's apartment on the Moika Canal (now Moika, 12), not far from the Winter Palace, quite alarming the Tsar and Count Benckendorf, ever vigilant against another Decembrist uprising. They reacted as always: repressively. Obituaries in the press were strictly forbidden. Only one journal, *The Literary Supplement*, dared print a headline on January 30, 1837 which read: "The sunshine of our poetry has gone out! Pushkin is dead!" Its editor was at once summoned and reprimanded personally by Benckendorf: "How dare you run a banner headline to announce the death of a civil servant of absolutely no consequence? 'Sunshine of our poetry?' Ha! What kind of position is that? Is that some kind of honour?"

Natalya sent invitations for a funeral to be held in St. Isaac's Cathedral (then in the Admiralty, not on what is now St. Isaac's Square). But the service was cancelled (supposedly, say some, duellers, like suicides, were deemed unworthy of Christian burial). This seems doubtful; Pushkin had confessed and received extreme unction. Perhaps the Tsar feared a large angry crowd passing the Winter Palace and his own windows?

Tensions grew, and the poet's body was already decaying as the Tsar finally granted his personal permission for the use of a small imperial church right by the Winter Palace, the Konyushennaya Church, "about which," Zhukovsky recalled, "we had no right even to dream." (In Soviet times the church would be turned into a taxi garage). Holding the poet's funeral in an imperial church effectively turned the rite into an act of state. Major bureaucrats, the General Staff, and members of the diplomatic corps were invited (so many, indeed, that even in death, the poet was alone in an alien throng).

To be fair to the Tsar, no church in the capital could possibly have fit all the mourners who wished to pay their last respects to their beloved poet. Still, the traditional bearing of the coffin into church was cancelled; instead, it was brought into the crypt from the poet's apartment in the wee hours of February 1, 1837, as troops blocked the streets.

The funeral took place on the morning of February 1, 1837. Admission was by tickets only. Prince Vyazemsky noted "there were more gendarmes than mourners." All teachers and students in the city were forbidden to miss classes to attend the ceremony. Yet police had trouble holding back the silent throngs by the church in the bitter cold.

To avoid further demonstrations of popular feeling, authorities had the poet's coffin removed from the church crypt in the dead of night on February 3, 1837 and placed on a fast police sleigh to be sent for burial in Svyatogorsky Monastery, by Mikhailovskoye. All show of grief or even respect for the national poet was strictly forbidden. As the sleigh's horses were changed in a small station not far from Petersburg, the wife of the censor Nikitenko asked a peasant about the sled. "Yeah... some guy named Pushkin got killed, and, dear Lord, they're shipping his body out like a dog's, in burlap and straw!" Only two persons were allowed to accompany the coffin on the long trip: the gendarme Rakeyev, and Pushkin's old friend Alexander Turgenev, by command of the Tsar. Yet Nikita Kozlov, the poet's devoted servant from cradle to grave, stayed by the coffin ceaselessly, and "neither ate nor drank for three days from grief." The "sunshine of Russian poetry" was buried at dawn on February 6, 1837. Just two of the Osipova-Vulf sisters and a few serfs joined Turgenev and Kozlov in mourning him.

Natalya visited her husband's grave only twice: first in 1841, when an obelisk was placed on his tomb, then finally in 1842. In 1844 she remarried General Pyotr Lanskoy. She later spent time together again with D'Anthès in the Slovakian country estate of her older sister, Alexandra Goncharova, who married Austrian diplomat Baron Gustav Friesonhof. Natalya died on November 26, 1863 in St. Petersburg.

Russia's first monument to Pushkin was only erected in 1880, in Moscow – an occasion for famous speeches about Russia's national bard by Dostoyevsky, Turgenev, and others. That monument stands in what is now called Pushkin Square.

If you chance to be there just before seven o'clock in the evening, it may seem to you that all the fretting lovers in the city are waiting by the poet's statue. Perhaps for an instant, before their dates, they imbibe a bit of his loving energy, his warmth, wit, passion, and intensity. Of course, there is a more prosaic explanation (his statue is directly over the hub connecting Moscow's three busiest subway lines).

Yet it is meet that lovers meeting should stand sometimes with flowers near where Pushkin stands, by those central arteries, in the very heart of Moscow, the heart of Russia, the city where the poet was born and married. When after construction his monument was moved, it ended up on a little mound, turned aside from the nearby Kremlin. As ever, he pays no heed to that great seat of power; instead, with majestic melancholy, he gazes at the constant stream of everyday humanity spilling in and out of perhaps the busiest single branch of McDonald's in the entire world.

As a poet myself, I am sentimentally attached to Pushkin Square; how much joy and grief it has brought me! Yet few places on Earth are quite as soulful and serene as the graveyard in the Svyatogorsky Monastery where Pushkin rests by his mother, where:

> Above the solid graves an oak stands, broad boughs spanning
> With quivering, rustling leaves.

What peacefulness and love abide there, what grace and dignity! A grave is ever a place of quiet mourning and wordless contemplation. Yet I have stood by Pushkin's grave, and felt an odd lightness in the heart, a mysterious warmth and inner comfort which no logic could explain... As if this great soul – this "soul in sacred lyre" – has there received at long last – at least from Mother Nature – that one true maternal, ever-caring, ever-feminine love he was always seeking.

> And though the body without feeling
> Will wither anywhere and keep,
> Yet closer to a place endearing
> Is where I feel I'd rather sleep.
>
> I'd like, if by my graveyard's entrance,
> A sweet young life would bloom and play,
> And nature, shining with indifference,
> Forever beauty would display.

SELECTED LYRIC POETRY OF ALEXANDER PUSHKIN

I. SONGS OF YOUTH

Have you not heard his voice through groves at night –
The bard of love, the bard of his own sorrow?

THE BARD

Have you not heard his voice through groves at night –
The bard of love, the bard of his own sorrow?
When silent fields did wake upon the morrow,
That sound so sad and simple of his pipe –
Have you not heard?

Have you not met in bare dark forest bleak
The bard of love, the bard of his own sorrow?
Did you his hints of tears, his smiles not follow,
His quiet glance, his eyes consumed with grief –
Have you not met?

Have you not sighed, hearing his quiet voice,
The bard of love, the bard of his own sorrow?
When you looked at that youth in wooded hollow,
And met the gaze of his despondent eyes
Have you not sighed?

My confidante of magical old times,
Friend of my fancies playful, melancholy,
I knew you in the springtime of my life,
In my first dreams and frolics jolly.
I'd wait for you; in evening's quiet rest
You would appear, a laughing, merry granny,
And sit by me, wrapped in your peasant dress,
Wearing huge glasses, playful rattle clanging.
And as you rocked my cradle tenderly
You captivated my young ear with song,
And in my cradle left a pipe for me,
Which you yourself entranced with magic charm.
As childhood passed by, light as a light dream,
You then loved a young man, a carefree spirit,
Of all great Muses you alone did he
Remember later, when you'd sneak a visit.
But was it really you, your dress, your form?
How sweetly now, how quickly you'd transformed!
What fire lit up your smile as – through my door –
What fire in looks of welcome blazed; what storm!
Your cape that swirled in stirred-up waves contrary
So slightly veiled your lithe frame, almost airy,
Sweet your locks flowed, wreathed once more in a curl,
Your face of an enchantress, fragrant sweetly,
Your bosom whitened 'neath a yellow pearl,
Blushed red and glowed, while seething quietly...

MY PORTRAIT*

My portrait you demand –
But true to life and pure;
My dear, it's coming, on command,
Albeit in miniature.

A young flibbertigibbet I,
Who must still sit in class,
Not dumb, though, I say, nor shy,
Nor fond of posed grimace.

There never was a babbler worse
Or Doctor of the Sorbonne
Who caused more trouble and more fuss
Than myself, *en personne.*

My height cannot be much compared
To much, much larger churls;
I have fresh skin, light reddish hair,
And my head in curls.

I love the world, all its events,
And I hate solitude.
I abhor quarrels and arguments,
And my (few) studies too.

I'm fond of balls and dancing – much,
Of going to a play,
I'd say what else is it I love...
Were I not still in Lycée.

By all of this, *mon cher ami,*
You'll recognize my portrait.
Yes! Just as our good Lord fashioned me
I'd still like to look always.

True demon in delinquency,
True monkey in his mien,
A lot – way too much – flippancy!
My word! Voilà Pouchkine!

* Translated from the original French.

THE PAGE, OR MY FIFTEENTH YEAR

C'est l'âge de Chérubin...

My fifteenth year I'll soon be reaching;
Will I last till that joyous day?
Oh! How it sets my head a-reeling!
No one again will dare be needling
Me, or look with scorn my way.

I'm not a boy now. No! Already
A moustache bristles o'er my lips.
Like toothless old men, haughty, heady,
I walk; my voice is rough and ready,
If you push me, it's you who trips!

I please the ladies me, shy and modest,
And one of them I too revere...
Her proud gaze is so tempting, luscious,
Her dark cheeks blushing give me rushes,
More than my life I prize her dear.

She's strict, loves power, is ambitious,
I'm quite astonished by her mind.
But it's too awful how she's jealous,
Yet fends the world off with pride zealous,
Yet just to me alone is kind.

Just yesterday to me she grandly
Vowed: if e'er again my eyes dare rove
With scapegrace freedom randomly –
She'll give me poison: so, you see,
Is just how madly she does love!

She'd fly with me to deserts lawless
And feel contempt for gossip's whirl.
You want to know who is my goddess,
My Sevillana, peerless countess?
No! I won't name her for the world!

A STATUE IN TSARSKOYE SELO

Dropping a water-filled urn from a cliff,
a young maiden did smash it.
Sadly that maiden now sits, holding the useless shard still.
Marvel! That water still flows:
from the urn that was smashed it's still streaming,
And, as its gush never ends, sadly that maiden still sits.

EUGENE ONEGIN. CHAPTER VIII
(From the Unpublished Verses)

I Back then, when in the Lycée's garden
I unrebelliously bloomed,
Read keenly *Elisey's Tale* charming,
Thought Cicero an old buffoon,
Back then, when even a rare poem
Meant less to me than balls well thrown,
And I thought schoolwork was a bore,
Into the park the fence leaped o'er,
When I at times could be quite zealous,
Lazy at times, other times tough,
Sometimes quite cunning, sometimes gruff,
Subdued at times, at times rebellious,
Sometimes be sad, in silence pent,
Sometimes heartfeltly eloquent,

II When I would daydream before lessons,
Sometimes my sight and hearing dimmed,
I tried with bass voice asking questions,
And shaved the first down off my lip,
Back then...back then, when I first noted
The traits and ways, with eyes devoted,
Of maids enchanting, and when love
Was always stirring my young blood,
And I, just sighing for love vainly,
Thrashed in the wake of passion's dreams,
I sought love everywhere, it seems,
And daydreamed just of love so gently,
All day for one fleet meeting yearned,
The joys of secret suffering learned.

III Back then, 'neath oak-groves' arching sadness,
By waters flowing quietly,
In my Lyceum's corner pathways
The Muse began to come to me.
My little student cell monastic,
Which, until now, had not known gladness,
At once was gleaming, and the Muse
Laid there a feast of songs to choose.
Farewell, farewell, cold sciences!
I'm now from youthful games estranged!
I am a poet now; I've changed.
Within my soul both sounds and silence
Pour into one another, live,
In measures sweet both take and give.

IV Still of first tenderness a dreamer,
My Muse could never sing enough
*(Amorem canat aetas prima)**
All about love, and love, and love.
I echoed Her, and my friends youthful
In leisured hours at ease, unrueful,
Would love to listen to my voice.
How passionately their souls rejoiced
With zealous brotherly enthusing:
They first of all did laurels bring
To me, that for them I might sing
The fruits of my still timid musing.
Oh, joy of innocence of old!
How sweet your dream is to my soul!

* "Let youth's song be of love." From Sextus Propertius, *Elegies*, Book II, x, line 7.

TO MY FRIENDS

For you the gods but briefly will
Give golden days and golden nights,
With languor lovely maidens still
Will cast upon you watchful eyes.
So sing and gambol, friends, the while!
Spend every hour of fleet eve's racing,
And at your carefree merrymaking
I'll look through my bright tears and smile!

IN THE ALBUM OF [THE ACTRESS] SOSNITSKAYA

You managed to combine a coldness very heartfelt
    With wondrous warmth of captivating eyes.
    Whoever loves you's certainly a dumbbell;
But he who loves you not's dumber a hundred times.

A St. Petersburg Actress

TO DORIDA

She loves me! I believe! The heart must keep believing.
No, never would my darling be deceiving!
There's no pretense in her dear languid passion swift,
Shy modesty, the Graces' priceless gift,
Her costume and her speech, charming in carefree manner,
The youthful way she calls me soft pet names so tender.

EPIGRAM ABOUT ARAKCHEYEV*

Persecuting all of Russia,
Even governors he'll torture,
And the State Council will lecture:
He's the Tsar's brother and friend.
Full of malice, full of vengeance,
Without wit, heart, honour, conscience,
Who's he? "*Unflattering in reverence,*"
And whore's toy solider, in the end.

*Count Aleksey Arakcheyev was Deputy President of the Council of Ministers, and effectively headed Tsar Alexander I's government from 1815—1825. An extreme reactionary and martinet who founded brutal military colonies, he chose "Unflattering in reverence" as the device for his coat-of-arms. His mistress, Anastasia Minkina, was so ill-tempered that it was said she was the only man Count Arakcheyev feared. She was murdered in 1825, it is believed, by her serfs.

Of foreign lands an inexperienced lover,
'Gainst my own land, though, constantly a mutterer,
I'd say out loud: in this country of mine
Where would one honest wit or genius find?
Where is a man who's civil, noble-hearted?
Who's fiery, free, outspoken and exalted?
Where is a woman's fairness not like ice,
But captivating, fiery, and alive?
Whose conversation's easy and unfrightened,
With brilliant wit that's happy and enlightened?
With whom are we not cool, empty, and bland?
My Fatherland I almost hated, really...
But then I saw Golitsyna last evening...
And – now – I'm fine with my dear Fatherland.

ODE TO LIBERTY

Begone, and vanish from my sight,
You Cytherean queen so feeble!*
But where are you, of Tsars the blight,
You songstress proud of heady freedom?
Tear off my laurel, cast it down
And smash my over-precious lyre!
I'll sing to all of Freedom's fire
And smash down vice upon its throne!

And show me now the noble road
You made for that inspired Gaul**
Into whose heart, 'midst glorious woe,
You hymns courageous did install.
You foster-sons of flighty Fate,
World's tyrants, tremble and take heed,
Whilst you – take courage, hear indeed –
Arise, arise, you downcast slaves!

Alas! Where'er I cast my gaze –
Always the scourge, the rod appears,
Of laws' oppressive deadly shame
And impotent caged peoples' tears.
And unjust power everywhere
In hazy prejudice does dwell,
Enslaves us through a genius fell
That but for deadly glory cares.

Despite crowned monarchs' majesty,
Alone those lands don't groan and cower
Where wed to holy liberty,
With ties that bind, are just laws' power,
Whose broad shield firm defends us all,

* Refers to Venus, goddess of love.
** Refers to the poet French André Chénier, guillotined in 1794.

Where, held in faithful hands unquiv'ring,
The sword of Justice, never slipping,
Impartial, fair, holds all in thrall.

Even the mighty's crimes are stayed
When that sword firm and fair appears,
Where hands that wield that sword aren't swayed
By selfish greed or yet by fears.
Rulers! Your crowns and laurels do
Not come from God, but from Law's hand.
Above the people you do stand,
But Law Eternal stands o'er you.

And woe to those unhappy lands
In which the law is slumbering,
Where either mob or crownèd king
Do take the law into their hands.
....
You tyrant rogue, 'gainst whom none dares!
You and your throne I hate with passion!
Your doom, the death of all your heirs,
With cruel joy I can imagine.
Upon your brow all find the trace
And stamp of countless people's curses.
You're nature's shame, world's blight outrageous!
That you exist is God's disgrace!

When on Nevá's dark gloomy flow
The star of midnight sparkles, prances,
To pillows carefree heads sink slow,
As calm sleep burdens them in trances,
The poet only stares till morn,
At dreaded outline, in mist skirted,
At tyrant's monument deserted,
A palace now forgot, forlorn.

The bard hears Clio's voice and cowers:
Beyond where that wall dreaded lies,
Our Tsar Caligula's last hours
He sees before his very eyes,
Sees how, with stars and ribbons strewed,
With wine and malice drunk, approaching,
The secret killers come, with loathing,
Fear in the hearts, their faces rude.

The faithless sentry silent stands,
The drawbridge lowering stealthily,
The gates to Treason's hired hands
In darkness ope relentlessly...
Oh shame and horror of our times!
Those janissaries, beasts, invaded,
Their blows rained down, inglorious traitors!
A crownèd villain murdered lies.

And hence, take heed, great heads of states!
Nor executions, nor promotions,
Nor altars, nor barred dungeons' gates
Defend you against heaven's motions.
But bow your heads first, willingly
Beneath the Law's unerring portal,
Then o'er your throne stand guard, immortal,
The people's peace and liberty.

Marianne, Spirit of Liberty

TO PRINCESS GOLITSYNA, SENT WITH AN ODE TO LIBERTY

A simple child of nature being,
I used to praise, in all my song,
The lovely sacred dream of freedom,
I breathed it sweetly, breathed it strong.
But when I hear you, when I see you –
What now? Oh weakling! Woe is me!
I'll nevermore again be free,
With all my heart love slavery.

TO TURGENEV* (EXCERPTS)

...Why do you mock me feverishly
When my hand, quivering feebly,
Lost on my lyre, only refined
And tender chords of dearest rapture
Of love, the heart's exquisite torture,
In its still untuned strings can find?
Yes, being given up to pleasure,
Most sweetly do I sweetly sleep –
Just you – an idler beyond measure –
For zealous work still ardour keep;
...Bearing your crushing duties' burden
Of empty, serious, heavy chores,
Alone you find the time for sermons
To mock my idleness and mores.

But summon me no more, I'm pleading,
To Work, forever dropped, despised,
Nor to poetic lack of freedom,
Nor yet to verses I've revised!
What is the point? Is it worthwhile
To weakly sing of how I pine?
Yet let Ninette but with a smile
Arouse this carefree love of mine,
While calming, setting it on fire!
But Work is cold and flat – not missed:
No epic poem e'er could rival
A smile from sweet and passionate lips!

*Alexander Ivanovich Turgenev was the poet's close friend (it was he who in the end escorted Pushkin's coffin for burial in Svyatogorsky Monastery). Though a fellow member of the jovial Arzamas literary society, Turgenev was Director of the Department of Religious Affairs in the government. By contrast, his brother Nikolay was a Decembrist firebrand who escaped execution only by fleeing to Britain. Pushkin wrote his *Ode to Liberty* at a party at the Turgenev brothers' home (20, Fontanka Canal, overlooking Tsar Paul I's Mikhatlovskiy Palace in St. Petersburg).

THE COUNTRY

I'm glad to see you, lonely barren nook,
Of calm and work my haven, full of inspiration,
Where my life's days stream by, flow in an unseen brook,
    Of sheer oblivion and elation!
I'm yours! I've fled our Circes' sinful reels,
Balls, sumptuous feasts, amusements, false temptations,
For rustling oak trees' peace, and silence in the fields,
For freedom's idleness, true friend of cogitation.
    I'm yours: I love this garden dark.
    I love its coolness and its flowers,
This meadow, where sweet hayricks make their bowers,
The light streams gurgling, banked by hedges gnarled.
Whichever way I look are paintings, always moving,
Before me two lakes' plains, agleam in their vast bluing;
Sometimes a fisherman hoists up his sail's white span;
Beyond, a row of hills, and golden harvest growing,
    Far off the wandering herds are lowing,
Above the lakes' moist banks, where scattered huts do stand,
Are wingèd windmills, byres, and barns for drying, smoky:
    Signs everywhere of peaceful works of man.

Here I, from chains of vanity, at last find freedom,
I'm learning how, in truth, bliss can at last,
In reverence for law my soul's freedom finds ground,
No mutterings of mob's benighted malice heeding,
With sympathy I hear each shy prayer that's made,
    Yet have no envy for the state
Of wicked men or fools who strut their grand injustice.

Oh oracles of time, now I call unto you!
    In this seclusion so majestic,
    Your joyous voice rings clearly through,
    Casts torpor off from tired grieving:
    For work a fever takes its stead,
    Creative thoughts from you and feelings
    Mature within my soul's own depths.

Yet here a horrid thought the heart forever darkens:
    For, midst the hilltops and the wheat field's golden mane,
A friend of mankind looks around and sadly hearkens
To inhumanity, to murderous, bloody shame.
    For, blind to tears and deaf to groaning,
As if chosen by Fate for people's doom and harm,
Here serfdom savage, neither heart nor true law knowing,
Has stolen for itself – by Violence's rod –
The work and property and time of peasants grieving.
Bent over others' ploughs, sullen, and cowed by whips,
Here scrawny slavery must drag through furrows rich –
    Just for the landowner unyielding.
Here everyone must bear harsh yokes until the grave;
To heed one's hopes, one soul's own voice, no one here's daring,
    Here every blossoming fair maid
    Gets forced to be a toy for villains cold, uncaring.
And here the dear support of fathers as they age,
Their younger sons, their friends in toil, in labour brave,
March off to multiply, teeming from poor huts dirty,
In courtyards shambling, a crowd of tortured slaves.
Oh, if my voice but knew how others' hearts to worry!
Oh why within my breast does useless fever sit?
And why has fate denied me rhetoric's great gift?
Friends! Will I live to see my people no more blightened
And slavery cast down upon the Tsar's command?
Above my fatherland by freedom's grace enlightened
– At last – is a dawn beautiful at hand?

TO CHAADAYEV

Of love, and hope, and quiet glory
Deceptions dear did not last long.
Our youthful games have vanished wholly,
Like dreams, like drifting morning fog.
But still in us desire's burning,
Oppressed by power's deadly yoke,
Impatiently our souls are yearning:
We hear the calling of our folk.
We wait with yearning, our hearts pounding,
For Freedom's sacred fleeting bliss,
The way young lovers fret while counting
The minutes to a secret tryst.
For while with freedom we do burn,
While in our hearts honour's still living,
My friend, to our land's aid let's turn
Our souls, impulsive beauty giving!
Comrade, believe: she will soar steep,
Our star of captivating rapture,
For Russia will arise from sleep,
And on the shards of slavery fractured
Our names will be writ large, and keep!

II. SOUTHERN IDYLLS

I see the shoreline in the distance,
The magic South, land of the noonday sun...

The day's last gleam fades out, is disappearing,
In evening mist the ocean blue is sheathed.
Make sound, make sound, you little breeze obedient!
Wave, worry under me, you gloomy, giant sea.
I see the shoreline in the distance,
The magic South, land of the noonday sun;
With turmoil and with grief my soul must thither run,
Aglow with recollections wistful!
My eyes again give birth to tears from God above;
My soul's aboil, and shudders, sighing,
My dream of old, so cherished, round me flickers, flying,
Remembered from years past it comes back: Crazy love!
And all I suffered from, all my heart finds endearing,
All hopes, and all desires that languorously deceive...
Make sound, make sound, you little breeze obedient!
Wave, worry under me, you gloomy, giant sea.
Fly on, my vessel, bear me off to distant shorelines,
By dreaded whimsy of the treacherous great seas,
Don't bring me back to bleak coasts pining,
To my own country's misty leas!
That land where passion's fire first seized
My heart, and feelings warmed my spirit,
Where tender Muses first did smile on me in secret,
Where in first storms the bloom did pall,
Of youth that now is lost forever,
Where joy betrayed, and fled with wings light-feathered,
Abandoned my cold heart to suffering and gall.
I, restless, searched for new sensations,
And fled from you, coasts where my homeland ends!
I fled from you, you fount of brief elations,
Of youth's brief moment momentary friends!
And you, you temptresses of sinful aberrations,

For whom I gave myself up, loveless, whole,
Gave up my rest, my glory, freedom, and my soul,
Yes, you're forgotten too, fair-weather girlfriends fleeting,
So young, of my gold springtime my best friends in secret,
Yes, you're forgotten too! Though still they live in me,
Old heart-wounds, wounds of love, that never healed, still bleeding...
  Make sound, make sound, you little wind obedient,
Wave, worry under me, you gloomy, giant sea.

Alas! Say, why is she so shining
With tender beauty brief, which soon
So noticeably fades, declining
In youth, just as it most does bloom?
T'will fade! The life her youth possesses
Will not be hers long to enjoy.
Not long will she be raining blessings,
Her family circle's greatest joy,
With carefree wittiness, endearing,
Our chats be sweetly brightening,
And with her soul so calm, all healing,
Assuage my soul that's suffering.
My melancholy woe concealing
With nervous thoughts, I, burdened, rush
To hear and hear her phrases cheering
And cannot look at her enough!
I watch each movement that she's started,
Each sound she utters take in whole:
The slightest moment being parted
Is sheerest torment to my soul.

The flying wisps of clouds are thinning, scattering far.
O star of melancholy, oh bright evening star!
Your ray silvers the plains, the vast steppe slowly fading,
The bay that dozes hushed, black cliff-peaks silver painting,
I love your feeble light in Heaven's height a-glimmering,
It wakens thoughts in me that long since had been slumbering,
Your rising clings to me, familiar shining sphere,
Above that peaceful land, where all to my heart's dear,
Where graceful poplars spring up tall in valleys steep,
Where tender myrtles and dark cypresses do sleep,
And sweetly soft the surf of southern waves is sounding,
There in those mountains I, wrapped up in my heart's pounding,
Did take my pensive ease, and loomed above the sea,
Watched night's soft shade lull huts to sleep there wistfully,
And through the mists, o star, for you, searching the ether,
With her own name a girl named you to girlfriends eager.

THE STORM

Have you seen, perched upon a cliff,
A maid in white, above the whitecaps?
In stormy mist the raging swish
Of waves that raced ashore in rising,
When rays from lightning bolts did shine
Upon her with a scarlet gilting,
And furious wind did beat and fly
From her in evanescent quilting?
The sea is fair in stormy mist
And fair the sky gleams in foul weather.
That maid, though, trust me, on that cliff,
Than waves or sky or storm is fairer.

GRAPES

No, I'm not going to mourn the roses
That faded with the slight fleet spring;
I'm fond of grapes before they're chosen,
On hillside vineyards ripening.
They make my fertile valley splendid,
Bring joy to autumn's golden whirl,
Caressing, thin, long, sweet, and tender,
Like fingers of a sweet young girl.

TO A GREEK GIRL

You have been born to set afire
Imagination in us poets,
To captivate it, to inspire
With lively greetings, charming habits,
With your exotic Eastern speech,
Your eyes, that like a mirror gleam,
Your tiny little foot so tempting...
Yes, you were born for blissful splendour,
For passion, living fervently.
But tell me, when the bard of Leila*
Was singing his celestial dream
Of his ineffable ideal,
Was it not you he made appear,
That bard of heartache so delightful?
Did, very far away, perhaps,
Beneath the skies of sacred Hellas,
That skald of griefs inspired, zealous,
Perceive you in a dream perchance?
And was your memorable visage
Concealed within his heartfelt depths?
What if, to his glad harp you, listening,
Let that magician's tempting skill
Make murmurs rise against your will
Within your breast so proud, yet quivering,
Which you, slight, on his shoulder, laid?...
No, no, my friend! Of jealous whispering
I do not wish to feed the flame;
For ages, no joy could I feel,
T'is new to me, this pleasure brief,
And sunk in a mysterious grief,
I fear what's lovely can't be real.

Calypso Polychroni, mistress of both Byron and Pushkin

* "The Bard of Leila" (Lord Byron).

A lantern in a Jewish hovel
Small in a corner, flickers, pales,
Beneath that lantern an old man
Re-reads the Bible. His grey hairs
In curled locks fall upon his book,
While a young Jewish woman weeps
Above a cradle lying empty.
Across the hut, in his thoughts steeped,
Head downcast, her young husband sits,
And ponders something very deeply.
And in that sad hut an old woman
Prepares the meagre evening meal.
Closing his Holy Book, the old man
Now folds it shut with clasps of brass.
His old wife sets down their poor supper
And calls the family to eat.
But no one comes, heedless of food.
The silent hours slip away.
All slumbers 'neath night's vaulting murky.
The Jewish hovel, all alone,
Withstands sleep's happy visitation.
The bell-tower of their small town
Strikes midnight. Suddenly a knocking,
Dread, pounding, startles them. They shudder,
The young Jew gets up, quite unnerved,
Opens the door with shock and horror,
And in lumbers an unknown wanderer,
Holding a heavy walking staff...

I have outgrown my aspirations,
No longer do I love my dreams.
I'm left with suffering in patience
My heart's own emptiness, it seems.

In Fate's cruel storms and pointless roamings,
My flowering laurel wreathe did fade.
And so I live in sadness, lonely,
And wait: is my end on its way?

Just so, by fall's last chills defeated,
When first cold winter snowstorms shriek,
Alone, on the bare branch depleted,
Trembles the long-delayed last leaf.

I will fall silent soon. But if, on days of sadness,
With pensive play my heart's harp-strings once answered,
If ever once bright youths my voice in silence heard,
And if they ever once admired my long love's torture,
If ever you yourself indulged in loving rapture,
And murmured mournful verse alone when no one stirred,
And loved the passion of my heart's own language...
If, if I still am loved, allow me, friend so dear,
To with my lyre give life and bring to ear
The name my beautiful and cherished love once carried.
But when the sleep of death takes me for evermore,
Utter above my urn, with tender resignation:
Oh, he was loved by me, for me his heart did pour
Forth songs and love with his last inspiration.

My friend, I have forgot all trace of passing years,
And all the torrents wild of being young, rebellious,
Don't ask me to tell more of what's no longer here,
Of what was given me in sadness and in pleasure,
    What I did love, by what I was betrayed,
Though not entirely of joy perhaps I taste,
Still you are innocent, and born to just be happy.
Believe in happiness, seize each fleet moment, trust:
Your soul's alive for friendship and for love,
    For kisses lingering with sweet passion.
Your soul is clean and pure, and never has known grief,
For light as a clear day's the adolescent conscience.
Why should you hear from me how crazy passions sear
    Some unsurprising story artless?
That tale, against your will, will stir your quiet mind.
Tears out of you will pour, your heart in pangs will tighten,
In carefree trusting soul, the carefree trust will blighten,
And then my love for you, perhaps, will only frighten,
Scare you, perhaps for good. Darling! No, let's just dally...
I am afraid to lose my last sensations pleasant.
Demand from me no more such dangerous confessions.
Today, today, I love; today, today, I'm happy.

A LITTLE BIRD

Though exiled, I observe, still heeding,
A sacred rite from upbringing:
I give a little bird its freedom
To mark the joyous birth of spring.

I'm worthy now of consolations.
Why unto God should I complain?
Since even one of his creations
Through me goes free, life's not in vain!

FRAGMENT FROM ONEGIN'S JOURNEY

I lived then in Odessa dusty,
The skies are clear and free down there,
And busy trade abounds, is fussy
Erecting broad sails in the air,
Of Europe all there hints and hearkens,
Breathes, has a southern shine, and sparkles,
Flaunts lively, vast variety:
The golden tongue of Italy
Resounds along its happy streets
Where proud Slavs strut, and Frenchmen preen,
Where Spaniard greets Armenian,
Where Greek, Moldavian fat with sweets,
Or Egypt's son walks by that sea,
Retired corsair, Moor Ali.

Odessa in melodious verses
Our friend Tumansky has described.
But he with passionate prejudices
Too much within his gaze imbibed.
He came, marched straight off, like a poet,
Lone o'er the sea to gaze with lorgnette,
And then wrote paeans with charming pen
Of green Odessa's garden glen,
All in a panegyric *thème.*
And that's all fine; there's just one thing:
Bare steppes around that point are ringed.
His work, like magic, forces, then,
On hot days, bare shrubs on the hill,
To spread broad shade against their will!

But where's my tale now run off, silly?
"Odessa dusty," I had said:
I could have said "Odessa swilly,"
And not lied, either, 't must be plead.
For five-six weeks a year's the norm,
By will of Zeus, Lord of the Storm,
The place gets drowned, drenched, mushed, and mashed,
Into a thick mud sinks at last.
All homes with yards of mud get flayed.
Only on stilts foolhardy walkers
Vainly attempt to ford streets swollen;
Coaches and people stall, dismayed:
Hitched oxen, their broad horns bent down,
Take feeble stallions' places now.

But soon the masons' hammers sound,
Set, soon, a stone pavement resounding,
Real stone covers the new, saved town,
Like smithies, horseshoes' bronzes pounding.
Although, in this Odessa humid,
There's one more problem, don't you know it?
Of all the things they lack! it's water!
It's going to be a frightful bother!
Although, it's no great cause to pine –
Especially when so much wine
Gets brought in free, evading customs.
But southern sunshine? Black Sea bright?
For what more could one ask, my friends?
A land the gods themselves have blessed!

When the dawn cannon shot got fired,
Called to the hills forth from its ship,
Straight down the dunes I'd race inspired,
At first light to the sea I'd slip.
And then, ah! through a hot pipe stave,
Enlivened by the salty wave,
Like Muslim gone to heaven and back,
I'd sip thick Eastern coffee, black.
Then off to stroll...By now, appealing,
The Casino starts. Cups clinking.
Can be heard, the croupier yawning
Comes to the balcony, half sleeping,
A broom in hand, and by the gate
Two merchants' terms by now are met.

And look! The whole square bursts with colours!
All's come alive: and to and fro
On business, or for fun, streets flutter –
Though more, it seems, on business go.
Scanning the flags of every nation,
The merchant, child of calculation
And risk, inquires if the skies
Send welcome sails home as his prize.
And what new goods now are required
To be declared in quarantine?
Perhaps it's come at last, fresh wine
In barrels? Where's there plague or fire
Or famine, perhaps, or a war?
Or something new like that in store?

But we, like kids who know no sadness,
Ignored the worried traders' woes.
We only wanted oysters brought us
From far Constantinople's coasts.
And have they come, our oysters? Wondrous!
Our happy ranks of youthful gluttons
Fly to devour, from ocean shells
Their captives lush, fat, and alive,
With just a bit of lemon sprinkled.
Noise, argument, and light white wine
Gets brought from cellars to be tippled
By Automne's* waiters, seeming kind,
(As time flies by, their bill of woe.
Invisibly the while does grow).

But dusky blue the sky is darkening,
The Opera awaits, we race,
There Europe's darling, ever-charming,
Rossini now our Orpheus plays!
He pays no heed to direst critics;
Always the same, yet new, and witty,
He pours forth sounds: and how they boil!
And how they flow and burn and hiss!
Passion'd as young lovers who kiss
In bliss, in happiness of love,
Like champagne, ever bubbling, rolling,
In streams and sprays of droplets golden
But folks, is it perhaps a crime,
With do-re-mi comparing wine?

* César Automne — The fanciest French restaurant in Odessa at that time.

Does naught else makes the evening charming?
Aren't opera-glasses fond of play?
Can't trysts be had in darkened corners?
And prima donnas? And ballet?
Can't we watch beauty in the *loge*,
Where trader's daughter flaunts and shows
Her youth and grace, her languor proud –
Around her willing slaves all crowd?
She hears and yet she doesn't hear
The cavatina, or the prayers,
The jokes and flattery mixed in layers...
Her husband slumbers, by her near,
Half-sleeping, he calls out "encores"
Then yawns, and once again he snores.

Finale played, the hall grows bare,
And bustling, rushing off, crushed, spars
The crowd, running about the square
Amid the gleam of lamps and stars.
And blessed Italy's bright sons
With their light touch croon playful runs
By heart, half automatically,
While we sob the recitative.
But now it's late. Odessa sleeps,
Soft is its warm and breathless night,
Numbed. The moon arises calm and bright,
Diaphanous its curtained light meets
And embraces heaven. All is still
But the Black Sea's murmuring rill...

And so, I lived then in Odessa...

NIGHT

My voice, only for you, affectionate and yearning,
The darkened silent lull of late night wakes, disturbing.
A candle by my bed with sadness lonely burns.
My verse begins to spring, pours bubbling out and churns,
And flows, a brook of love, it flows, full of you, brimming,
Your eyes before me shine, in darkness gleam, a-shimmering,
And when they smile at me, my love, you voice implores:
My friend, my tender friend...I love!... I'm yours... I'm yours!

For one last time, my friend so tender,
I come again to your sweet bower.
To love and happiness surrender,
In peace with you share one last hour.
Henceforth no more with hopeful longing
Pass dark night just to me belonging,
No more, until the sun's first rays,
Let candles blaze.

Night's soft breeze
Streams easeful; clear
And foaming
Flows
Guadalquivir.

Mark the golden moon appearing,
Hush! As a guitar sings free...
As a youthful señorita
Leans against her balcony.

Night's soft breeze
Streams easeful; clear
And foaming
Flows
Guadalquivir.

Cast your shawl off, darling angel,
Show yourself, as bright as day!
Through grilled bars of wrought-iron tracery
Slip your sweet foot through, and play!

Night's soft breeze
Streams easeful; clear
And foaming
Flows
Guadalquivir.

By a noble señorita,
Spanish beauty, stand two knights,
Both are daring, both are freely
Looking straight into her eyes.
Both with handsomeness are gleaming,
Bright of mind, of fiery hearts,
Both of them alertly leaning
With strong hands upon their swords.

Dearer than their lives they prize her,
Bright as glory shines her star,
But just one her heart replies to:
Who has won this maiden's heart?
"Who, decide, is your beloved?"
To the maiden say both knights,
Standing both with hopes so young and
Looking straight into her eyes.

Beneath the light blue skies of her own native land,
In languor languishing and pining,
She faded out at last, till faithfully she spanned
Her shadow young above me flying.
Yet twixt us looms a bound beyond our ken:
In vain I sought for feelings searing.
I heard from lips indifferent of her death,
The news indifferently hearing.
But is this whom I loved with all my fiery soul
In constant, burdened consternation?
For whom my tenderness and grief did endless flow,
With so much craziness and torment and elation?
And now? Where's woe, where's love? Alas! My soul can find
For that poor shadow trusting, hoping,
For memories sweet of days forever left behind,
No hint of tears or self-reproaching.

Amalia Riznich

Bound for your homeland's distant shoreline,
Our distant foreign land you left.
That hour of memory, hour mournful,
Long time in front of you I wept.
My arms, as they were growing number,
Tried, tried to hold you tightly tucked,
And separation's frightful suffering
My moans prayed you'd not interrupt.

But you from our caressing bitter
Pulled back your lips and tore them free.
And from this land of exile wistful
To a new land were calling me.
You said: "that day reunion graces,
Beneath a sky that's always blue,
Where olive trees give shade, love's kisses,
We'll once again, my friend, renew.

But there, alas, where heaven's vaulting
Is sparkling light cerulean blue,
Where olives' shades lie on the waters,
Your final sleep has come to you.
Your suffering, your beauty fleeting,
Into the grave's urn vanished then,
With them the kisses of our meeting...
But I still wait; you owe me them.

INVOCATION

Oh, if it's true that in the night,
When sleep embraces all the living,
And, down from heaven, moonbeams bright,
Play on the tombstones, tripping, slipping,
Oh, if it's true that then, indeed,
The silent graves are oped, and empty,
I call Leila's shade, I'm waiting:
To me, my friend, come here, come here!

Appear, oh shade that I have loved,
The way you were before we parted,
Like winter's day, cold, pale and dulled,
By final agonies distorted.
Shine like a distant star, appear
Like a light sound or wind's soft swishing,
Or like a dreaded apparition:
I do not care, come here, come here!

I do not call you to reproach
The guilty ones, whose malice needless
Did kill the dearest friend I know,
Or to discover the grave's secrets,
Nor yet because my heart's still seared
With doubts and griefs, sometimes... No! Mourning,
I want to say, I still, still love you,
I'm still all yours, come here, come here!

THE CAPTIVE

Imprisoned, I'm caged in a dungeon that's dank,
A young eaglet, fed but on slavish grains rank,
Then aggrieved, my companion flies nigh, flaps his wings,
And fresh prey, still bloody, to my window brings.

He pecks, casts it through my caged bars with his beak,
Then stares at me, as if his heart heard me speak,
With looks that are calling, with calls that would say,
If shrieks could find words, "Come! Let's fly, fly away!

We're free spirits, brother, let's go, the time's right!
Let's rise through the clouds to the peak ever white!
Let's soar to the borders of blue sea and sky,
And stroll on the wind where just wind strolls – and I!"

If sweet and youthful hope infused my every breath,
If I believed my soul might somehow after death
Escape from mere decay, preserve its thoughts eternal,
Keep memories, keep love past the abyss's portal,
I swear! I would have left this world long, long ago!
I would have snuffed out life, let it, base idol, go,
And flown off to a land of freedom, peace, and pleasures,
A land where there's no death, nor prejudices' tethers,
Where purest thought in Heaven's pureness streams...

Yet vainly do I drift in such deceitful dreams.
My stubborn mind objects, scorns hope that follows doom.
Mere nothingness awaits me once I'm in my tomb...
What? Nothingness? No thoughts, not even my first love?
I'm frightened... And with sadness once more I look on my life
And want to live long, long! so long one face endearing
Might set ablaze in secret my soul dreary.

THE DEMON

Back when, to me, all things shone newly,
All the impressions of this life.
The looks of girls, the wind in oak trees,
The nightingale that sings at night,
When all the loftiest of feelings
Of freedom, glory and of love,
Of arts inspired, just set me reeling,
And powerfully stirred my blood.
Those days of hopes and pleasures easy,
And shocks revealed by sudden grief,
Were when a certain evil genius
In secret came to visit me.
And melancholy were our meetings,
Because his smile, his look so bold
And charming, his sarcastic speeches
Poured chilling poison in my soul.
With slander that was ever-biting,
He taunted, tempted Providence.
He called the beautiful a pipe-dream,
For inspiration had contempt,
And he did not believe in freedom.
He doubted love, held life in scorn.
He could not see the slightest reason
To bless one thing this world had born.

Nikolai Rayevsky

TO THE SEA

Farewell, farewell, free force of nature!
This is the last time I will see
You cast and hurl your breakers azure,
Your beauty proud, your sparkling sheen!

Like friends when parting, moaning, whimpering,
When time has come to say goodbye,
Your sound's so sad, your sound sighs, whispering,
For the last time I hear you cry.

O bound of all my soul's desire!
How often by your shores I've roved,
With silent misty dreams afire,
With languor, full of cherished hopes!

And how I loved your echoes precious,
Your voice of the abyss, dull pounds,
Your calm, when evening stills all sounds,
Your moods, your roaring gusts capricious!

A fisherman's meek sail is cowed,
And so protected by your whimsy,
And slips through towering waves, stays proud,
But then you play, with untamed frenzy,
And fleets of mighty ships are drowned.

Alas, I could not leave forever
My boring, dull, unmoving shores
To celebrate your joys, and quiver,
Tossed by your wave-crests, hither-thither,
Escape, poetic, my locked doors.

You called, you waited, but imprisoned,
I tore my soul in two, and moaned.
Your utter power charmed, impassioned
Me, by your shores left alone.

Why such regret indeed? And whither
Would I now set my careless course?
There's still one object in your desert
That strikes within my soul a chord.

One distant cliff, the grave of glory...
There into cold oblivion
Great memories did sink, deeds storied,
For there did fade Napoleon.

He passed away in suffering, grieving.
Soon after, sudden as a squall,
Another genius disappeared then,
Another ruler of our thoughts.

Lord Byron

He vanished, mourned by tears of Freedom,
But left this world his laurelled art.
So rise up, howl, you storm-winds shrieking!
For he, oh Ocean, was your bard.

Your image all his work was moving:
His soul was fitted to your frame.
Like you, he too was strong, deep, brooding,
And he, like you, could not be tamed.

The world's gone bare. So where now, Ocean,
Where would you wildly carry me?
Man's fate's the same the whole world over:
Where some good's left, it's guarded ever
By Progress or by Tyranny.

Farewell, my Ocean! I'll remember
Your beauty, your triumphant grace!
I'll hear and hear and hear forever
Your roar when evening lights do blaze.

To forests, wildernesses silent,
I take with me, my spirit raves
But of your cliffs and gulfs, your tides and
Your sheen, and shades, and speaking waves!

III. RUSTIC EXILE: MIKHAYLOVSKOYE

I was just born for this life peaceful,
For stillness pastoral, it seems...

A drizzly day's fizzed out; a drizzly night's dull haze
Across the heavens spreads like leaden clothing;
Like a dread ghost, beyond the pine grove roaming,
        The misty moon disperses rays...
As always, gloomy grief upon my soul it's casting...
Way far off, there, the moonrise glitters, glancing,
Down there the air gets drunk, and fills with gloaming warmth,
Down there the sea heaves sheathes of sumptuous foam in swarms
        Beneath the light blue heavens swelling...
Right now's when down the mountainside she likes to roam
To shores completely drowned by waves' roaring and yelling,
        There, underneath the black cliffs blessèd,
In melancholy now, she's sitting there, alone...
Alone! And near her no one's crying, no one's grieving,
No one kisses her knees in bliss, bereavement;
Alone! To no one's lips does she give up
Her shoulders, soft lips moist, her snowy-white soft bosom.
. . . .
. . . .
. . . .
Of her love heavenly no one on earth is worthy.
You are alone, aren't you? You're crying... I won't worry.
. . . .
But if, though. . . . .

THE TALISMAN

Where the ocean comes careening
Against desolate, bare cliffs,
Where the moon is warmly gleaming
On the evening hour's sweet mists,
Where, in harems, at his pleasure,
Days spends the Mohammedan,
There a sorceress gave me treasure,
Kissed me, gave a talisman.

She caressed me in our bower,
Said: "My talisman you'll keep.
It is full of hidden power
And t'is given with love deep.
From disease, the grave, storm's rages,
From the hurricane's dread wave,
Your sweet head, my own, my angel,
This, my talisman, won't save.

Of the Orient the riches,
None my talisman can bring.
Where the Prophet's faithful preaches,
This, my gift, won't make you King.
Longing for your dear friend's bosom,
Forth out of a sad, strange land,
Homewards, northwards, o! my true one!
No speed gives my talisman...

But should cunning eyes behold you,
Suddenly bewitch your mind,
Some dark night, if lips too bold should
Kiss unloving and unkind –
My sweet friend! From sin heart-rending,
From new wounds the heart can't stand,
From betrayal, from forgetting,
Saves you then my talisman!"

THE BURNT LETTER

Farewell, letter of love, farewell. It was her order...
How long I have delayed! How long my poor hand dawdled,
Refused to drag my joys to flame... Enough!
The time has come: burn up, letter of love.
I'm ready; not a thing now is my soul perceiving.
The greedy flame will soon your pages be receiving...
One minute! Sparks fly up, it's blazing, light smoke flares
And winds itself around, gets lost with all my prayers.
Of faithful seal the former evidence,
The melted wax, boils up... Oh, Providence!
It's over! Pages darken, curl, and crest,
In ashes light, now twirling their last traces blest,
They whiten. How my breast is tightened! Dearest ashes,
Poor joy and comfort of my fate's bleak, hopeless passions,
Remain forever with me on my grieving breast.

Yelizaveta Vorontsova

WISH FOR GLORY

When full of love and bliss I felt complete elation,
And on my knees, at you in silent supplication
I looked and looked, just thinking: "You are mine!" –
You know, my dear, was glory on my mind?
You know how I just fled society's fuss showy,
Bored with my gossipy vain title as a poet,
Tired out by endless storms, I paid no heed at all
To distant buzzing praise, or to catcalls.
How could I even care for critics cruel pronouncements
When, leaning close to me, so languorously glancing,
You, slightly, on my head, laying your hand, your glove,
Would whispering, ask me, "Are you happy? Do you love?
Could you love someone else the way you love me ever?
Tell me the truth, my friend: will you forget me never?"
But I an awkward silence then preserved,
And being filled with pleasure totally, inferred
That what would come won't come, that the dread day, us sundering,
Would never ever come. Instead: what? Tears and sufferings,
Betrayal, slander, all on my head now land
All of a sudden... Who am I and where? I stand,
Like a wanderer struck by lightning in the desert.
And all's grown dark before me now; all's altered.
A new desire cooks me in its flame:
I wish for glory now, I wish that with my name
Each hour would e'er confound your hearing, so by me
You'd be surrounded e'er, so with loud, plaintive, crying...
All, everything around you sounded with my noise,
So, in the silence, hearkening to my faithful voice,
You'd not forget my last lorn supplications to you, broken-hearted,
That night in garden's shade, when we were being parted.

SCENE FROM FAUST

Faust and Mephistopheles by the seashore.

Faust

Demon, I'm bored.

Mephistopheles

What of it, Faust?
Such is the bound you're bound to bear.
And there is none who oversteps it.
All clever creatures end up fretting:
Some boredom bores – and some affairs,
One's faithful, one has lost all faith.
One never got of lust his share,
One's shares of pleasures was too great.
Yet all are yawning, all live on,
And for them all the grave does yawn.
So you yawn too.

Faust

How dry that joke is!
Find me some manner nonetheless
To keep amused.

Mephistopheles

Just be content
At this, the proof of your own reason.
Write in your album, if you please,
Fastidium est quies. Tedium
In truth is but the soul's release.
I'm a psychologist: It's science, really!
Tell me: when was it you weren't bored?
Think well. Search in your memory. Own up!
Remember how o'er Virgil you once snored
And only caning woke your wit up?
Or how once roses from you poured
Forth, on eager girls to shower over,
Carousing loud, for them songs roared
With lust from last night's hangover?

Or when you'd disappeared, it seemed,
To the great dreams your great soul dreamed
Into the darkest depths of science?
Yet weren't you bored then? Do confide it!
Like Harlequin forth from the flame
You summoned me at last by name.
I fluttered in, a petty demon,
Endeavouring to make you cheery,
Brought you to witches' dens, to ghosts,
For what? For trifles, nonsense gross!
You wanted glory? And – you got it!
Would fall in love? You did! What of it?
You took from life all life puts out
But were you happy?

Faust

Cut it out.
Poison me not with hidden ulcer.
In deepest knowledge there's no life.
I've cursed the sciences' false light,
And glory... Its rays random, glancing,
Are meaningless as sleep. But there's
Still one good thing left: the joining
Of two souls.

Mephistopheles

And the first tryst's enjoyment,
No? But if inquiry won't offend,
Just whom were you remembering then?
Not Gretchen, now?

Faust

Oh dream so wondrous!
Oh pure and perfect flame of love!
There, where the shady grove soft flutters,
Where sweetly purling streams do rush,
Upon her breast so marvelous
When I my raptured head did lay
I was happy...

Mephistopheles

Oh Father, save us!
You're raving, Faust, by light of day!
Your memory is too convenient
And you deceive yourself, it seems,
Was it not I whose striving eager
Got you your wondrous, beauteous queen,
And in the depths of midnight murky
Brought her to you? And then
I was amused alone to spend
That time, finding my labours worthy.
As you two were ensconced, enthralled,
And as that fine beauty of yours,
Ecstatic, shuddered in elation,
Your soul stayed in a worried state,
Had sunk by now to contemplation
(And you and I did demonstrate
That contemplation's boredom's seed).
So, my dear Sophist, need I state
What you were thinking at that time
When no one thinks?
Should I say?

Faust

Say it! Tell me! Well?

Mephistopheles

You thought then: my meek lamb obedient!
How hungrily I longed for you!
How slyly in a simple maiden
I caused dreams of the heart to stew!
To selfless, helpless love repining,
She gave herself with blameless will...
So why's my own breast now so full
Of grief and boredom so despisèd?

I see the victim of my whim
And look on, sated with my pleasure,
And my contempt now knows no measure,
Just so, a heedless fool might grin
Vainly determined on some evil,
Knifing a beggar in the wood
And curse the cut-up corpse with fever:
So at some venal tart one would,
Sating one's lust on upon her, hurried,
From lechery look askance, now worried.
And you, from all of this delight,
Could only draw one cruel conclusion...

Faust

Begone, hell-hound and dark illusion!
Begone, and vanish from my sight!

Mephistopheles

Gladly – just give me an assignment.
Without one, as you know, I can't
Just separate from you like that –
My time is never frittered idly.

Faust

Say! What's that gleams white from afar?

Mephistopheles

A Spanish galleon, with three masts,
That's reaching Holland now, at last:
Aboard three hundred villains are,
Two monkeys, and gold bullion also,
Of chocolate, too, quite a rich cargo,
Plus one disease... It's stylish, though,
You got its gift not long ago.

Faust

Drown everything.

Mephistopheles

At once.

(Disappears)

A WINTER EVENING

Snowstorm, gloom-filled, heavens drowning,
Wild the snowy whirlwind flies:
Sometimes, like a beast, it's howling,
Sometimes, like a child, it cries,
Sometimes, on our roof's frayed border
With a gust the straw resounds;
Sometimes, like a lost late wanderer,
On our little window pounds.

Our ramshackle hut, half-ruined,
Feels so dark, by sadness crushed,
Why do you, my dear old woman,
By the window sit so hushed?
Say, my friend, has the storm's muttering
Worn you out, brought you to heel?
Or are you just somewhat slumbering,
As you click your spinning wheel?

Let's just drink, my dear old friend (from even
When I was a poor, small boy);
Where's your mug now? Drink from grieving,
And the heart will feel more joy.
Sing for me your song, how bluebird
Lived in peace beyond the sea.
Sing how one morning a girl heard,
As to fetch water went she.

Snowstorm, gloom-filled, heavens drowning,
Wild the snowy whirlwind flies:
Sometimes, like a beast, it's howling,
Sometimes, like a child, it cries.
Let's just drink, my dear old friend (from even
When I was a poor, small boy);
Where's your mug now? Drink from grieving,
And the heart will feel more joy.

Iván, dear coz',* if we start drinking,
Surely we must toast, I'm thinking,
The three Matryonas, Peter, Luke,
And Pakhomovna to boot!
Long we've lived with them and, truly,
All such friends, no matter what,
Must be toasted, ne'er forgot!
Must be toasted, absolutely!
If we're drinking, then let's drink!
Glasses clinking, then let's clink!
Pouring pour, with froth brims brimming,
Let's begin, my dear, in truth!
The three Matryonas, Peter, Luke,
First with beer we'll toast, head swimming,
Then Pakhomovna as well,
After pies, with wine – and tell –
Just to show how much we love her –
Fairy tales of that fair mother –
Oh, how sweet and bright her tongue!
Where did all her tales come from?
Where'd she get her plots so witty?
All her proverbs, songs, and ditties,
Wonders, wives' tales, gifts galore
From our ancient faith's true lore!
How the soul rejoiced in hearing!
I'd not eat or drink a week;
I'd just sit and hear her speak!
Who spun such grand tales endearing?
Don't forget those elders true!
(That they're gone's a pity, truly)
Yet they must be toasted too,
Must be toasted absolutely!
Listen, I'll begin, my dear:
Next, your fairy tale I'll hear.

* The word *сват* literally refers to a relative, who might be the father of the son-in-law or daughter-in-law. It also means "matchmaker." Ah, well... all relationships blur a bit "if we start drinking"...

[THE PROLOGUE TO RUSLAN AND LYUDMILA*]

A green oak tree's by a cove curving;*
A gold chain on that oak is found,
And night and day a cat most learnèd
Walks by that chain, around, around,
When he walks right, sweet songs intoning,
When leftwards, tells a fairy tale.

Wonders are there, wood-sprites are roaming,
Mermaids from branches hang their tail,
On paths of which no one has knowledge
Of unseen beasts there lurk the spoors,
On chicken legs, a little cottage
Stands without windows, without doors.
With visions wood and dale are yawning,
There waves come crashing at light's dawning
Upon the sandy, empty beach,
And thirty knights, in armour gorgeous,
The clear sea one by one disgorges
With their sea-sword-coach, them to teach.
And there a king's son, that way chancing,
A frightful Tsar does captive seize,
There past the people, past clouds passing,
Right through the woods, right through the seas,
A wizard bears a knight with ease.
A princess there's in prison pining,
A brown wolf faithful by her lying,
There Baba Yaga's mortar dread
Itself, with her inside, does tread.
There Tsar Kashey on his gold moulders,
There Russian scents of Rus' give odours!

* It is the first two lines of this poem that the character Masha in Chekhov's play *The Three Sisters* repeats to herself obsessively.

And there I've passed, and honey quaffed,
And seen the oak by that cove curving,
Sat under it, and the cat learnèd
His fairy tales to me repassed.
I've one remembered, and this story
Through me now comes to light, world, glory...

My blood is blazing with desire.
My stricken soul for you does pine.
Oh, kiss me now! Your kisses' fire
Is sweeter far than myrrh and wine.
Incline your head to me but softly,
And tamed, I'll linger with you calmly,
Until the cheerful light of day
Chases the gloom of night away.

A WINTER MORNING

It's frost and sunshine – morning wondrous! –
My lovely friend, that sweetly slumbers –
It's time, my beauty, ope' your eyes!
Ope wide your bliss enveloped gazing,
And to the North's Aurora blazing,
As the North Star come forth, arise!

Last night, remember snowstorm's raging?
In murky skies that gloom rampaging?
The moon was but a faint, pale stain.
Through gloomy clouds it yellowed, flitting.
And, oh, how sadly you were sitting!
And now – look out our windowpane!

'Neath blue cerulean heavens' gleaming,
In wondrous carpets, softly keening,
In sunlight sparkling, the snow lies.
Transparent woods are all that darkens.
The fir greens o'er the frost and harkens,
The river shines beneath the ice.

And our whole room, with amber sparkling,
Gleams in the dawn. With merry gargling
The hearth-stove crackles, wood piled high.
It's pleasant lying in bed thinking.
But say, though, shouldn't we be ringing
To yoke the brown mare to the sleigh?

As we on morning snow go sliding,
My darling, feeling the full riding,
As our horse runs impatiently,
We'll see the fields, their barren bleakness,
The woods which recently were leafy,
The lakeshore, that's so dear to me.

TO***

A wondrous moment I remember:
Before me once you did appear;
A fleeting vision you resembled
Of beauty's genius pure and clear.

By grief and languor hopeless rendered,
Beset by noisy vanity,
Long time in me your voice rang tender,
Of your dear features were my dreams.

Years passed. Rebellious storm winds sundered
And scattered hopes that used to be,
And I forgot your voice so tender,
Your features dear and heavenly.

In gloom of backwoods' isolation,
My days dragged by, a silent drudge,
Without God's spark or inspiration,
Or tears, or any life, or love.

My soul awoke in precognition:
And once again you did appear,
Resembling a fleeting vision
Of beauty's genius pure and clear.

And now my heart beats in elation!
And resurrected soar above
The spark of God, and inspiration,
And life, and tears at last, and love.

CONFESSION

To Alexandra Ivanovna Osipova

I love you so – though it's distress,
And work in vain and shame most fruitless,
And in this silly suffering foolish
Cast at your feet I must confess.
It doesn't fit me; I'm too old now,
It's time that I got smarter, please!
Yet all the signs have clearly told now
That in my soul is love's disease.
I yawn with boredom when without you.
I'm sad when with you, wait with woe,
And I've no strength, I want to tell you,
My angel, how I love you so!
When from your hall I hear emerging
Your rustling dress, your steps so fine,
Or voice so innocent and virgin,
I suddenly quite lose my mind.
You smile at me – joy, heaven's praises!
You turn away – and I'm in grief.
For all day suffering my pay is
Your little hand so pale and brief.
When to embroidering you render
For hours and hours yourself, and bend your
Eyes and curls down, a bit wild,
I'm so endeared, in silence tender,
Admiring you just like a child!
And should I tell you of my misery,
And of the jealous grief I feel
When you sometimes, in weather drizzly,
Decide to wander far afield?

Your solitary tears' immersions?
Your little corner têtes-à-têtes?
And to Opochka your excursions,
Your piano, when the evening frets?
Alina, pity me my suffering!
I do not dare to seek your love.
It may be I have sinned so much,
My angel, I am not worth loving.
But just pretend it! Your look sweet
Sublimely says all things demurely!
Oh dear! It isn't hard to fool me!
I'm glad myself to be deceived!

OCTOBER 19th

The forest casts its scarlet garments off,
The frost bedecks the withered fields in silver,
The light of day peeps out, as if unwilling,
And hides in the surrounding mountaintops.
Blaze up, o hearth, in my bare cell and prison.
And you, dear wine, friend of the fall's sharp frost,
Pour joyous tipsiness into my bosom,
Oblivion brief, make bitter cares seem lost.

For I am sad, and without any friend
To drink with, healing woes of separation,
Whose hand I'd clasp in heartfelt admiration
And wish good cheer for many years on end.
I drink alone. Imagination lonely
In vain calls out for comrades who aren't here.
No steps familiar can I hear approaching.
My soul gives up on waiting for friends dear.

I drink alone, and on the Nevá's banks
Today my gathered friends my name are naming.
But – even there – aren't many of you failing?
Who isn't feasting now in your glad ranks?
Who's not kept faith with our tradition charming?
Whom has the cold *beau monde* stolen away?
Whose voice is stilled midst brotherly catcalling?
Who didn't come? Who's not here, couldn't stay?

Our frizzy-haired free singer hasn't come.
His cycs afire, with his guitar sweet-sounding.
In some Italian myrtle grove abounding
He sleeps in peace*. No friendly local son
Carved out with care upon a Russian gravestone
A few brief words in his own native tongue
To give a gloomy greeting and sad haven
To northern sons lost, wandering far from home.

*This refers to Nikolai Korsakov, 1800—1820, a Lycée classmate and bard, who died while travelling in Italy.

Are you now sitting 'midst your group of friends
You restless lover of strange skies and lees?*
Or still crossing Earth's steamy tropic ends,
And endless ice on midnight Arctic seas?
Godspeed to you! From our Lycée's gates striding,
You, full of jokes, boarded a ship, set forth,
And since that time, the ocean is your highway,
Beloved child of seething waves and storms!

Wherever Fate did cast you on the seas,
You kept those morals taught in first, fair years.
Lycéen fun, pranks' clamor, yearning, tears
In stormy waves came back to you in dreams,
And o'er the seas your hand to us extending,
In your young soul our memories are kept,
And you'd repeat: "to parting never-ending
By secret destiny we are, perhaps, condemned."

My friends, how beautiful our union is!
Eternal like the soul, it can't be broken.
It withstands all, free, careless, and outspoken,
Our links were formed by friendship and the Muse.
Where'er we're cast by Fate, whate'er it's storing,
Wherever happiness might let us roam,
We're still the same: the whole world's strange and foreign,
And Tsarskoye Selo is our true home.

*Fyodor Matyushkin, 1799—1872, another classmate, circumnavigated the globe and became Admiral of the Imperial Russian Navy.

From place to place, though chased by lightning dread,
In nets of cruel fate caught, uncomprehending,
I'd quaver in the bosom of new friendship,
And sink caressingly my weary head...
Midst upstart angry prayers melancholy,
And trusting hopes of my first eagerness,
My tender soul, which other friends sought really,
Unbrotherly made greetings' bitterness.

And now, stuck here, in this abandoned hole,
This shrine of desolation, frost and snowstorms,
A sweet reward was given me, rejoicing:
With three of you, three dear friends of my soul,
I have embraced. My outcast place of pining,
Pushchin, my dear, you were the first to grace!
You sweetened one more day in exile writhing,
Transformed it to a day of our Lycée.

You, Gorchakov – born lucky to the end,
Praise be to you! For Fortune's chilly gleaming
Have not traduced within your soul your freedom;
You're still the same for honour and your friend!
Completely different paths strict Fate assigned us;*
We parted soon, once we set forth in life.
And yet by chance upon a country crossroads,
We met, and like two brothers clasped arms tight.

When I was chased by wrathful Fate so cruel,
Estranged to all, an orphan with no home,
I'd sink my dreamy head down all alone,
Awaiting you, the Muses' herald true,
And then you came, inspired dawdling's offspring,
Delvig**, my dear, your voice did then awake
My heart's own warmth, so long stilled in me, slumbering,
And cheerfully I then did bless my Fate.

*Prince Alexander Gorchakov would become Foreign Minister, then Chancellor of the Russian Empire.
**Baron Anton Delvig, 1798—1831, a poet and Pushkin's friend.

Since youth, in us Song's spirit ever burned,
With a divine disquiet us inspiring;
Since youth towards us two Muses fleet came flying,
Sweet was our lot caressing them in turn.
But I already loved applause, shouts feverish.
You proudly sang just for your Muse, your heart.
My gift, like life, I frittered away heedless,
While you in silence honed your perfect art.

The Muses' service brooks no vanity.
The beautiful must always be majestic.
Deceitful guidance gain we from youth frantic.
In noisy daydreams we rejoice, are free.
Then we awake – too late though! And now grievous
We gaze back whence we came, yet cannot see.
Say, Wilhelm*, isn't that how life did treat us,
My brother in the Muse, in Fate's decree?

It's time, it's time! Our heartaches unallayed
Aren't worth this world; let's leave behind illusions!
Let's hide our life away in shade's seclusion!
I wait for you, my friend so long delayed...
Approach, and with the fire of magic Story,
Revive the heart's true teaching deep in us.
We'll speak of snowy Caucasus peaks stormy,
Of Schiller, and of glory, and of love!

For me too, now, it's time. My friends, feast on!
Within I feel a joyful premonition:
Remember my poetical prediction!
When one year's passed, we'll meet again anon!
Then will come true my dearest aspirations,
When one year's passed and I come back to you!
How many tears, how many declamations!
How many cups raised high towards Heaven's blue!

* Refers to Wilhelm Küchelbecker, 1797—1846, a poet and Decembrist.

Refill your cups, friends, fill them up, I say!
Drink each last drop in honour of our union!
Now bless us with your jubilation, Muses!
Now bless us all, and long live our Lycée!
To all our tutors, our youth's noble keepers,
All honours to the living and the dead!
As we with gratitude lift up our beakers,
All ills forgot, give thanks for blessings yet.

Refill, refill with passion, from your heart,
Again now, bottoms up, drink each drop blessèd!
And yet for whom? O friends, I'll let you guess it!
Hurrah! Our Tsar! Yes, let's drink to the Tsar!
He's but a man, a slave to time's illusion,
Of rumours, doubts, and passions but a slave,
So let's forgive his unfair persecution:
He captured Paris, founded our Lycée!

Feast on, feast on, while we are all still here!
Alas, our circle hour by hour is thinning.
Who sleeps in coffin now, who's orphaned, distant?
Fate sees us fade as our days disappear.
We bend invisibly, and chill, are fading,
Drawn back to our beginnings, to our home...
Which one of us in old age on Lycée Day
Will be obliged to celebrate alone?*

Unhappy friend! Amidst new generations,
Unwanted stranger, guest who just won't leave,
He'll think of us united in libations,
With shaky hand he'll close his eyes, and grieve...
Yet may he still be joyous in his sadness,
And pass that day but with his goblet old,
As I today, disgraced, locked in my fastness,
Have passed it without worry, without woe.

* It was Prince Gorchakov.

SCENE FROM BORIS GODUNOV

NIGHT. A GARDEN. A FOUNTAIN

The Pretender

(enters)

The fountain's here. And here is where she'll come.
It seems to me I wasn't born a coward;
Flashing before me close I have seen death.
And before death my soul has never quavered.
By slavery forever I've been threatened,
I've been chased down; my spirit was unfailing,
With daring I escaped unfreedom's bonds.
So now what is it so stops up my breathing?
What is this tremor I can't overpower?
Is it suppressed desire that in me trembles?
No – it is fear. The whole day I did wait
For this brief secret tryst now with Marina,
And weighed within my mind all I would say,
How I'd seduce her proud and haughty mind,
And christen her the Empress of great Moscow,
But now's the time, and I remember nothing.
I've quite forgot those speeches I made up,
And love casts murk on my imagination.
But something just flashed by! It's swishing!.. Quiet!
No, it's the light of the deceitful moon,
A little breeze blew lightly by...

Marina

(enters)

Tsarevich!

Pretender

It's her! Now all the blood's stopped up inside me!

Marina

'S that you, Dmitry?

Pretender

Oh voice, so sweet, so magic!
(walks towards her)
Oh is it you at last! Is that you whom I see,
Alone with me in evening's silent stillness?
How slow the wheel of boring day did turn!
How slow the gleam of twilight was in fading!
How long I waited for the gloom of night!

Yekaterina Orlova
("My Marina Mniszek is a real Yekaterina Orlova!")

Marina

The hours race, and every minute's precious.
And I instructed you to meet me here
Not to subject myself to tender speeches
A lover makes! I don't need words. I'm certain
That you do love. But listen: I've decided
That to your fate both stormy and uncertain
I'll link my own. And so I have the right,
Dmitry, to demand of you one thing:
And I demand that you open your soul,
Tell me your secret hopes and aspirations,
Reveal your plans and even apprehensions,
So hand in hand with you I could with valour
Set forth in life – but not blind as a child,
Or merely slave to slight whims of my husband,
Nor yet to be your silent concubine,
No, but as wife to you, who's fully worthy,
A helpmeet to the Tsar of Muscovy.

Pretender

Oh let me for a single hour forget
My destiny's unending cares and worries!
Please, just forget that you are looking at
The Tsar's own son. Marina! See in me
A lover, and a man whom you have chosen,
See someone whom your slightest glance makes happy.
Oh hear me out! Oh hear my prayer of love!
Let me express what in my heart is brimming!

Marina

But not now, prince. You dawdle – all the while
The ardour of your followers is cooling,
And hour by hour the dangers and the toils
Become ever more dangerous and hard.
And doubtful rumours already are spreading.
The latest news supplants the latest news,
And Godunov is also taking measures.

Pretender

Who's Godunov? Does Boris have the power
To rule your love, my only bliss and blessing?
No, no! In truth I look with pure indifference
Upon his throne and his imperial might.
Your love alone! What is my life without it?
Or glory's gleam, or all the power of Russia?
In barren steppe, in bare mud hut with you–
–You would replace my regal crown – more precious
To me's your love!

Marina

For shame! Do not forget
Your lofty errand and your sacred mission!
To you your rank must ever dearer be
Than all the blandishments and joys of living.
With power there is naught that can compare.
I'll have no seething youth who bubbles madly,
Kept by my looks in plaintive captive state,
Know: I have pledged my hand in troth most solemn
But to the one true heir to Moscow's throne,
The Tsar's own son, preserved and kept by Fate.

Pretender

Don't torture me, dear ravishing Marina!
Don't say that it's my rank instead of me
That you did choose. Marina! You've no inkling
How painfully you sear my heart with that.
How – for what if? Oh! What frightful doubt I feel!
Do say: had I not chanced to be born royal,
Had blinded Fate not so appointed me,
If I were not the son of dread Iván,
His outcast child, by this world long forgotten,
Say then... then would you love me still? Or not?

Marina

Dmitry's who you are. You're not some other.
Some other I could never love.

Pretender

No! No more!
I've heard enough! I'll not share with a corpse
A lover who belongs to him entirely.
No, that's enough imposturing: I'll tell
The whole truth now! So listen: Your Dmitry
Is long since dead and buried, gone forever.
But would you like to know just who I am?
In truth, I'm but a poor black-robed monk-novice
On whom monastic discipline grew boring.
Beneath my cowl I plotted my grand project:
I planned how I'd present the world a wonder.
And finally I fled from my dark cell
To the Ukraine, where dwell the rowdy Cossacks.
I learned to ride a horse and wield a sabre,
Then I came here and called myself Dmitri,
And so deceived your silly Polish courtiers,
What do you say now, arrogant Marina?
Are you not pleased with what I've just confessed?
Why won't you speak?

Marina

Oh shame! Oh woe is me!

(Pause)

Pretender (quietly)

Where has this vexing outburst lured me?
The happiness I'd built up with such labour
I have perhaps forever cast away.
What did I do? Oh madman!
(out loud)
I see! I see!
You are ashamed of love that isn't princely..
So go ahead, pronounce your final verdict.
For now my fate lies only on your hands.
Decide! I'll wait! *(falls on his knees).*

Marina

Rise, miserable pretender!
Do you imagine just because you're kneeling
As if before a trusting girl, a weakling,
That you could win my proud, ambitious heart?
You're wrong, my friend! For, at my feet prostrated,
I've seen my share of counts and knights and nobles,
And coldly I rejected all their prayers
But not so that some runaway ex-monk should –

Pretender (gets up)

Do not despise or scorn the young pretender;
For it may be that valour hides within him
That's worthy of the mighty throne of Moscow,
That's worthy of that hand of yours so priceless...

Marina

That's worthy of a shameful noose, man shameless!

Pretender

It's my fault that ambition overweening
Made me deceive both God and courts of kings.
To all the world I lied, and yet you can't, Marina,
Dare punish me; to you I've acted fairly,
For you are someone I would not deceive.
The thought of you for me is all that's sacred,
I'd never dare dissimulate with you.
For love, oh love! A jealous love, a blind love!
T'was love alone that ever could impel me
To tell you all.

Marina

You're boasting of this, madman?
Who asked for such confessions out of you?
If you're indeed a nameless, wandering beggar,
Who managed to keep blinded two great peoples,
Then at the very least you always must
Stay worthy of your fraudulent success,
And must secure your own deceit audacious
By keeping it a deep, eternal secret.
How could I ever give myself to you,
Forget my birth, my shame that keeps me virgin,
And merge my destiny with that of yours,
When you yourself, as simply as just now,
So flippantly your scandal go revealing?
Because of love he bubbled out his secret!
I am amazed that in my father's court
You haven't yet revealed yourself through friendship,
Or out of joy when brought before our King,
Or spilled your tale to Father Wisnowiecky
Out of the faithful zeal with which you serve!

Pretender

I swear to you that you alone could force
And torture my wracked heart to its confession.
I swear to you, at no time, and in no place,
Not at great feasts, while quaffing folly's goblets,
Nor yet with friends while preciously discoursing,
Threatened by knives, spread on the rack, tormented,
My tongue won't give these secrets dread away.

Marina

Oh? So you swear? That means I should believe you?
Oh, I believe! But first, might I inquire,
By what you swear? Not by our Lord's name holy,
Devoutly as a Jesuit-schooled foundling?
Or on your honour, like some knight gone questing?
Or do you merely pledge your royal honour,
As the Tsar's heir? Is that it? Won't you speak?

Dmitry

(proudly)
The shade of dread Iván himself did choose me,
And christened me Dmitry from his grave.
That shade did stir our peoples up, unruly,
Judged doom on Boris, whom I will replace.
I'm the Tsar's heir! Enough! For it is galling
To stoop so to a haughty Polish maiden!
Farewell for good! The game of war most bloody,
And vast concerns of Destiny all-touching
Will dim, I hope, love's grief within my heart.
Oh! How I will begin to hate you truly
When passion's shameful fever shall have passed!
Now I shall go – though whether Russia crowns
With doom or laurel-wreathes my expectations –
If I find death in battle like a warrior,
Or like a villain on the scaffold block,
You nevermore shall be my faithful helpmeet.
No more shall you of my fate be partaking.
And yet, perhaps, one day you may regret
That destiny you with such scorn rejected.

Marina

But what if I reveal your shameless hoax
And warn the world about you ere you go?

Pretender

How could you fancy I'm afraid of you?
Whom will the world believe? Some Polish schoolgirl?
Or the Tsar's son of Muscovy? Yet know
That nor your King nor Pope nor nobles
Could slightly care whether I speak the truth.
Am I Dmitri? That's not their concern!
I'm but a pretext for their feuding war,
Just the excuse they looked for. As for you,
Rebellious wench! Be sure, they'll curb your tongue!
Farewell!

Marina

No, wait! Tsarevich! Now at last
I hear the speech of real men, not of schoolboys.
It reconciles me to you, my dear prince.
Now, I forget your outburst of sheer folly
And see Dmitri once again. But – listen:
It's time! It's time! Stir up! And no more dawdling!
To Moscow march and lead your armies on,
Clean out the Kremlin, take the throne of Moscow.
Then send your nuptial envoys back to me.
But – God's my witness! Till those feet of yours
Have not ascended up the throne-room staircase,
Until at last you've cast out Godunov,
I'll listen to no speeches about love.

(Exits.)

Pretender

No! With Godunov it's easier to battle,
It's easier testing cunning with court Jesuits
Than – with a woman! – Damn them! I've no strength!
Confusing me, she weaves and winds, and crawls,
Slips from my hand, and hisses, threatens, stinging!
A snake! A snake! No wonder I did shake!
She very nearly brought about my ruin!
But now I'm firm. Our armies march at dawn.

The last late flowers are more dear
Than gorgeous first queens of the field.
They melancholy daydreams wistful
Do stir more strongly in our heart.
Just so, the hour when we must part
Evokes more than the sweetest trysting.

If, perchance, life should deceive you,
Be not gloomy, be not riled!
To sad days be reconciled;
Days of joy, believe, are near you.

In the future the heart lives,
Though the present is not cheering:
All's but a moment, passing swift;
What has passed will be endearing.

IV. THE STORMS OF FATE

And only I, mysterious bard,
Was cast ashore by storm and lightning...

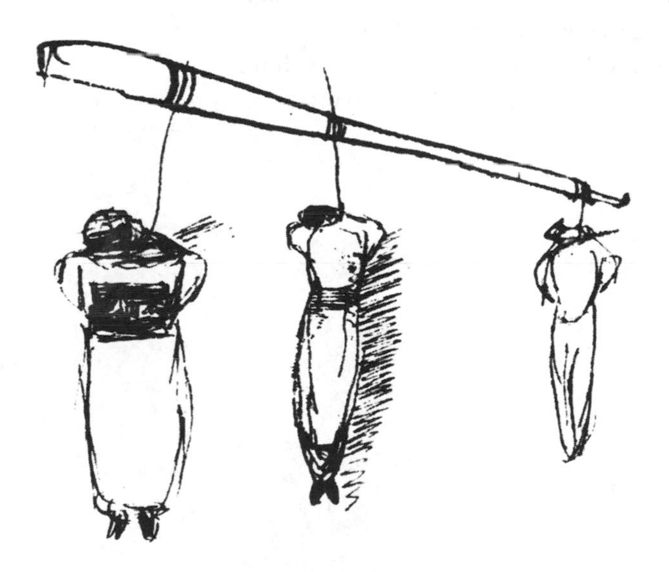

The hanging of the Decembrists

ARION*

A lot of us were on that skiff.
While some of us broad sails were spanning,
The rest were amiably manning
Great oars beneath. And still and stiff,
Hunched o'er our tiller, our sage captain
Our crowded skiff in silence steered.
But I, by carefree faith e'er cheered,
Sang to my mates. Then great waves sheered
Up, swept, smashed, whirlwinds blasted, crashing,
Our captain and his mates were lost!
And only I, mysterious bard,
Was cast ashore by storm and lightning.
I sing the hymns I sang before,
And my drenched raiment on that shore
In sunshine under cliffs am drying.

* In Greek mythology, the shipwrecked poet Arion sang to the storm-waves, and was rescued and brought ashore by a dolphin.

TO IVAN IVANOVICH PUSHCHIN

My very first, my priceless friend,
I too gave blessings to strange Fate,
When through bleak snowstorms she did send
Your sleighbell-heralded advent
To my secluded courtyard gate...

To blessèd fate I make oration:
Let my voice too, in future days,
Return your gift of consolation,
Shine light through your incarceration
From our Lycée's clear loving rays.

The Lycée

A MESSAGE TO SIBERIA

Deep in your dark Siberian mine
Preserve with pride your stubborn patience.
Your toil of grief is not in vain,
Nor are your lofty aspirations.

Misfortune's loyal sister, Hope,
Will find your underground so gloomy,
Both cheer and joyousness renewing;
The time you've longed for shall approach:

Of love and friendship true, the joys
Break through all locks, cross all dark spaces,
As through your hard-barred convict cages
You hear my free, resounding voice.

Your heavy shackles to the floor
Will fall, your jails will crumble. Liberty
Will joy to see you step forth free,
Your brothers will return your sword.

The Bronze Horseman without the Horseman

Behold, a sower went forth to sow.*

In lonesome wasteland freedom sowing,**
Ere morning-star I walked, ere sun.
With hands still clean, pure and unknowing,
In earth where slave-drawn furrows run,
I cast the freeing seed of life –
But I was only wasting time,
Good aspirations, deeds – for none.

So graze on, graze, you peaceful peoples!
You will not wake to honour's call.
What need have herds for gifts of freedom?
They're used to shears and butcher's stall,
For ages to their heirs bequeathing
Just yokes with ringlets, whips that gall.

Greek Rebels in Kishinev

* *Matthew*: 13, 3.
** Some consider this Pushkin's meditation on the Greek and Rumanian struggles for freedom from the Ottoman Empire (the poet's drawings in this period show pictures of Greek rebels, as above). Yet it is also about political apathy in the face of slavery and tyranny — or perhaps just reminds us of the enduring consequences to ourselves of our indifference to the plight of others.

THE POISON TREE*

In fearsome desert, barren, dead,
On sands that from the heat are blazing,
The poison tree, like sentry dread,
Stands, lone in all the world remaining.

For Nature of these thirsting steppes
One day of wrath caused its conception,
And made its greening leaves all dead,
And filled its roots with purest poison.

The poison seeps right through its bark,
By noonday's heat is boiling, melting,
And by the evening chill grows hard
Into a thickened tar transparent.

And to this tree the bird flies not;
The tiger flees it. Just a whirlwind
That's black to this death-tree runs up –
And races past, but now accursèd.

And if a cloud by chance bedews,
Lost on its wanderings, those thick branches,
Down from its leaves a poisoned juice,
Like rain, falls which the hot sand catches.

* The literal and correct translation of the Russian word "анчар" is actually "upas." In turn, as the Oxford English Dictionary relates, the word "upas" means "poison" in Malaysian. In 1785, the British botanist Erasmus Darwin (grandfather of Charles Darwin) described the "dread Upas": "Fierce in dread silence on the blasted heath, fell upas sits, the hydra-tree of death." Around it supposedly nothing lived for fifteen miles in any direction — it was said to be near Batavia (now Djakarta) on the isle of Java, Dutch East Indies (now Indonesia). Byron, in *Childe Harolde* IV, cxxvi, referred figuratively to: "This uneradicable taint of sin, This boundless Upas, this all-blasting tree." I would normally never hesitate to use Byron's words for rendering Pushkin, especially as the Oxford Russian-English dictionary gives no other entry for "анчар." Yet such Oxonian erudition risks puzzling those of our readers whose reading knowledge of Malaysian is as rusty as mine. Besides, "The Poison Tree" just sounds better!

But once, one man sent out a man,
Off to the death tree with glance awesome,
Who trudged, obedient, through the sand,
And next morning brought back the poison.

He had brought back the tar of death,
The branches with their leaves all withered,
And on his forehead pale the sweat
Dripped down in rivulets, but chilly.

Brought them – and then lay down, grown weak,
On rough rush mats 'neath those vaults tented.
The poor slave died then at the feet
Of his invincible potentate.

The prince then with that poison fed
His arrows sharp and to him slavish,
And then with them sent doom and death
In distant lands to all his neighbours.

"Who trudged, obedient through the sand"
(the slave in The Poison Tree)

OCTOBER 19, 1827

God help you all, my dear, dear friends,
In all life's cares, in Tsarist service,
In friendship's wild carousing fervent,
In all sweet Love's mysterious beds!

God help you all, my dear, dear friends,
Through storms or everyday griefs blowing,
In foreign lands, in desert ocean,
Or in Earth's dark, abysmal ends!

Decembrist Wilhelm K

TO YEKATERINA NIKOLAYEVNA USHAKOVA

If they send me far from you,
Still I'll never, ever, leave you.
Luscious lips and deep eyes true
In my memory will be keeping.
Bored and pining silently,
I'll not wish to find new gladness.
Say though, will you sigh for me,
If, one day, they ever hang me?

EPIGRAM ON FADDEY BULGARIN*

There's nothing wrong with being Polish:
Kosciuszko is, and so's Mickiewicz.
Were you a Tatar, that's no crime;
In this, again, I see no shame.
Be Jewish? That's no cause for blame.
What's wrong, Boulevardin,** is your spying.

*Faddey Bulgarin, originally from Poland, was editor of the Northern Bee, a newspaper funded and guided by the Tsarist 3rd Section (secret police). He mocked Pushkin's African origins, and compounded his racism with copious denunciations of the poet to the secret police, greatly harming the poet's ability to get published.

**In order to preserve the rhyme and rhythm, I have taken some liberties here with the original Russian text. Фигляр in Russian means a poseur. Видок refers to Vidocque, the head of the French secret police. In short, this epigram reminds us that it is not the origins, but the actions of a person that count.

In this world's plain that stretches sad and endless,
Mysteriously three springs have risen up.
The spring of youth, a spring quick and rebellious,
Does bubble, race, and sparkling flow and run.
Next, the Castalian* spring gives wondrous vision;
From it the exile in that plain partakes.
The final spring's the cold spring of oblivion:
Sweetest of all the heart's hot thirst it slakes.

*The Castalian brook flows down Mount Parnassus to Delphi. Its sacred springs' gaseous vapours helped the Pythian oracle to see prophetic visions.

BACCHANALIAN SONG

How is it that Joy lost its voice?
Ring out, Bacchanalian singing!
And long live the maidens appealing,
The lovely young wives who're so loving of us!
So fill up your goblets, now, higher!
With bright, clinging chime
Into the thick wine
Let's drop rings of heartfelt desire!
Let's raise up the glass, with one gulp, relieve it!
And long live the Muses, and long live sweet Reason!
May you, holy sun, long burn on!
As this little lamp pales and flickers
Before the clear rising of Dawn,
So every false wisdom but glances and withers
Before your immortal mind's spark!
And long live the sunshine, and vanquished be dark!

V. MEDITATIONS

The way I used to be, that way I still am now:
In love with love, carefree...

Tel j'étais autrefois et tel je suis encor.

The way I used to be, that way I still am now:
In love with love, carefree... My friends, don't you know how
At beauty I can't look without feeling affection?
Without shy tenderness and secret pangs of tension?
Has love not played enough in life with me, untaught?
Have I not thrashed enough like a young hawk that's caught
In nets of treachery that Venus has been casting?
But having nothing learned from hundred wounds in passing,
Unto new idols I still bring and bring my prayers.

TO NANNY

My friend through my travails, woes hardest,
My dear bedraggled little dove!
Alone you pine, in deep pine forests,
And wait for me, so long, so long!
There, by the window of your bower,
You grieve and wait as if entranced,
Your knitting needles, by the hour,
Are slowing in your wrinkled hands.
You stare out past the gates forgotten,
Look towards a long black path outstretched,
And grief, foreboding, cares, do tighten
And tug each hour in your breast.
And visions come to you . . . .

Arina Rodionovna, the poet's nanny, in youth and old age

Oh spring, oh spring, oh time of love,
How cruel and heavy is your coming!
What lang'rous worry and what longing
Are in my soul, are in my blood!
My heart's estranged to pleasure wholly.
All that exults and, sparkling, shines,
Leaves me but cold and melancholy...

Give back my blizzards, snowstorms bleak,
And long dark gloom of winter nights!

Winter's chill blasts of wind are still blowing,*
Morning frost on the meadows still strewing,
Yet on spring's thawed earth, shy midst the snowdrifts,
Still the very first blossoms came blooming.
And, as if from some magic wax kingdom,
From its honeycomb cell so sweet-scented,
The very first bee has come flying,
O'er the very first blossoms flies, flitting,
As a scout of the beautiful spring.
Will that dearest friend soon be arriving?
Will the meadow soon green and be thriving?
Will the curly-leafed birch soon be wavy,
Will it sprout silver-light slight leaves sticky?
Will the wild cherries bloom with sweet fragrance?

* This is said to have been Fyodor Dostoyevsky's favourite poem.

THE PROLOGUE TO THE BRONZE HORSEMAN

By coasts where desolate crash the waves
Stood he, filled full of grand thoughts brave,
And looked afar. Before him only
The broad flood flowed, bare river – save
One poor skiff on its whitecaps lonely.
By such thick mossy, swampy clay
Just god-forsaken mad Finns stay,
Just here and there their black huts dotting.
The woods, kept secret from all rays
Of sunshine that the fog was swathing,
Stirred, rustling round.

And then he thought:
From here the mighty Swede we'll menace;
Here we will build a city up
To spite our haughty neighbour jealous.
Here Nature has decreed that we
To Europe force a window free,
With mighty step bestride the ocean.
And o'er these waves which no one knew
The whole world's flags will stream hereto;
We'll feast on this vast space in motion.

A century's past, and this young town
Is now the midnight-sun-lands' wonder.
From deep dark woods, swamps' soggy ground
A sumptuous beauty rose in grandeur.
Where once some Finnish fisherman,
Bleak nature's melancholy stepson,
Alone stood in the shallow sand,
Casting his tattered net unresting
In murky waters, now look round!
All bustles by the river's bounds;

Great gleaming giants crowd in, graceful,
Of towers and palaces! And boats
From every one of this world's coasts
Throng to our wealthy dockyards, racing.
In granite our Nevá is clad,
And bridges drape over our waters;
With rich dark-green grand lawns and gardens
Have claimed the river's islands back.
Next to our new capital splendid
Our ancient Moscow dimmed, did fade,
Stands, by a beautiful young Empress,
A dowdy dowager old maid.

I love you, place of Peter's making,
I love your stern and stylish face,
The Nevá's mighty current breaking
On her embankments' granite grace,
The patterns on your wrought-iron fences,
Your twilight's clear and thoughtful gloom
On summer evenings, shining moonless,
When I sit sleepless in my room,
And write and read and need no lanterns:
How gleam the buildings, sleeping monsters,
On streets deserted! And I see
The Needle of the Admiralty.
And not allowing murk nocturnal
Into the heavens' golden bower,
Each dawn relieves each dawn eternal:
That race leaves night but half an hour.
I love your winter's cruel broadsides,
Unyielding air and frosts that bite,
Across the broad Nevá the sleigh rides,
The girlish faces rosy bright,

At balls: the gleam, the hum, the chatter,
At feasts, where bachelors make their fame,
The foaming champagne-glasses' clatter,
The punch-bowl's light blue tongue of flame.
I love the warlike animation
Upon the Fields of Mars displayed,
The troops of horse and foot arrayed,
Their beauty lacking variation,
The rows that sway and then grow tight,
Victorious banners' tattered remnants,
The glittering bronze of soldiers' helmets
Shot through by bullets in the fight,
I love, war-capital, your fortress,
Your smoke, your cannons' sudden boom
To mark when midnight-sun-land's Empress
Brings forth a son to the Tsar's home,
Also when victory o'er the foe
Is hailed with Russia's celebration,
Or, from its blue ice breaking free,
Nevá flows, bears it to the sea,
Feels spring days coming with elation.

Be gorgeous, Peter's town, steadfast!
Remain unconquerable, like Russia!
And may the elements at last,
With being tamed, make peace, be hushed.
And may the Finnish waves not keep
Their grudge 'gainst being tamed forever,
And may their futile malice never
Rouse Peter from eternal sleep!

THE FEAST OF PETER THE GREAT*

Over the Nevá whip, flapping,
Gaily-coloured flags of ships,
You can hear the boatmen laughing,
Singing gaily in their skiffs.
In the Tsar's home joy's resounding,
Drunken guests rejoice, make sound
The Nevá, from cannons' pounding,
Quivers far and wide around.

What has caused our great Tsar's feasting
In our town of Petersburg?
Why such salvoes, fired by cheering
Battleships at river's curve?
Is our Russian standard greeted
With yet one more triumph new?
Are the Swedes severe defeated?
Does for peace our dread foe sue?

To this land we've seized from Sweden
Has Brandt's boat docked, rickety?
Are we honouring how our "Skipper"
Sired our young fleet's family?
Are his warlike grandsons gathered
In proud ranks by the Old Man?
Is it Science being honoured
By choirs' hymns and cannon blasts?

*In 1688, the teenaged Tsar Peter the Great personally refitted an old boat built by Dutch shipbuilder Karsten Brandt, delighting in sailing it all over the Silver Grape Pond in Izmailovo (now about 10 minutes' stroll from Moscow's "Partizanskaya" Metro stop). So keen became Peter's lifelong passion for all things nautical that he later fought the Great Northern War with Sweden, to gain Russia an outlet to the Baltic Sea, where he built a grand new capital, St. Petersburg. "Brandt's boat," thereafter affectionately called "the grandfather of the Russian Navy," can be seen to this day in St. Petersburg's Naval Museum – a splendid classical building whose depiction graces the Russian 50-ruble note.

Do we celebrate Poltava's
Anniversary, feast great,
When our land from Charles' dread onslaught
By the Russian Tsar was saved?
Is an heir born, big, proud, burly,
To our Empress Catherine?
Does our giant Wonder-Worker*
Feast the birthday of his queen?

No! With rebels our Tsar's feasting,
Letting go of every grudge,
Making merry, he's forgiving,
Drinking healths from common cups.
On their foreheads he plants kisses,
And his heart and face do glow
As he celebrates forgiveness
Like a triumph o'er the foe.

That's what's caused the cries and cheering
In our town of Petersburg,
And the cannons' choirs from reeling
Battleships at river's curve.
That's what's caused this joy resounding –
Our Tsar's cup's by froth becrowned!
The Nevá, from cannons' pounding,
Quivers far and wide around.

* Peter the Great was nearly 7 feet tall and loved to work with his own hands.

Town resplendent, town of beggars,
Air of slavery, splendid face,
Pale green archway of your heaven,
Boredom, cold, and granite grace.
Yet I'm sad for you too, truly
Because, sometimes, here, a girl
Walks with sweet small foot alluring,
Waving, soft, a golden curl.

Oh blessed he picked with choice capricious,
By all your dreams so full of rue,
Whose love your obvious sighing wishes,
Whose looks have power over you.
But woeful he, whose silence zealous,
Afire with the flame of love,
His head down drooping slightly, jealous,
Hears what you can't confess enough.

I loved you once, and still, perhaps, love's yearning
Within my soul has not quite burned away.
Yet may that nevermore you be concerning;
I would not wish you sad in any way.
My love for you was wordless, hopeless cruelly,
Wracked now by shyness, now by jealousy,
Yet I loved you so tenderly, so truly,
As God grant by another you may be.

Karolina Sobanskaya

WRITTEN ON A SLEEPLESS NIGHT

I can't sleep, fire's out, no light.
All is bleak, rests restless, tiresome.
Just the clock near me sounds lonesome,
Ticks on with no end in sight,
Ticks the Fates' cruel chitter-chatter,
Drowsy night's dull pitter-patter,
Mouse-life's darting busily...
What's your point in bothering me?
What's your meaning, droning ticker?
Are you of reproach a flicker
Of the way I waste my day?
What is it from me you're needing?
Are you calling or foreseeing?
Oh, to glimpse your truth, to peek!
Sense in you is what I seek...

THE FLOWER

A dried-out flower, without fragrance,
Forgotten in a book I see;
My soul's somehow already racing,
And fills with a strange reverie.

Where did it bloom? In which spring? When?
Did it bloom long? Who picked it then?
Was it a stranger or a friend?
Who put it here and to what end?

In memory of tender trysting?
Or else of fateful parting day?
Or else perhaps of lone walk wistful
In silent fields and wooded shade?

Do he and she still live, I wonder?
And where now is their little nook?
Or have they faded, lost their lustre,
Like this small flower in this book?

I still remember school when life began,
We were a throng, we carefree children glad,
A boisterous and brashly boyish clan.

A woman there, in modest raiment clad,
And yet magnificent in grandeur meek
Kept strictest watch upon us schoolboys mad.

Surrounded by our wilful impish shrieks,
She wisdom with a gentle voice imparted
And gently with us children would she speak.

A veil diaphanous did grace her forehead,
Her eyes were light with heaven's radiance,
Yet little thought to her words I allotted.

I would grow shy, seeing her solemn grace,
Her visage, full of calm and consolation,
And sacred language full of holiness.

Shrinking from her reproachful meditations,
I often used to make sarcastic quips
And twist the sense of truthful conversations.

And often on the sly I liked to slip
Into the splendid murk of a forbidden garden
'Neath vaulting artificial purple cliffs.

I was caressed in there by shadows calming.
I gave my youthful mind up to my dreams
And idle musing was my joy and balsam.

I loved the rustling leaves, the sparkling streams,
'Neath shaded groves the alabaster idols,
Unmoving thoughts on their fair faces gleamed...

And all of these grand marble spheres and lyres,
Swords, scrolls in marble hands, and heroes bright
By laurels crowned, in regal purple attired,

All this brought certain sweet and sensuous fright
Into my heart, and tears of inspiration,
Beholding them, were born within my eyes.

And two other miraculous creations
Just drew me in with other-wordly grace:
Two statues captured my imagination.

One was the Delphic idol, young in face
Yet furious in noble pride most dreadful.
With sacred fire his marble chest did blaze.

The other one was feminine and youthful:
A sweet and sensuous, sly and false ideal –
Enchanting demon – false, yet beautiful.

Before these two I would forget myself,
My young heart pounding; chills in me would run
Right down my spine, standing my curls on end.

A dark desire for unknown pleasures strung
Taut my wracked heart, by gloom devoured whole,
Just riveting me...vainly was I young.

Lost to the other lads all day I'd stroll
In mournful silence: ever the Park's idols
Would cast their shade mysterious on my soul.

*May 26, 1828**

Gift so futile, gift so random,
Life, why were you given me?
Or else why has Fate unfathomed
Doomed you to Death's penalty?

Whose malevolent attraction
From the void has called me out,
Filled my soul with so much passion,
Racked my mind with raging doubt?

No grand purposes are sent me:
Empty-hearted, idle-brained,
Always a dull grief torments me,
Sounds monotonous life's strains.

* On the occasion of his 29th birthday according to the Julian calendar. May 26, 1828, or June 6, 1828, by the Gregorian Calendar.

REMEMBRANCE*

When to most mortals sounds of noisy day do fade,
And on the city's streets grown silent,
The half-transparent night casts down its shade,
And sleep rewards the day's toil mildly,
I, in that time, in silence toss and turn:
Those wakeful hours sorely try my patience.
Through night's inaction stronger in me burn
Of heartfelt self-reproach the serpents.
With dreams aboil, oppressed, beset with grief, my mind
Into a crowd drives thoughts appalling...
And silent recollections pass before my eyes,
The scroll in which they're writ unfolding:
And, with repulsion, as I'm reading there my life,
I tremble, cursing with rue awful;
Complaining bitterly, with bitter tears I cry,
Yet don't wash off the lines so mournful.

* This was Leo Tolstoy's favourite poem; he would declaim it to himself loudly, at the end, however, substituting for the word "mournful" the word "shameful."

REBIRTH

A savage artist, brushstrokes sleepy,
The painting of a genius mars,
With sacrilegious scrawl unseemly
A senseless mess on it he tars.

But as the years pass, colours foreign
Fall off, like snakeskin's ancient flakes,
What genius wrought once gets reborn
Again, and former beauty takes.

Just so, my erring ways do vanish,
And in my wracked soul leave no trace,
Then visions rise up with a flourish
From pure and innocent first days.

SOMETIMES WHEN MOODY REMINISCENCE*

Sometimes when moody reminiscence
Gnaws at my heart with silent grief,
And suffering comes back from a distance,
And like a spectre chases me,
When everywhere I look are people,
And in a desert I would hide,
Feeling I hate their voices feeble –
Then I forget myself and fly –
Not to that blessèd land, whose heaven
So sparkles deep, mysterious blue,
Whose ocean waves splash warmly through
Embankments marble, faded, yellowed,
Whose laurel, and whose cypress dark,
Grew up in freedom, splendour, art,
Where once Torquato sang majestic,
Where, even now, in gloom of night,
'Neath cliffs that echo in the bight
His octaves boatmen aren't forgetting.

Instead, it seems I'm always yearning
For grey and chilly northern waves,
Amidst their crowded whitecaps churning
I see a barren island's capes,
A saddened island's savage shores,
Where wintry berries grow in scores,
'Midst faded tundra, melting snow,
And washed at times by chilly foam.
At certain times you'll see arriving
A northern fisherman, tough breed:
He stretches out his nets for drying,
And stokes a campfire by the sea.
It's always there the whitecapped weather
Casts up my frail and flimsy boat...

....

*Anna Akhmatova's favourite poem

VI. ON THE ROAD

Grey time, wild coachman ever steady,
Drives on, won't leave his driver's seat...

Let's leave, I'm ready now! Wherever you, my friends,
Have whims you'd like to go, even to the earth's ends,
I'll gladly follow, from haughty maid flying:
Unto the distant foot of the Great Wall of China,
To Paris bubbling, or – at last! to that land yet
Where Tasso's quatrains gondoliers at night forget,
Where ancient cities' ruins beneath the ash are slumb'ring,
Where cypress groves' sweet scents set all the senses humming:
Wherever! Let's go now! But friends, say, by and by,
In all these pilgrimages will my passions die?
Will I that maid, that proud tormentress, be forgetting,
Or, at her feet cast down, her youthful rage begetting,
Will I, as if paying a common debt, bring love?
(.................)

A WINTER ROAD

Through a mist that's waving, rolling,
Breaking through, the moon does pass;
On the meadows melancholy
Melancholy light does cast.

On a winter road so dreary,
Fleet my troika runs its route;
Of its little bell I'm weary,
Clinking with but one dull note.

Something strikes a chord within me,
In the coachman's endless song:
Sometimes fiery, daring, cheery,
Sometimes grieving in my heart.

Not one light, no black hut looming,
Barren snow round barren path,
Just the milestones striped and gloomy
Are the only things I pass.

Dreary, sad... Tomorrow, Nina,
I'll be back by your dear fire,
Lose myself and clutch you nearer,
Look and look, and never tire.

When the sonorous clock's arrows
Keep their measured rounds so hard,
Fleeing all things dull and shallow,
Midnight won't keep us apart.

I'm sad, Nina: my path's dreary,
Hushed, my coachman nods, apace,
From his little bell I'm weary,
Wrapped in mist is the moon's face.

THE CART OF LIFE

Although at times the burden's heavy,
The cart rides with a rhythm fleet.
Grey time, wild coachman ever steady,
Drives on, won't leave his driver's seat.

We mount the cart when morn's arising,
We'd gladly break our head in two,
Our haste, comfort and ease despising,
Leads us to yell: "let's go! ....!"

But when it's noon, we've lost that valour
And fear more, having rattled through
The little rolling hills and valleys,
We yell: "Ease up there, silly fool!"

But still the cart keeps rolling, rolling,
By evening we're quite used to it.
As towards our shelter we ride dozing:
Time drives the horses with a whip.

SUPERSTITIONS

I rode towards you, and waking dreams
Did wind in playful thought around me.
The moon, on my right side, cast beams
On our race ardent, hoofbeats pounding.

I rode away, and other dreams
Made my soul lovelorn, melancholy.
The moon, now on my left, cast beams
With gloomy gleams, on me, despondent.

Removed in quiet reverie,
We poets ever are capricious;
And thus traditions superstitious
Live with our hearts in harmony.

THE STEED

"Fiery steed, why are you neighing?
Why does your head droop and sink?
With your mane, why aren't you waving?
Why don't you champ at the bit?
Don't I give you all you're wanting?
Don't you eat oats in abundance?
Is your hasp not fair, bright, bold?
Aren't your reins soft, smooth, and silky,
Aren't your horseshoes made of silver?
Aren't your stirrups gilded gold?"

But the steed replies with sadness:
"I am feeling worn and wan:
Far off I hear armies tramping,
Martial horns and arrows' song.
So I neigh, with nostrils flaring,
Not for long can I still dance
On green fields, so blest with caring,
Flaunt my harness, preen and prance!
Soon an enemy most heartless
Rudely will remove my dress,
And strip off my silver horsehoes
From my lithe and supple legs;
That is why a wild grief gnaws me:
Soon I'll lose my saddlebags,
And your flayed skin will be sprawling
On my sweaty, frightened flanks."

Round Izhora I was riding,
When I looked up at the skies.
For your glances I was pining,
For the dark blue of your eyes.
Though most sadly I am smitten
By your beauty chaste, austere,
Though it's "vampire" I am christened
In the provinces of Tver',
Still on bended knee before you
To offend I would not dare,
Or with lovelorn pleas implore you.
I've no wish to cause you care.
So I'll revel, pointless, clueless,
In society's vain fuss.
Soon, it's likely, I'll be heedless
Just how sweet your face once was,
Lithe your build, graceful your movements,
Prudent speech, quite by the book.
Your mild calm, so unassuming,
Cunning laugh and cunning look
I'll forget... If not, be certain,
I'll ride back quite soon enough
In a year to your sweet province
And – till November – fall in love.

"And – till November – fall in love"
(Katya Velyasheva)

(November 2nd)*

A country winter. What's to do here? I am greeting
My servant, as he brings my morning teacup
With questions: Is it warmer? Has the storm died down?
Is there powder or not? Should I go riding now,
Abandoning my bed, or till dinner's at table
Should I just fuss with the old journals of my neighbour?
It's powder. We get up, and on the horse we ride
And gallop through the fields just at the day's first light,
And carry hunting whips, the dogs behind us racing,
Our eyes with fervour scan pale snow, keep gazing,
We circle, trot around, and it has gotten late
When, having missed two hares, we ride back to our gate.
Oh what a joy that was! It's evening. Snowstorm's crying...
A candle darkly burns, my heart is gnawing shyly.
Of boredom, drop by drop, I slowly poison sip
I want to read; my eyes over the letters slip;
My thoughts are far away... I close the book, despairing,
I take my pen, I sit, with violence am tearing
Disjointed words out of my grudging, slumbering Muse,
But sound does not match sound, and soon all rights I lose
To Rhyme, to old maid muse gone balmy,
My poem weakly drags, is getting cold and foggy.
I'm tired; and with my lyre my quarrel I stop,
Go to the living room, and there I hear the talk:
Elections on their way, some sugar factory's founding,
And very weather-like, the house mistress is frowning,
As she her steel needles for knitting nimbly darts,
As she tells fortunes for a certain king of hearts...
How dull! Thus day by day goes by in solitary,
But if, one evening time, upon our village dreary,
When, in my corner, I'm half-sleeping over checkers,

*I.e. November 14th, by our Gregorian Calendar. And it was already winter!

When, from far off, a covered sled or carriage enters,
A family by surprise: two maidens with one spinster
(Two curly-haired sweet blondes, two slender, graceful sisters),
How lively, suddenly, these boondocks get!
How life, my God, fills up, seems hopeful yet!
First passing glances, looks full of attention,
Then a few words, and then free conversation,
Then friendly laughs, songs in the evening reel,
With waltzes rollicking, and whispers at the meal
Then looks all languorous, light-hearted, airy speeches,
And lingering, on narrow stairways, meetings:
One girl at twilight on the porch does pace:
Her neck and breast are bare – the snowstorm's in her face!
But northern storms are to our Russian rose not fazing!
How warm – even in frost – the kiss she gives is, blazing!
How fresh the Russian maid when snowflakes fly!

"A family by surprise: two maidens with one spinster"
(with little demons dancing attendance on them)

TO A KALMYK GIRL

Farewell, dear, pleasant Kalmyk maiden!
For, nearly spoiling all my plans,
My good old habit almost played me,
Seduced me in this broad expanse
Of steppes, where your broad tent did span.
Your eyes, of course, are rather narrow.
Your nose is flat, your forehead's broad,
Your grasp of French is rather shallow,
In silk your legs you don't swathe taut.
You don't, o'er samovar, o'er campfire,
Make English patterns of your bread,
By Cinq-Mars feats* you're not inspired,
In Shakespeare you're a bit unread.
You do not lose yourself daydreaming
When there are no thoughts in your head,
You don't sing arias: *Ma dov'è,***
Or dance galopes in gatherings teeming.
Who needs that? But for half an hour,***
While they were hitching up my team,
My heart and spirit were o'erpowered
By your wild grace and look so keen.
My friends! What does it really matter
Just where our idle heart gets rent?
In ballrooms bright, smart box-seat chatter,
Or in a nomad's wicker tent?

* *The Plot of Cinq-Mars against Louis XIII,* a popular historical novel by the French Romantic poet Alfred de Vigny, was published in 1826.
** "But where is … ?" (*Italian*).
*** See page 86 for more details about this "half an hour."

THE MONASTERY OF MOUNT KAZBEK

High o'er mountain family,
Kazbek, your vault majestically
Shines rays eternal, blessed and airy.
Beyond the clouds, your monastery,
An ark in heaven fluttering,
Steams o'er the peaks, is seen but barely.

Goal strived-for long in wandering!
To climb, leave in ravines all crowds,
To rise to freedom, high, aloft!
To you, my cell beyond the clouds!
To hide, and neighbours be with God!

Oh beauty, do not sing* to me
More songs of melancholy Georgia.
For they bring up, evoke in me
Another life, a distant shoreline.

Alas! You call forth in your tune,
In your cruel melody's refraining,
The steppe, the night, and 'neath the moon
The face of a poor, distant maiden.

That darling fateful spectre – when
I see you – I'm forgetting.
But then you sing, and, once again,
Before my eyes it is engendered.

Oh beauty, do not sing to me
More songs of melancholy Georgia.
For they bring up, evoke, in me
Another life, a distant shoreline.

* There are countless romances and songs set to Pushkin poems. This poem is actually a rare case of the reverse. It was written by special request as the lyrical accompaniment to a Georgian melody improvised by Pushkin's friend Alexander Griboyedov, the poet, playwright, diplomat and composer, during a musical evening with the composer Mikhail Glinka. In turn, this poem was set again to hauntingly beautiful music by Rachmaninoff.

Dawn drums sound... From my hand tips
Dante's epic, now in tatters,
And a verse, sprung to my lips,
Unsaid, into stillness slips –
Farther still my spirit scatters.
Beat familiar, beat alive,
Say, how often were you booming*
Back in days of quiet blooming,
Once upon a distant time?

*Refers to the reveille drum of the Lycée.

DELIBASH (The Turkish Captain)*

Shots ring out beyond the hillocks:
Their camp looks down; so does ours.
On a hill before the Cossacks
A red Turkish standard glowers.

Hey there, Turk! Don't charge our horse charge;
Have some pity for your life.
Poor amusement deaths in war are:
You will end up on a pike.

Cossack, hey! Race not to battle:
For the Turk, with gallop dread,
Curving scimitar a-rattle,
Will cut off your daring head.

Charging, both sides screaming, crashes...
Look! You see what's happened yet?
Speared straight through their Delibash is,
– And our Cossack's lost his head.

A Cossack and his horse

*Alexander Blok's favourite poem.

THE CLOUD

O very last cloud of the storm that has scattered!
Alone, you are borne off along the clear azure,
Alone, you are casting a bleak shadow grey,
Alone, you bring sadness to joy felt by day.

Just recently you had all heaven surrounded,
And lightning and thunder all round you resounded.
Mysterious rumbling from your billows came,
And then the parched earth you did slake with your rain.

Enough, though, be hidden! That storm now is chastened,
The earth has been freshened, the squall has passed, racing,
The wind, now caressing the tips of the trees,
From skies that are calm now does chase you with ease.

FOREBODING

Once again the black clouds gather
In the silence overhead,
Ever-envious Fate unhappy
Once more sends me a new threat...
Shall I scorn predestination,
In its face look, keep aloof,
Patient, with determination
From the proud days of my youth?

I, of stormy life so tired,
Wait indifferent for the storm:
Yes, perhaps, it may transpire,
Safe again, I'll find the shore.
But foreseeing separation,
That dread hour I can't escape,
Just to press your hand, my angel,
Just for one last time I race.

Angel mild and unrebellious,
Gently murmur then: "Farewell!"
Let, with sadness, your look tendrest
Be downcast, or rising, swell.
And of you those memories' fires
In my soul will then replace
All my strength, pride, hopes, desires,
And brave heart of younger days.

The more we do commemorate
Our Lycée's sacred founding day,
The shyer our group of old friends great,
Does press into one family fray,
The more it thins, the more it does
In merrymaking make us gloomy,
The hollower our feasting cups;
Sadder the old songs we are crooning.

So has the breath of earthly storm
With freak winds buffeted us, starkly,
That we, twixt youthful feasts till morn,
Have our own souls been changing, darkly.
We've come of age, and Fate has willed
That we encounter all she offers.
And Death has strolled through us and killed,
And made appointments for more slaughters.

Six places are no longer here,
Six friends we had – and see no longer,
And scattered here and there they sleep:
Some on the battlefield now slumber,
Some home, and some abroad are dead,
Some by disease, and some by keening
Sadness to moist earth were led...
And over each we have been weeping.

And now it seems, it is my turn.
I hear my dear friend Delvig calling,
My friend from youth, when I did yearn,
My friend from youth, when I was lonely,
My friend of all my youthful songs,
Of feasts and purest thoughts imagined,
He calls our crowding shades beloved,
That genius lost for good, impassioned.

Close in, come closer, my dear friends!
Tighten our group of old friends great,
My song of those who've perished ends:
Survivors we congratulate
With hope that soon again we'll face
A feast of our Lycée's good cheer,
That all still here will still embrace
And learn new losses not to fear.

The poet, Baron Anton Delvig

THE DEMONS

Clouds are racing, clouds are writhing,
And, invisibly, the moon
Lights the snow up as it's flying;
Gloom's in heaven, night's in gloom.
In a bare field I am riding.
Din-din-din! the bell complains,
I can't help but being frightened,
'Midst these strange and unknown plains.

"Coachman! Hey! Let's go!" ... "I can't, sir,
See the horses walk so slow.
Blizzard's blown my eyes in, blasting,
All the roads are drowned in snow.
Kill me, but I see no traces,
We're quite lost. What shall we do?
For it seems a demon leads us
Round these fields and whirls us through.

Look right there, right there he's teasing,
Blowing, spitting at me, coarse.
There, towards a ravine he's leading,
With a push, our lonely horse.
There, like a fantastic milestone,
He before my eyes did lurk.
There he flashed with a spark tiny,
Vanished in the empty murk."

Clouds are racing, clouds are writhing,
And, invisibly, the moon
Lights the snow up as it's flying,
Gloom's in heaven, night's in gloom.
We've no strength to circle longer.
Suddenly the horses froze,
Bell fell silent. "What's that yonder?
Tree-stump or a wolf? Who knows?"

Snowstorm rages, snowstorm weeping,
Snorting horses ill-at-ease,
There! There! – off he darts now, sweeping,
But his eyes in this gloom blaze.
Horses start off in a lather,
Din-din-din! the bell complains...
Now I see the spirits gathered
In the ever-whitening plains!

Never-ending, ugly, formless,
In the gloom that this moon weaves
Demons whirl around me, various,
Like November's falling leaves.
Hosts! What hounds them! Where to their flight?
Why this singing, plaintive screech?
Are they burying a house sprite?
Are they marrying off a witch?

Clouds are racing, clouds are writhing,
And, invisibly, the moon
Lights the snow up as it's flying;
Gloom's in heaven, night's in gloom.
Demons racing, boundless, mounting,
Row on row, high, long, and far...
With their mournful, plaintive howling,
They are tearing up my heart...

VII. FROM THE HEART

There is a heart where I'm still living.

MADONNA
A Sonnet

Of all the great old masters' paintings, few, indeed,
I'd decorate my home with – if at all,
To cause my visitors sheer superstitious awe,
Impressing those who to grand critics pay blind heed,

O'er my meek little nook, which slothful labour crowds,
There's just one picture whose sight I would ever savor,
Just one, from canvas glancing down, as from the clouds,
Our purest Maid, with Heaven's Son, our Saviour,

So She'd with majesty, and He'd with reason gaze,
With looks of meekness, soft, yet with bright glory's rays,
No angels near, alone, 'neath Zion's green palm fronded...

My dream's come true. Our Lord Creator sent
You down to me, sent you, my own Madonna,
Of purest grace the purest monument.

What is there in my name for you?
It will die out, like sad waves sounding
Their last, on distant shorelines pounding,
As in deaf woods night's sounds ring through.

Within your album it will leave
A deadened trail, like in description
To tracings on a grave's inscription
In a strange language you can't read.

What's in't? Forgotten long ago,
By new rebellious passions rendered,
It will not give your soul a glow
Of recollections pure and tender.

But in still sadness, undisturbed,
Pronounce aloud my name while grieving;
Say: I'm remembered in this world;
There is a heart where I'm still living.

Upon the Georgian hills there lies the haze of night.
  Aragva's river foams beside me.
I feel both sad and light; my melancholy's bright;
  My melancholy's full entirely
Of you and just of you... This gloominess of mine
  Nothing's tormenting, nothing's moving.
My heart's again afire and loving, because – why?
  It simply cannot not be loving.

"Upon the Georgian hills..." (manuscript)

When in the grasp of my embrace,
I wrap your slender waist, enfold you,
With tender words of love and grace,
With raptured words and arms I hold you,
You're silent, from my arms extend
Your own, freeing your body supple,
Then answer me, my dearest friend,
But with a smile that's slight, untrustful...
So diligent, your memory
Collects sad tales of treachery,
So uninvolved and listlessly
You listen gloomily to me.
I rue then my past cleverness,
My reckless, sinful, youthful days,
The wakeful waiting for the trysts
On silent nights in garden glades,
I rue then words that lovers whisper,
How poems mysterious in me sing,
How carefree maids caress and cling,
And how they cry, and later whimper.

FROM THE TALE OF TSAR SALTAN

...By the blue sea our prince, moving,
From blue sea eyes not removing,
Looks – and where its waters flow,
A white swan appears, swims slow.
"How are you, my lovely princeling?"
Why so still, like a day drizzly?
What is it that makes you sad?
Says the swan to him at last.
Prince Guidon to her makes answer:
"Grief eats up my heart with sadness.
All get married, yet I see,
Still unmarried only me."
"But just whom is it you're seeking?"
"On this earth somewhere lives, breathing,
A Tsar's daughter, so they say,
From whom eyes can't look away.
During day than sun she's brighter,
Nights, she makes the world shine lighter.
In her locks bright moonbeams are,
In her forehead gleams a star.
And herself, majestic, precious,
Like a peacock stately, paces,
When she speaks, her sweet speech seems
Like the murmuring rush of streams.
But enough, could this be right?"
Asks the prince, and waits in fright.
For a long time the white swan
Hushes, thinks, and then goes on:
"Yes, indeed, there's such a maiden,
But a wife's no mitten braided,
Can't be shook from your white wrist,
Pinned upon your belt, then missed.

Let me give you some good counsel,
Listen, think before you answer,
Think again, and think it through,
Lest you'll later rashness rue."
Then the prince got down before her,
Swore his readiness, implored her,
Said he'd marry and be true,
Said he'd thought the whole thing through,
For his princess lovely he
Was prepared most passionately
To march miles no measure spans
Forth beyond the thrice-nine lands...
Deeply the swan started sighing:
"Why so far?" she asked, replying,
"Know: your fate is close nearby,
For that princess true – am I."
Then she flapped her wings in motion,
Flew up high above the ocean,
Back to shore did, diving, rush,
Landed in some underbrush.
Shook her wings with fuss auspicious,
Then she turns into a princess:
In her locks bright moonbeams are,
In her forehead gleams a star.
And herself, majestic, gracious,
Like a peacock stately, paces,
When she speaks, her sweet speech seems
Like the murmuring rush of streams.
Prince then princess hugs, caresses,
To his bosom pale close presses,
Then in great haste takes her home,
To his mother dear, his own.

At her feet he fell, imploring:
"Mother, our land's queen, who bore me,
I have found myself a wife,
Your new daughter true, for life.
Your permission we're requesting
To be granted your full blessing.
Bless us, may we live like doves,
In true harmony and love."
As their heads bent in orison,
'Neath her magic-working icon
Mother poured forth tears and cried:
"God, my children, be your guide."
Not for long did our prince tarry
Till his princess he did marry,
Soon they settled, loving, mild,
Soon they did expect a child...

Maria Pushkina, the poet's daughter

No, I do not hold dear that pleasure so rebellious,
That joy all sensual, insane, frenzied, delirious,
The groans, the crying out a young drunk nymph may make,
When, winding round in my embraces like a snake,
With gusts of kisses, wild, caressing, feverish, smoth'ring,
She hurries up the flash, last moment's final shuddering!

How much more dear are you, meek, sweet subduer mine!
Oh, with what tortured joy for you alone I pine,
When you, at last yielding to lengthy supplication,
Give yourself tenderly to me without elation,
Feeling ashamed and cold, my joyousness within
But scarcely answering, not feeling a thing.
Till livening with time, you too start thrilling –
Till more and more at last my flame you share unwilling!

BEAUTY

(in the album of ****.)

She is all harmony, all marvel,
All far above mere worldly lust,
With girlish modesty she dawdles,
In her majestic grace untouched.
And when she gazes all around her,
She has no rivals, has no friends.
Our beauties' meagre circle ends
And flees the first gleams of her splendour.

No matter where you might have raced,
Even to tryst and meet your lover,
Whatever myth your heart still graced,
What sacred daydream in you hovered,
Yet meeting her, you'll blush and pine;
Unwittingly you'll stop and stay there,
With reverence and pious prayer
Before her sacred beauty's shrine.

I thought my heart had long forgotten
Its ease in suffering of yore.
I told myself: all that has happened
Can come no more, can come no more!
The joys are gone, with sadness racing,
And trusting dreams so fanciful,
But once again they quiver facing
The power of the beautiful.

TO***

No, no, it isn't right, I cannot, I don't dare
Give myself madly up to love's worry and anguish;
My peace of mind I strictly guard with care,
And don't permit my heart to blaze with searing passion.
No, no more love for me! ...Although, why not, betimes,
Just daydream, for a minute's contemplation,
When just by chance, before my very eyes,
A young and pure and heavenly creation
Passes and disappears? Am I really forbid,
Charmed by a maid, with passionate sweet sadness,
To follow her just with my eyes, and when all's still,
To bless her, wish her joy, just wish her gladness?
Wish her, with all my heart, all blessings in this life:
Happiness in her soul, carefree leisures abundant,
All! – Even joy to him she chose, who'll call her wife,
Who'll give that maiden fair a brand new name – as husband.

It's time, my friend, it's time! For peace the heart is calling.
Day flies by after day, and every hour is tolling
A bit of being away: together you and I
Suppose that we will live – but see! Just then – we die.

There is no joy on earth, but there is peace and freedom:
Long time of enviable fate I have been dreaming,
Long time, I, tired slave, have dreamed of secret flight
Unto a distant shrine of toil and pure delight.

In mournful storms I have become a man.
The stream of all my days, for so long murky,
Has stilled now with a moment's slumber quirky,
And now reflect the heavens' azure span.

Is it for long? Somehow it seems they've gone,
Those bleak storm days, days bitter in temptations...

If not for something murky gnawing
Within my something-seeking soul,
I'd gladly stay, sheer pleasure drawing
In this mysterious silence whole.
Forgetting deep desires' murmuring,
I'd call the whole wide world a dream,
Just hear your babble sweet, not stirring,
And kiss and kiss your darling feet...

Will you forgive my jealous reverie,
My love's tormented crazy agitation?
Why be so fond – if you're faithful to me –
Of always frightening my imagination?
Surrounded by admirers in a crowd,
Why must you always try to be everyone's "darling"?
Why are all others' empty hopes always allowed
Now tender, and now bleak, your glances charming?
You've dimmed my mind; I'm taken, all your own!
You're certain of my constant love unhappy...
Can't you see how, midst throngs round you impassioned,
Shunning all chatting, silent and alone,
I writhe in lonesome agony distressing?
From you no word, nor glance! Cruel friend, tormenting!
If I would flee – with worry or with plea
Your eyes never attempt to follow me.
And if some other beauty towards me coming
Starts chatting, fills her speech with playful hints,
You are so calm, your gay reproachful squints
Kill, stop me cold, without expressing loving.
As for my constant rival, also, tell me true,
Whenever he sees me alone with you,
Why does he greet you far too casually and slyly?
Who's he to you? Explain it! By what right's he
Allowed to pale, and have a jealous fit?
Between nightfall and dawn, at hours and times immodest,
Mother not watching by, alone, only half-dressed
How is it you receive him, let him sit?
But I'm your love. When we are by ourselves
You are so sweet, your kiss, caressing, rough,
So fiery! The words that speak your love
Are so sincere, so soulful, and so heartfelt!
Yet at my sufferings you laugh and mock;
But I'm your love, we understand each other.
My darling, don't torment me, please, enough!
You do not know how powerfully I love;
You do not know how bitterly I suffer.

VIII. AND I FORGET THE WORLD...

...Filled by the silent Muse,
Above the waves' abyss with bliss his wake he hews.

Near lands where sovereignty of golden Venice rules,*
A lone nocturnal gondolier his way plies through the pools.
By evenstar's soft light, he – singing – turns his oars
– Of Reynald, Godfred, and Erminia – by their shores.
He loves singing his song, for pleasure sings his story,
Lacking all further plans, he sings heedless of glory,
Of fears heedless, of hopes...Filled by the silent Muse,
Above the waves' abyss with bliss his wake he hews:
So, in this sea of life, where cruelly the tempest
In darkening gloom to my lone sail grants no rest,
Not minding what men say, I sing and I rejoice,
Dreaming up secret poems with my secret voice.

* Based on André Chenier's *Près des bords où Venise est la reine de la mer.*

May God forbid I go insane.
No, better beggar's pouch and cane!
  No, better work and starve.
Not that my faculties of mind
Are dear to me, for I'm inclined
  With them to gladly part.

If only I were left alone
With what a lively gait I'd roam
  'Neath darkest forest's trees!
I'd sing, deliriously ablaze,
And lose myself all in a daze
  Of blurred and wondrous dreams.

And I would hear and hear the waves,
And full of gladness I would gaze
  At Heaven's empty crown:
And strong and wilful would I reel,
A whirlwind, stirring up the fields
  And casting forests down...

Alas, though, if you go insane,
Then like the plague you'll be a bane,
  Indeed, they'll lock you up.
And to a fool's chain you'll be leashed,
And when you're caged up like a beast,
  They'll come to tease and mock.

And I won't hear at night in jail
The clear voice of the nightingale,
  The oak grove's muffled strains.
Instead I'll hear my cell-mates' shrieks,
The night-watch cursing as it peeks,
  And rattling, clanking chains.

THE POET

Until the poet by Apollo
To sacred sacrifice is called,
In this world's cares, so vain and hollow,
He is faint-heartedly enthralled.
His holy lyre's hushed; songs – unwritten:
Cold sleep his soul tastes bitterly,
And 'midst this world's unhappy children,
Unhappiest, perhaps, is he.

But once, divine, the word, the prize,
So slightly nuzzles his keen ears,
The poet's soul stirs up and rears,
Like an awakened eagle, cries.
He grieves at this world's pastimes idle,
He flees the rumour of the crowd.
Before the feet of all men's idol
He does not bend his head so proud.
But stern, but wild, away he roves,
And wracked by sounds and turmoil raves
By coasts where desolate crash the waves,
By spreading, rustling oak-leaved groves...

THE ECHO

If in thick woods a wild beast roars,
A horn gets blown, or lightning storms,
If fair maid sings o'er green hill's bourn,
  To any sound
Your answer in the air forlorn,
  Cries newborn round.

You heed the thunder pealing loud,
The voice of storms, the billows' howl,
  And rural shepherds crying out,
And send answer true.
Like you, to whom reply's not found,
  Are you, poet, too.

THE PROPHET

With thirsting soul wracked, worn and thin,
I marched through bleakest desert onwards,
And a six-wingèd Seraphim
Appeared to me upon a crossroads.
With fingers light as sleep then he
But grazed my eyes most gracefully,
And my foreseeing eyelids started,
Like a young frightened eaglet, startled.
And to my ears then he reached out,
And filled them with a ringing shout:
To Heaven's shuddering I hearkened,
And to the lofty angels' flight,
To slithering things in deep seas' night,
To valley grapes grown dull, cold, hardened.
And then upon my lips he clung,
And then tore out my sinner's tongue,
That babbles, idle, cunning, moody.
In my mouth, numb now to all things,
He placed the sharp wise serpent's sting,
He placed it with his right hand bloody,
Took sword, in my breast cut a hole,
Took out my feeble heart a-quaking,
Then, while it blazed, put in a coal,
The gap in gaping breast replacing.
In desert sand I corpse-like lay.
Then God's voice called to me, to say:
"Arise, thou Prophet, see and hearken,
By my will let your soul be stirred,
And, wandering by lands and waters,
Burn people's hearts up with my word."

TO THE POET
A Sonnet

Poet! Care not for love through fame, now or hereafter.
Elated cheers will pass after a minute's din,
You'll hear judgments of fools, and hear the crowd's cold laughter:
But you must just stay firm, stay ever calm and grim.

You're king: so live alone. Walk freely on your pathway:
Wherever your free spirit leads you, go,
Perfect the fruits of favourite thoughts until they glow.
For no rewards for noble deeds be asking.

For they're inside of you. You're your own highest judge.
Strictest of all praise for your work you'll grudge.
Does it content you, artist true, demanding?

It does? Then let the crowd scoff, spurn,
And spit upon the altar where your flame does burn.
Let them in childish rage your easel-stand be rattling!

AUTUMN
(A Fragment)

What thought won't at that time walk in my slumbering mind?

*Derzhavin**

I

October has arrived. The grove's already shaking
From branches stripped all bare the very last few leaves.
Fall's cold breath blows. With frost the road's now flaking.
The brook behind the mill still runs and, bubbling, breathes,
But ice quiets the pond. Meanwhile, my neighbour's taking
Out to the hunting fields his pack of dogs which seethes.
The winter wheat gets trampled in that furious larking;
The sleeping woods wake up to the sound of hounds barking.

II

Now is my time of year. I do not love the spring:
The thaw's a bore to me: smells, dirt... spring gives me ailment,
Blood stirring, feelings, mind restrained in longing's sling.
From winter's bitter blasts I find much more contentment;
I love her fallen snows, the moonlit sleighbell's ring!
So quick and free the sleigh rides with a girlfriend,
When, wrapped in sable furs so warm and fresh, you race;
She gives your arm a squeeze, both shivering and ablaze!

III

What fun it is, with skates of sharpened steel strapped on me,
To glide on mirrorlike stilled rivers' even glow!
And winter holidays so glittering, alarming?
But honestly, enough: half the year snow and snow –
Why even, in his lair, the hibernating bruin
Gets sick of it at last! You can't just always go
Out sleigh-riding, entranced by Armida the maiden,**
Or sour by the stove by double windows hidden!

*From *To Eugene: Courtly Life* by Gavrila Derzhavin, 1743—1816, famous Russian poet who hailed Pushkin's *Memories in Tsarkoye Selo* (1815), which Pushkin declaimed before Derzhavin at a public examination at his Lycée; this incident was immortalized by the painter Repin, and is referred to in *Eugene Onegin*, Chapter VIII, ii. See Biography at page 52.

**Armida was an enchantress and seductress of the knight Rinaldo in Torquato Tasso's *Gerusalemme Liberata*.

IV

Oh, summer beautiful! I'd be in love with you –
But for the heat, the dust, and the mosquitoes, horseflies,
You, leaving all our spirit's faculties sapped through,
Torment us: like the fields, with suffering our mind dries:
Save how to freshen up, and drink and drink anew,
We have no other thoughts. And old hag Winter's now prized:
With pancakes and with wine our leave of her we take,
With ice-cream and with ice we celebrate her wake.

V

The days of autumn's end most scorn when they're upon us,
But she is dear to me, and makes my heart her own
With beauty still and mild, so brilliantly modest,
Just so a child unloved in her own home
Draws me near her. And, to be truly honest,
Of all the times of year I joy in fall alone.
There's so much good in her! I, lover, not much preening,
Found something meet in fall for my capricious dreaming.

VI

How can it be explained? I'm fond of fall, at length,
As, somehow, maybe, a consumptive girl's weak waning
Sometimes appeals to you. She is condemned to death:
The poor thing bows her head, not angered, uncomplaining:
Her smile's still visible on lips all out of breath,
The yawn of grave's abyss she can't hear through her straining:
Yet on her shining face, soft velvet light's still caught,
Today her spirit's still alive, tomorrow – not.

VII

Oh, gloomy season mine! My eyes' delight, enchanting!
How pleasant to me is your beauteous farewell grace!
I love the sumptuousness of nature softly passing,
In velvet raiment and in gold the forests dress:
Their treetops sound so light with wind's fresh breath but glancing
And waves of misty fog beshroud the skies like lace,
The sun's rays, so rare now, and the first frost upon us,
And seeming far off now, dread winter's greyhaired menace.

VIII

And with each autumn chill my heart blossoms anew.
The bitter Russian cold upon my health works wonder,
For everyday, plain life my old love I renew.
I sleep at the right time, at dinner I feel hunger.
How light and joyous in the heart is my blood's stew
Of boiling desires! And I feel happy, younger,
And full of life again! Such is my organism!
(I do hope you'll forgive this needless prosaism).

IX

They bring a horse to me: through open fields, he, shaking
His mane, and riding off, far off his rider bears,
The echo of his hooves, so brilliantly quaking,
Sounds through the frozen vale; ice under hoofbeats tears.
But short day fades away, and in the hearth forsaken
A fire burns again: now brilliant light it flares,
Now sputters, ebbing slowly. I sit before it reading –
Or ling'ring thoughts within my soul I'm feeding.

X

And I forget the world, and in a silence sweet,
I sweetly lull myself by my imagination,
And deep inside of me awakens poetry.
My soul is shy of its own lyrical elation,
And trembling it resounds, and dreamlike, tries to be
With words, poured forth at last, expressed in free creation:
A throng of guests, invisible, then at me streams,
Old friends of mine, the fruits of all my dreams.

XI

And thoughts within my head rise up and boldly quaver,
And rhymes so easily to meet them lightly go!
My fingers seem to seek my pen, my pen seeks paper...
One minute! – and how free the verses flow!
Just so a docked ship sleeps in harbour's waters tapered –
But ho! The sailors up and down the ship race, throw
Themselves, and then the sails fill up, in the wind heaving,
The monster leaves its berth and moves, the waters cleaving...

XII

And sails... Where shall we sail? ....
....
....
....
....
....
....
....

...I came back again
To that small plot of land, where once I spent
Two years living in exile and unnoticed.
By now ten years have passed since then, and many
Have been the changes coming to my life.
I too, to universal law submissive,
Have changed myself, but, once more here,
All of my past embraces me with vigour,
And so it seems but yesterday I walked
Through these groves, wand'ring.
Here's the forlorn cottage
Where with my poor old nanny I did live.
The old lady has gone. Beyond the wall now
I cannot hear her footsteps heavy tramping,
Nor her devoted, always-caring snooping.

And here's the wooded hillock, on which often
I used to sit, not moving, and look down
Into the lake, remembering with sadness
The look of other waves, of other shorelines....
By crops of gold, and pastures gently greening,
Dark blue, and sparkling broadly, the lake's gleaming,
And through its waters deep, unknown, mysterious,
A fisherman sails by and, dragging, pulls behind him
His net in tatters. On the shorelines sloping
Some villages are scattered; there, behind them,
The mill is crooked now; its wings with effort
Are flutt'ring when the wind blows...

On the border
Of grandfather's old lands, in that same place,
Right where the road climbs up into the mountain,
All potholed by the rains, right there three pines
Do stand – the first off farther, the two others
Right close together – here, when I would pass them,

When I'd ride by on horseback in the moonlight,
Their rustling treetops whisperings, well-known, soft,
Would send me greetings then. On that same pathway,
Now I rode past them; before me they stood
And I saw them again. They're just the same still,
Still whisp'ring in my ear the same soft greetings,
But yet, about their roots ancient and withered,
(Where everything before was bare and naked)
By now a new young grove is growing up,
A family of green, its bushes thickening,
Sheltering beneath like children. Further off,
Their brooding gloomy friend is still there, standing
Like some old bachelor, and all around
Him, still, all is deserted.

Greetings, youngsters!
So young, and so unknown to me! I won't
Be blessed to see your greening growth in fullness
When you outgrow and pass my old companions,
And hide their ancient heads with your new boughs
From sight to passersby. But, one day, may
My grandson hear your greeting whispered soft,
When riding back from chatting at a friend's house,
Filled in his heart with happy, pleasant musings,
And, passing by your shade in gloom of nighttime,
Then think of me, remembering.

A page from Pushkin's notebooks

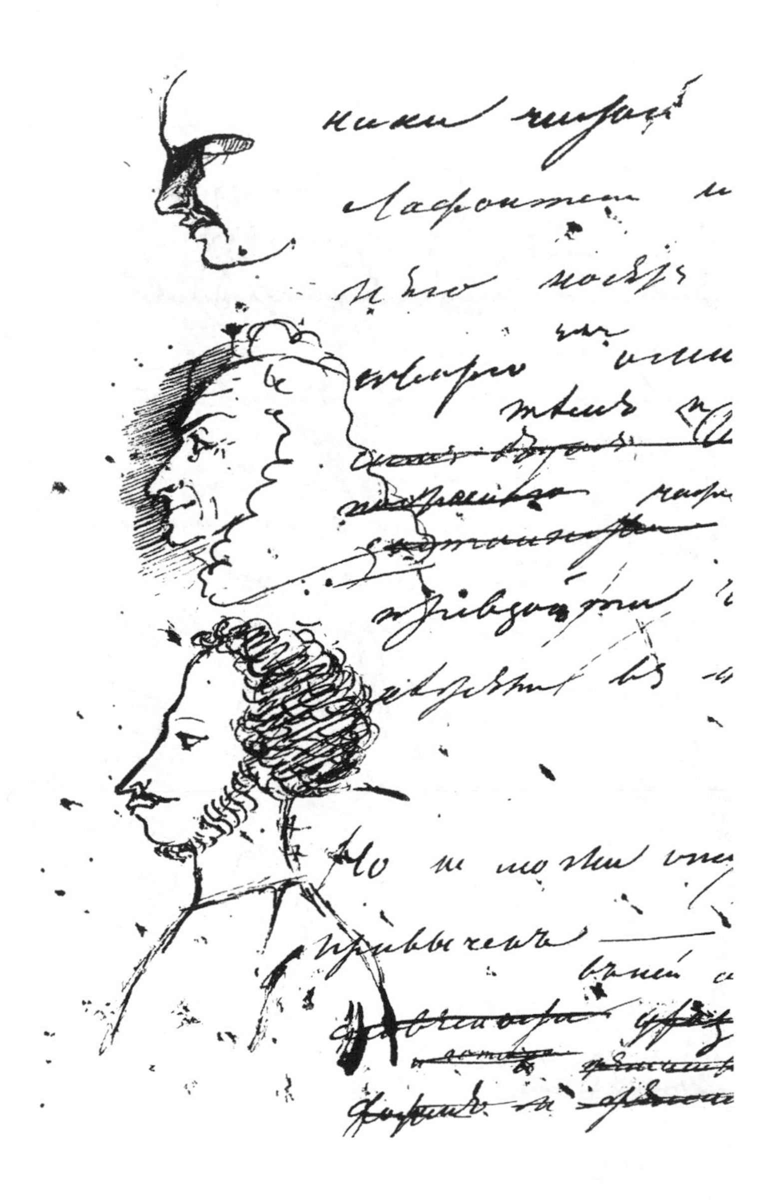

A manuscript page with a portrait of Voltaire (second from top) and self-portrait

FROM EGYPTIAN NIGHTS

The poet walks... his eyes are open,
But no one else around he sees;
Yet, by him, tugging on his clothing,
A passerby his hem does seize.
"Explain your ceaseless, senseless wandering!
You've barely scrambled to the heights,
Already though, your gaze is dropping,
For quick descent your spirit cries.
You see the world of beauty dimly;
A fruitless fever wears you down;
A minor object for a minute
Distracts you, tempts you, lures you out.
A genius ought to seek the heavens;
A real poet is obliged
For his inspiring compositions
To seek a subject that's inspired."
"Why does the wind swirl in the valley
And lift the leaves and raise the dust,
When stuck in doldrums ships do languish,
And wait for a slight breath with thirst?
Why, flying down from peaks that tower,
Do soaring, solemn eagles glower,
Then swoop down on a stunted stump?
Ask! Why such passion for her Moor?
Why does she love, young Desdemona,
The way the moon's in love with dark?
Because, in truth, a maiden's heart,
Like wind, like eagle, knows no owner.
The poet, like the wind, is thus:
He picks up anything he wants –
And, like an eagle, soars in flying,
And asks of no one where to dart,
As Desdemona chooses blindly
An idol for her loving heart."

CLEOPATRA

The palace gleamed. A chorus thundered
And flute and lyre sweet songs released.
The Queen's rich voice and dark eyes wandered,
Enlivening the sumptuous feast.
All hearts to her grand throne were flying,
Yet o'er her golden cup of wine,
She suddenly grew pensive, sighing,
With sadness drooped her head divine.

It seems the sumptuous feast is sleeping:
Hushed are the guests. The choir falls still.
Yet she lifts up her head, locks sweeping,
And a clear light her eyes does fill:
"For all of you my love is bliss!
This bliss, however, you can buy.
Would you be equal to me? Hear this!
Be equal to me till you die!
Who'll bid in passion's trade today?
I sell my love quite openly;
Say, who amongst you men will pay
His life to spend one night with me?"

She spoke. With horror all are seized
With passion every heart does race.
The cowering shudders she perceives,
A challenge chills upon her face;
She looks at her admirers coldly
And thinks them cowards, dull and dim.
Then from the crowd a man steps boldly;
Two others rise and follow him.
Bravely they walk; their eyes are bold.
She rises up to greet them all.
It's settled now; three nights are sold;
Their bed of love and death does call.

The priests praise them with murky blessings,
Now quivering from the fatal urn
(The shocked guests' slightest stir arresting)
Their lots are drawn, each one in turn.
The first was Flavius, warrior fearless,
A grizzled Roman soldier peerless
Who from his wife could bear no more
The haughty scorn and taunting galling.
He hearkened unto pleasure calling
As once he heard the call of war
And fighting savage and appalling.

Next came Criton, a youthful sage,
Nurtured in groves Epicurean,
A bard and acolyte and page
Of Eros, Grace, and Cytherea,
Who charmed the eyes and heart beneath
Like spring's first green the meadows crowning...
The last of them did not bequeath
His name to history. First downy,
Tender stubble his cheeks grazed
And ecstasy in his eyes blazed.
With innocent young passion quivering
His boyish heart did boil and steam,
And with a melancholy lingering
The proud queen's eyes caught his and gleamed.

"I swear, mother of sweet sensations,
To You – worship unmatched give I!
Upon my bed of wild temptations
As simple hired whore I lie.
Hear me, most potent Aphrodite,
And you fell lords of Hades' lair,
Gods of the depths of Hell almighty,
Until the break of dawn, I swear

My rulers' least whim and desire
In every way to please and sate
With all love's mystery and fire
I'll sate with blissful Heaven's state.
Yet when the dawn's first shy glow basks
In purple porphyry, night's bliss stops –
I swear, a sharp and deadly axe
My happy lovers' head then chops.

Now day has vanished. Hanging low
A golden crescent moon now gleams.
The Alexandrine palace dreams
In moonlight's soft, sweet haunting glow.
By purling fountains, torches bright
Play as soft puffs of incense whirl...
Sweet fruits that cool and give delight
Await these new gods of our world.
In luscious tranquil murk are spread
Out many wonders ravishing...
Neath purple curtains' lavishness
Now gleams the lovely golden bed.

When past the city gates in wistful thought I roam,
When I the public graveyard enter, footsteps slown,
See grates, small obelisks, smart pedestals, graves arty,
'Neath which the corpses of the capital are rotting,
In this thick swamp somehow together tightly bound,
As greedy guests at beggars' dinners crowd around,
See sleeping bureaucrats' and merchants' mausoleums,
Cheap-cut clumsy attempts to imitate museums,
And read inscriptions on them, both in verse and prose,
Supposed good deeds, and who in rank and service rose...
The amorous laments of widows for old cuckolds,
The urns ripped off by thieves, the obelisks unbuckled,
The graves gone slippery, that also, slanting sheer,
Yawn, waiting for new guests next morning to appear,
Such dark and dire depressing thoughts then come upon me,
An evil fit descends of gloom and melancholy.
To hell with it, to flee!

And yet, how dear to me
When autumn twilight comes, in evening reverie,
To walk past country graves where all my kin are buried,
Where still in solemn grace the dead slumber unhurried,
Where there is space for all the simple gravestones bare,
Where no pale sneaking thieves attempts at them would dare,
Where by those age-old stones, by yellow moss all covered,
A peasant passes by, says prayers with sighs smothered,
Instead of pompous urns and petty pyramids,
And noseless geniuses and frayed Caryatids,
Above the solid graves an oak stands, broad boughs casting,
With quivering, rustling leaves...

Our hermit fathers and our nuns blessèd and blameless,
To let their hearts fly up into the heavens nameless,
To keep their spirits strong, in storms of wind and war,
Composed a multitude of sacred hymns and lore.
But there's not one of them which gives me so much comfort
As one prayer our priest repeats and utters
Upon the melancholy days of Lenten Fast.
Unbidden, more than other prayers does it pass
My lips, bracing my fallen soul with strength mysterious:
"Lord of my days! Keep me from sloth that hides in bleakness,
From pride, greed, arrogance, and serpents therein hid,
Let not my tongue in idle gossip slip,
But, Lord, show me my own faults and transgressions,
And may my brother never hear my condemnations,
May I for grace, patience, and love forever strive,
And wisdom's innocence within my heart revive."

"May I for grace, patience, and love forever strive..." Drawing on the manuscript of this poem

FROM PINDEMONTE*

I do not value much those rights hailed with such din
From which so many people's heads just seem to spin.
I don't complain and grouse about the gods' sharp practice
Denying me sweet rights to argue about taxes,
Or make it hard for Tsars to war with Tsars.
It little riles me if the press is free to charge
And torment idiots, or tender censors' humours
Offend themselves in every ragsheet's rumours.
Oh! Can't you see that all of this is "words, words, words?"**
By other, better rights my soul gets stirred,
Another, better sort of freedom I am seeking.
Depend upon the Tsar? Depend upon the people?
Isn't it all the same? Who cares?
No, to none
To have to give account! Only myself alone to
Serve, to powers that be and servants at their beck,
Bend neither thoughts, nor conscience, nor my neck,
But, flitting here and there as my whims may incline,
Enthralled by beauties of great nature most divine,
Before creations of fine arts and inspiration
To quiver joyously in deeply moved elation...
– That's happiness!... Those are rights!...

*The Veronese poet Ippolito Pindemonte (1753—1828) wrote two books of Arcadian verse, *Le stanze* and *Poesie campestri*, and translated Homer's *Odyssey* into Italian. By presenting this poem as a "translation," Pushkin hoped to avoid problems with the censors.... in vain. This poem was banned from publication until long after Pushkin's death.

** *Hamlet* (Pushkin's own footnote; see *Hamlet*, — II, ii, line 194).

ELEGY

The faded gaiety of past years' frenzies
Clouds up my heart, as if hung over, heavy.
But like a wine, of days gone by the woe,
While aging in my soul, does stronger grow.
My way ahead is bleak. Of work and grieving
The ocean of my future worries, heaving.

But, oh my friends, I do not want to die;
I want to live, to ponder, wrack, and pine.
I know there will be moments of elation
Amidst my mourning, cares, and tribulation,
When revelling I'll drink harmony again,
And art forth from my eyes new tears will send,
And it may pass, on my sad twilight dying,
That love may blaze its rays in farewell smiling.

When through the noisy streets I wander,
Walk in cathedral's throng that teems,
And sit by crazy youths, I ponder
And give myself up to my dreams.

And then I say: the years are passing,
And multitudes though we seem here
We'll all pass 'neath the vaults e'erlasting
And someone's hour's already near...

I see an oak alone in autumn:
This forests' patriarch, I think,
Will quite outlive my time forgotten
As he my father's time outlived.

When I caress a child's head tender,
I think already: Farewell soon:
To you my place I now surrender:
For I must wither, you must bloom.

Each day and year now I'm amassing,
I like to see off in my mind,
Guessing the dates of my own passing,
Trying the right one to divine.

And where will fate send me my dying?
In battle, wanderings, or waves?
Or will the valley nearby lying
Receive my ashes in its graves?

For though the body without feeling
Will wither anywhere and keep,
Yet closer to a place endearing
Is where I feel I'd rather sleep.

I'd like, if by my graveyard's entrance,
A sweet young life would bloom and play,
And nature, shining with indifference,
Forever beauty would display.

Exegi Monumentum*

I've built myself a monument mere hands can't topple.
The people's path to it won't be o'ergrown with grass.
For it has raised itself above the crown unconquered
Where Alexander's column stands.

No, I won't fully die: my soul, in sacred lyre,
Will yet survive my dust, and, despite with'ring, thrive:
I'll glorious be as long's in moonlit world entire
One single bard is still alive.

Word about me will pass through all of Russia mighty.
My name in every one of her tongues will be penned:
By Slav's proud grandson, and by Finn, by savage, flighty
Tungus, and Kálmyk, the steppes' friend.

And many years will I be favoured with the people
For waking up good feelings by my lyre's thrall,
Because in my cruel age I praised and gloried Freedom,
For mercy to the fallen called.

Be to the Lord's command, oh Muse, forever heedful,
Fear not offense and shame, care not for glory's rule,
Take praise and calumny indifferently, not needful –
And never argue with a fool.

*From Horace Book III Ode XXX (see page 39)

LABOUR
(upon completion of *Eugene Onegin*)

Finally, now the time's come! I have finished my many years' labour.
Why, strange and secret, does sadness so trouble me now?
Is it, the deed being done, that I stand like a day-worker, useless,
Having been given my pay, foreign to all other toil?
Or do I pine for my work, for my silent companion at nighttimes,
Friend of my dawns swathed in gold, friend of my home's holy shrine?

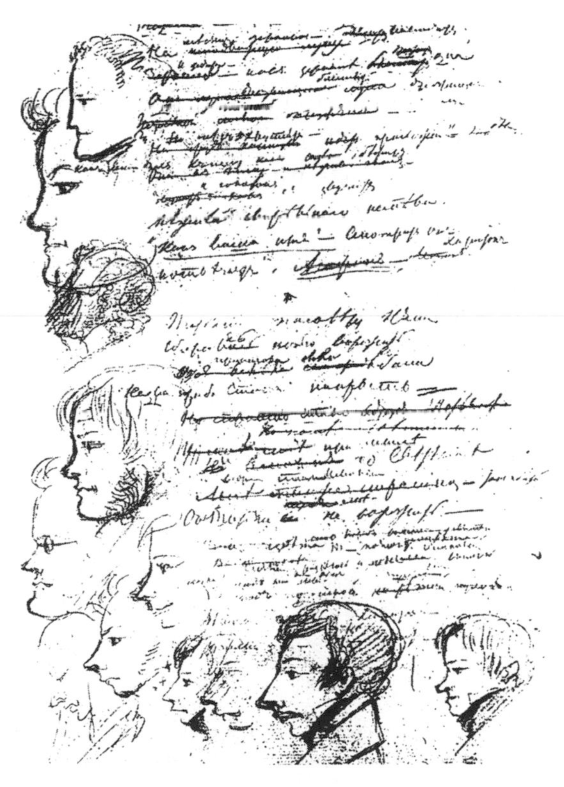

Page from the manuscript of "Eugene Onegin"

EUGENE ONEGIN
(Excerpts from the novel)

Pétri de vanité il avait encore plus de cette espèce d'orgueil qui fait avouer avec la même indifférence les bonnes comme les mauvaises actions, suite d'un sentiment de supériorité, peut-être imaginaire.

*Tiré d'une lettre particulière.**

For smiles from lofty halls not daring,
But caring just for friendship true,
I wish I here could be presenting
A gift much worthier of you,
More worthy of a soul that's lovely,
In whom there dwells a holy dream
Of poetry that's clear and lively,
With lofty thoughts, simplicity.
But be it so, with your hand biased
Accept these brightly coloured songs,
Half-humorous, half sad indeed,
Part folksy, and yet part ideal,
The breezy fruit of my free fun,
My sleepless nights, light inspirations,
My youth naïve, now faded far,
My intellect's cold observations,
And grieving notes straight from my heart.

* Suffused with vanity, he also had that sort of pride that led him to avow with equal indifference both his good and his bad deeds alike, due to a possibly imaginary sense of superiority.

From a private letter

CHAPTER I

To live he hurries and to feel he flies.

Prince Vyazemsky

I

"My uncle, man of rules, most honest,
When he fell ill beyond all joke,
Respect for himself forced upon us
(Better than that could not be hoped)
Let others learn from his example,
But Lord, how deathly dull to sample
The patient's sickbed night and day,
And never take a step away!
What execrably base dissembling
To keep someone half-dead amused,
Prop up his pillows, sadly brood,
With melancholy bring him medicine,
Sigh – as you ask yourself – all through –
When will the Devil come for you!"

II

Such were the thoughts of our young scapegrace,
Flying on post-coaches through dust,
By Zeus Almighty's sudden grace
The heir of all the family trust.
My friends of *Ruslan and Lyudmila*!
Allow me, to my novel's hero,
Without more rigmarole or fuss,
To introduce you, all at once.
Onegin – my good pal in "Peter"* –
Was born there, on the Nevá's banks.
Where you were also born, perhaps,
Or else just sparkled, my dear reader.
I strolled there, had my flings, before,
But I'm allergic to the North.

* As the Russians themselves call their most graceful of cities.

III

By serving "honestly and nobly,"
His father lived, from debt to debt,
And gave three balls a year – and so he
Did squander all, broke in the end.
But fate was kind to our Eugene:
At first *Madame* looked after him;
Monsieur then came and took her place.
The boy was frisky, but quite nice.
Monsieur l'Abbé, a threadbare Frenchman,
To keep the lad from suffering,
While teaching, joked of everything,
On morals strict and dull not dwelling.
He'd slightly scold each impish lark,
And walk him in the Summer Park.

IV

But when that age of youthful madness,
Rebellious, to Eugene first came,
That times of hopes and tender sadness,
They kicked *Monsieur* right out the gate.
Now my Onegin's free and dashing,
His hair cut to the latest fashion,
And like a London dandy dressed,
He joined society at last.
In French he absolutely brightly
Could speak and write most fluently,
And danced mazurkas easily,
And bowed with grace and ease unfrightened.
What more d'you need? The social sphere
Judged him quite smart and quite a dear.

V We all did study (more or less so)
Something or other at some time.
In education, God be praised, though,
With us, it isn't hard to shine!
Onegin was (such was the ruling
Of many judges strict, unmoving)
Just somewhat learnèd, yet a pedant.
He had a very happy talent,
Quite naturally, with a light touch,
To chat of all things *en passant*,
And looking sage, like a savant,
Hear weightiest disputes and hush,
And then incite smiles from *les dames*
With sparks from surprise epigrams.

VI Latin has now gone out of fashion.
Well, if I have to tell you true,
He barely knew enough of Latin
In epigraphs to have some clue,
To speak of Juvenal not wincing,
And write "*vale*," at letter's ending,
And knew, fibbing not much, I hope,
Two lines from the *Aeneid* by rote.
He really did not have much passion
To scour great tomes on ancient times,
Leaf through vast tracts with dust begrimed,
Yet various snips of history passing,
From Romulus to the last word,
Were in his memory preserved.

VII But lacking in that lofty passion
That for sweet sounds would give up life,
From trochees couldn't tell an iamb,
However much we'd beat and try.
He panned Homer, Theocritus,
But read with pleasure Adam Smith,
And was a deep economist,
That is, he could the reasons list
By which a nation thrives and prospers,
What makes it live, get rich, and grow,
And why it has no need of gold,
When it makes good cheap, *basic products.*
His father couldn't understand,
And went and mortgaged off his land.

VIII All my Eugene knew quite tedious:
Retelling it would bore me too.
But where he really was a genius,
And better than all science knew,
What, since he was a little boy,
Had been his labour, bane, and joy,
What occupied entire days
When he in torpor sad would laze,
Was that same art of passions tender,
Which Ovid used to celebrate,
For which, a traitor to the state,
He ended his bright age a rebel,
In bare Moldavian steppes and scree,
So far from his dear Italy.

X How he learned to dissemble early!
To hide his hopes, feign jealousy,
Shatter belief, then force believing,
Then seem to sigh most gloomily,
Then seem now haughty, now submissive,
Now full of care, and now indifferent!
How languid, too, his silence was!
How fiery his eloquence!
And, in his love letters, how reckless,
Breathing of love and nothing else!
How well he could forget himself!
How quick and tender were his glances,
Now shy, now brazen, time to time
With an obedient tear he'd shine!

XI How well he modelled innovation,
Could joke, with innocence bemuse,
Then scare with studied desperation,
With pleasant flattery amuse,
Alertly seize first tenderness,
Defeat a young girl's prejudice
With passion and intelligence,
Against her will gain a caress,
Demanding, wheedling her confession,
Snoop as her heart skipped gingerly,
Pursue her love, then suddenly
Obtain a secret trysting session,
Then, catching her now her on her own,
Give lessons in the silence lone!

XXIX On days of joys and of obsessions
Balls used to make me lose my mind:
There's no place better for confessions
Or slipping love notes, you will find.
Attention, husbands most respected!
I'm at your service: please, expect it!
Please mark this well, my little speech,
My warning's meant to keep your peace.
You, Mummies, too, be strict! Get with it!
Watch carefully your daughter's steps,
And hold on tight to your lorgnettes!
If not, if not... oh Lord forbid it!
I'm telling all this only since
It's long ago since I last sinned.

XXX Alas, on various amusements
I've wasted much, for good or ill.
If only morals would permit it
I would be crazy for balls still.
I love their youthfulness and madness,
Their crowding, and their spark, their gladness,
The gowns the crafty ladies spout!
I love their feet also – yet doubt–
Search all of Russia, you won't find
Three pairs of lovely ladies' feet.
Oh! I could not forget indeed
Two sweet feet... Sad now, cold, resigned,
I still remember. In my dreams
They still trouble my heart, it seems.

XXXI Oh, when and where, and in what desert
Oh madman, where will you forget?
Oh sweet feet, sweet feet that I treasured!
Where now do you spring flowers tread?
In Far East's bliss caressed so gently,
In sad North's snows, you evidently,
Could not so much as leave a trace!
You loved the feel, softer than lace,
Of carpets sumptuously mild.
How long since I for you those days
My thirst for glory and for praise
Forgot? – and home and exile wild?
My joy of younger years did pass –
Like your light footsteps on the grass.

XXXII Diana's breast, and Flora's cheeks
Delight the soul, my dear, dear friends,
However, Terpsichore's feet
To me are more enchanting yet.
How she to prophesying glances
Hints at your yet unmeasured chances
And with of beauty but a sign
Stirs, swarms, Desire's capricious mind!
Nymph-like Elvina, how I love her!
Under long table's tablecloth,
On springtime lawn's abundant swathe,
By fireplace-screen in winter warming,
On ballrooms' shimmering parquet floor,
On granite cliffs perched by the shore.

XXXIII Before the lightning, I remember
So envying the waves at sea,
Racing, in stormy ranks assembled,
With love to lie down at your feet!
I wished – as rush! – wave crashes, hisses,
To cover those sweet feet with kisses!
No, never in my wildest days,
A-boil with youth's mad glow and craze,
Was ever I so wracked with fire
To kiss bewitching young girls' lips,
Their rosy flaming cheeks, their hips,
Their bosoms, seething with desire,
No, ne'er so much did passion's gust
So tear and rip my soul with lust!

XXXIV Another time now I'm remembering!
Sometimes, in my most cherished dreams,
I hold her happy stirrup, trembling,
And in my hands, her foot real seems:
Again, imagination's boiling,
Again slight touch, all passions roiling,
The blood burns in my faded heart,
Again I grieve, again I love!
But no more praising haughty maidens
With my incessant, babbling lyre!
They're worth nor songs nor passion's fire,
Of which they're yet the inspiration.
These witches' words and gazes sweet
Are trickery... just like their feet.

XLVI Whoever lives and thinks can't help but
Despise most people in his soul.
Whoever feels, is e'er perturbèd
By spectres of lost days of old:
No more enchantments from a temptress,
Instead, the serpent of remembrance
Gnaws ceaselessly with cruel remorse.
Quite often this accords, of course,
Enormous charm to conversations.
At first Onegin's biting tongue
Embarrassed me; then I was drawn
To his sarcastic condemnations,
Got used to jokes and gall by halves,
And gloomy bitter epigrams.

XLVII How often, in the summer nights,
When, with a faint transparent glow,
The sky o'er Nevá's banks still lights,
And on its happy, glassy flow
Diana's face is not reflected,
By love affairs of old affected,
By early love's sweet memories,
We'd feel again, carefree, at ease,
We'd drink kind night's breath to the lees!
And in that blissful stillness pale,
Like as to forest green from jail
A drowsy convict just released,
So we were borne back in a dream
To life's beginnings young and keen.

XLVIII So, as regret in his soul seethed,
And leaning on the granite bank,
Eugene did stand in reverie,
As "poet" paints himself, in prank...
And all was quiet; just night watchmen
Saluted to each other, lonesome,
And distant drozhkys' hoofbeats pound
From the Millionaya* did sound.
Drifting that sleepy flow along,
A rowboat lazed, its oars becalmed,
While from a distance we were charmed
By horns blown, then a rousing song...
Yet sweeter, midst the joys night brings,
Torquato Tasso's octave sings!

"And leaning on the granite bank"
Pushkin (at left) and Onegin on the Palace Embankment in St. Petersburg

* The Millionaya, an elegant and fashionable street in St. Petersburg, runs beside the Winter Palace from Palace Square to the Field of Mars.

XLIX O billows of the Adriatic!
O Brenta! No, I'll see you yet!
With inspiration once more frantic,
I'll hear your magic cherishèd,
Your murmur, hallowed to Apollo's
Grandsons, which my own heart knows
Through Albion's proud lyre, and loves.
Let golden Italy's nights come,
In freedom's bliss just revelling
With a Venetian beauty young,
Now very chatty, now struck numb,
In a gondola's mystery!
With her my lips will soon acquire
The tongue of Petrarch and love's fire.

L But is my freedom's hour approaching?
It's time! It's time! I call to it!
Above the seashore I pace, roaming,
I wave to sails, wait for my wind.
Ah! Cloaked in storms, with waves disputing,
On oceans' crossroads, wild, free, gloomy,
When will I make my free escape!
It's time this dull land to forsake,
This earth, which is my enemy,
And then, by southern ripples sweet,
My Africa's clear skies beneath,
To sigh for gloomy Russia's lee,
Where I so suffered, loved so hard,
Where I did bury my own heart.

LV I was just born for this life peaceful,
For stillness pastoral, it seems...
My lyre in backwoods rings out clearer,
More life's in my creative dreams.
To leisures innocent, devoted,
Across a lonely lake I'm roaming,
And *far niente** is my law.
Each morning I wake up and yawn
With the sweet bliss of ease and freedom.
I read a little, sleep a lot,
And fleeting fame I have forgot.
In former years, was I not leading
Just such a life? Neath shade I'd laze...
The happiest of all my days!

LVI O flowers, love, sweet sloth, and country
Fields! with you my soul does dwell!
I'm always glad of contrasts sundry
Between Onegin and myself,
So that some ever-mocking reader –
Or publisher and eager feeder
Of most deliberate calumnies –
Would not spot here my qualities,
Would not proclaim, incorrigible,
That I my portrait scribbled here,
Like Byron, bard of pride, most dear,
As though it were impossible
To write a poem on anything –
Except but of oneself to sing.

* Italian — to do nothing.

LVII I note in passing that all poets
Are friends of dreamy wistful love.
I used to dream of love's sweet objects:
My soul had visits from above,
Then kept these images in hiding;
Then, afterwards, my Muse revived them:
So, I might spin a carefree reel
Of mountain maiden*, my ideal,
Or slave-girls by the Salgir River**.
But now, my friends, I hear too often
A question always in the offing:
"For whom now does your lyre quiver?
From whom, midst crouds of jealous swains,
Have you poured forth new sweet refrains?

LVIII Whose glance excites your inspiration,
Invokes a dear caress inside?
With wistful pensive incantation
Whom has your verse now deified?"
And friends, the truth is, no one, honest!
My crazy loves' wild cares aren't missed.
I've suffered quite enough, and pined.
Blessed is a poet who's combined
Love's ache with Rhythm's, doubling thus
Poetry's sacred ravings free!
As Petrarch did before, so he
Becalms his heartswell torturous,
And all the while gains great repute.
But, loving, I was dumb and mute.

* Refers to *The Prisoner of the Caucasus.*
** Refers to a lyrical poem by Pushkin about the palace of the Crimean Tatar Khans, *The Fountain of Bakhchisarai.* The Salgir is the longest river in the Crimean Peninsula.

CHAPTER II

O rus!..
Horace
O, Rus!*

VII From this world cold, depraved, deformed,
Having no chance to wither yet,
His soul was cosseted and warmed
By friends, by girlish tenderness,
In matters of the heart knew nothing,
Hope comforted his heart's young running,
New spark and bustle in this world
Still kept his youthful spirit thrilled.
He stilled, with daydreams sweet, amusing,
The doubts he felt deep in his heart.
The goal for him of this life hard
Was an enigma, mist alluring...
On it he pondered all the time,
In all things miracles did find.

VIII A kindred soul, he was believing,
Was meant to meet him on life's way,
That joylessly alone and grieving
She waited for him every day,
And that his friends were true, and ready
To don, for his name's sake, chains heavy.
Unwavering would be their hand
Against which slander could not stand,
That by the Fates there had been chosen
For us alone, some holy friends,
A family that never ends,
Whose light uncanny's always glowing,
Whose rays will someday shine on us,
And to the world bring blessedness.

*Play on words: "*O rus!*" means "*Oh, the country!*" (From Horace's *Satires*, II, vi), but Rus is also the poetic name for the land of Russia itself.

IX And indignation and compassion
And purest love for doing good,
For glory's agony sweet passion,
From early days roused up his blood,
With lyre his wandering ways did ply
Neath Goethe's and 'neath Schiller's sky,
Exposed to their poetic fire
Which then his own soul did inspire.
The Muses of these arts exalted
He, happily, did not disgrace,
In all his cantos, full of grace,
He kept his feelings lofty, vaulted
Aloft with gusts of virgin dreams,
With charming, simple, serious scenes.

X He sang of love, to love submissive,
And clear and limpid was his tune,
As innocent maids' thoughts are, pensive,
Or boyish dreams are, or the moon
In heaven's desert calm appearing,
Goddess of tender sighs and secrets.
He sang of partings and of griefs,
Of "something"... "Distant, misty heaths..."
And – of course – roses (most romantic).
He sang of a lost distant shore
Where, wrapped in silence, long before,
His tears rolled down his cheeks quite frantic...
He sang of life's frayed, yellowed page,
While scarcely eighteen years of age.

XI

But in that desert where Eugene
Alone could recognize his gift,
Landowning neighbours' feasts of plenty
Were ordeals he would rather miss.
He fled from all their noisy chatter,
From their good-natured, endless prattle
Of wine, of bringing the hay in,
Their kennels and their kith and kin,
Which doubtless did not shine with feeling,
Nor with the spark of poetry,
Or wit, or clever repartee,
And with no hint of art was breathing...
But as for what their dear wives said –
T'was even less intelligent!

XII

But Lensky, being rich and handsome,
Was thought a suitor everywhere.
All planned – such is the country custom –
To hitch up, to their daughters fair,
This neighbour new, this "semi-Russian."
If he walked in, at once discussion
Was focused only on the theme
How dull unmarried life did seem...
Round samovar they'd sit at tea,
While Dunya poured it clumsily,
They'd whisper "Dunya, carefully!"
Then bring out her guitar, so she
(Good God!) could shriek and caterwaul:
"Come, darling, to my golden hall!"

XIII But Lensky, having no desire,
Of course, to put on marriage chains,
With all his heart wished to draw nigher
To Onegin – and become his friend.
They got quite close, though wave and stone,
And ice and fire, and prose and poem
Are not so different as they were.
At first, these differences disturbed,
They thought each other dull, then drolly
They rather liked each other, then
Together daily riding went,
Were soon inseparable wholly.
So we (I will confess first too)
Make friends from having *naught to do.*

XIV But no such friendship our dear land knows...
Though prejudice we've killed and shun,
We think of all others as zeroes,
And of ourselves alone as one.
We all would be Napoleons:
Two-legged beasts, in millions,
We'd boss and keep as naught but tools.
Feelings for us are quaint, for fools.
Eugene provoked far less objections
Than most, though he knew people well,
And so despised them, truth to tell,
But (there's no rule without exceptions)
Some he distinguished quite a lot,
Respecting feelings he'd forgot.

XV He heard out Lensky's feelings smiling.
The poet's passion, feeling, ire,
His wavering judgments undecided,
His look, as if forever inspired.
Onegin thought it fresh, appealing...
Cold quips, a poet's hope congealing,
He did his best never to vent,
And thought "it's silly to prevent
His momentary state of blessing.
He'll learn, even unhelped by me,
But just for now I'll let him be
Believing in the world's perfection.
So let's forgive a fevered youth
Young fever and young nonsense too."

XVI Disputes between them, often heated,
Arose, and led to thoughtfulness.
The ancient pacts of bygone peoples,
The ways of virtue, wickedness,
The fruits of knowledge, prejudice,
The secrets of the grave, of death,
And Fate, and life, all one by one,
Before their court in turn did come.
Our bard, who found his own thoughts heady,
Recited, read, waving his hands,
Extracts of poems from Northern lands.
Eugene listened, condescending,
Though comprehending fitfully,
He'd listen quite assiduously.

XVII More often, though, the human passions
Distracted our young hermits' minds.
Onegin spoke of them as passing,
Their violent power left behind –
Yet with unbidden sighs regretful:
Blessed is he, who's left their fretful
Grip, of passions weary grown,
Blessed he, who them has never known,
Who has cooled off his love in parting,
His hate, with bitter words, not strife,
Yawned with his friends sometimes, or wife,
From jealous fits was never smarting,
And never staked his parents' all
Upon some deuce's treacherous fall.

XVIII When we ourselves flee towards the banner
Of reasonable tranquillity,
And when our passion's spark grows dimmer,
And sillier now seem to be
Our passions' gusts and willful longings,
Their quirky and belated callings,
Which we ourselves could scarcely tame,
We sometimes like to hear the tale
Of other people's stormy passions,
And let our heart be stirred by it.
Just so, an aged invalid
Will eagerly bend his attentions,
Being forgot, in bare hut cooped,
To tales told by some mustached youth.

XIX But young men's fiery rowdiness
Can never hold back anything:
Of hatred, love, grief, happiness,
Their ready tongue keeps babbling.
Thinking himself in love a cripple,
Onegin heard, sage-faced, unquivering,
The poet tell all of himself,
In love with his own heart's distress,
As he his over-trusting conscience
With bare simplicity released.
Eugene recognized with ease
The tale of his young love's experience,
The feelings full, splendiferous,
That long since aren't new for us.

XX Oh, he did love, as we already
No longer love, as only bards'
Insane poetic souls unsteady
Condemned to love forever are!
Just one dream, always, everywhere,
Just one wish haunting, always there,
One ever-present, endless grief.
No distance cools, far though she be,
Nor many years of being parted,
Nor hours devoted to the Muse,
Nor foreign beauties' tempting hues,
Nor science, nor good cheer light-hearted,
Could tame his soul's dear love inspired,
Warmed with an innocent, pure fire.

XXI While still a boy, with Olga taken,
Still ignorant of heartfelt pains,
He was a witness charmed, elated,
To all her childish, playful games.
Beneath the safe shades of the forest
He shared her happiness and frolics.
Their wedding wreathes by now were made
By parents, friends from near estates.
Plain, backwoods-raised, far from the city,
Thus graced with charming purity,
In her own parents' eyes it seemed
She bloomed like hidden valley-lilies,
That under thick weeds no one sees,
Not even butterflies and bees.

XXIII Forever meek, forever humble,
Forever happy as the dawn,
As poets are, sincere and simple,
As dear as kisses of first love,
Her eyes as light blue as the sky,
Her flaxen locks in curls, her smile,
Her voice, light step, lithe frame, her look,
All Olga's features... But take any book –
All novels paint her portrait dear:
The picture's nice, it must be said.
I used to love it once myself,
But now it bores me quite to tears.
So, reader, let me, anyhow,
Turn to her elder sister now.

XXV And so, Tatyana was her first name:
Neither her sister's beauty prized,
Nor fresh and rosy cheeks aflame
Would ever draw you to her eyes.
Unnatural, saddened, and withdrawn,
As frightened as a forest fawn,
She seemed in her own family
A foundling, strange entirely.
No cuddles could this girl display
To Dad or Mum. Instead she'd pout,
A child alone in childish crowd.
She didn't want to skip and play;
She'd sit, and let whole days just wane
While staring out the windowpane.

XXVI And thoughtfulness was her best friend
Since first in cradles she was laid;
T'would to her rural rest extend
Sweet flights that dreams did decorate...
Her tender, fragile fingers graceful
Knew not the needle or the lace-frame,
No silken pattern did she weave
To make a piece of linen breathe.
Showing the urge to domination,
With an obedient doll, a child
At play prepares the while
For well-brought up subordination,
And solemnly to it repeats
Laws, lessons that her Mummy speaks.

XXVII But even in her girlish days
Tatyana never touched a doll.
Whatever fashions were the rage
She shared none with her dolls at all.
The usual childish escapades
To her were foreign. Frightful tales
Instead, through winter nights' bleak dark,
Were all that thrilled her youthful heart.
When Nanny gathered Sister Olga
And all her little friends around
To meadows greening in a crowd,
She played no "hide and seek," unbothered.
Dull to her did their laughs resound;
Dull did their silly pleasures sound.

XXVIII She loved, upon the balcony,
To wait the coming of the dawn.
When first in the pale firmament
The dance of stars goes faint, is gone,
With quiet light Earth's edges glow,
And morning's herald wind, does blow,
And gradually the day grows bright.
In winter, when the shades of night
Take over, lengthening half the world,
When longer, in a languorous fit,
The quiet moon through mists does flit,
Until the lazy East is stirred,
In waking, she would make a rite
Of getting up by candlelight.

XXIX She was quite early fond of novels.
They replaced all, were all she'd know.
She fell in love with the false troubles
Of Richardson and of Rousseau.
Her father wasn't a bad fellow,
Though in the previous century wallowed.
In books he didn't see much harm,
Though he himself read not at all,
He thought of them as toys, as shallow,
And wouldn't give a second look
To check what kind of secret book,
Dozed with his daughter 'neath a pillow.
Meanwhile, his wife, for quite some time,
For Richardson quite lost her mind.

XXX Mum had been fond of Richardson
(Whom she in fact had never read)
Not because she thought Grandison
Another Lovelace, better yet,
But in her time Princess Alina,
Her Moscow cousin, wouldn't leave her
Alone – with talk of nothing else...
Her husband now was still back then
Her fiancé, against her will;
She'd pined for someone else, more dear,
In heart and spirit far more near,
Whom she liked much, much better still...
That Grandison was a gay fop,
A gambler, Guardsman, sergeant – top!

XXXI She dressed up just like him, alluring,
In perfect style and fit, of course,
But no one asked for her opinion:
They dragged her to the church by force.
And, hoping to relieve her mourning,
Her husband shrewdly took her shortly
Off to his country seat where she,
Bereft, stuck in obscurity,
At first, wept, raged, railed, wailed, tormented,
And very nearly got divorced,
Then drowned her woes in household chores,
Then with new habits grew contented.
From high on habits come to us
And take the place of happiness.

CHAPTER III

Elle était fille, elle était amoureuse.*

Malfilâtre

XV

Tatyana, oh my dear Tatyana!
I cry with you in sympathy;
You're captive to a stylish tyrant;
You've given him your destiny.
You're doomed, my sweetheart, yet – one instant –
Enjoy your blinding hope resplendent,
And call your darkest error bliss:
If there is joy in life – it's this.
You drink desire's magic poison
And let yourself be chased by dreams:
No matter where you go, it seems
You've found a place for sweet liason,
And it seems everywhere you walk,
Your fateful ravisher does stalk.

XVI

The grief of love pursues Tatyana;
She seeks her garden out to pine,
And suddenly her own eyes fail her,
She cannot walk, can't even try...
Her breast is heaving, cheeks are blushing,
With momentary fire flushing,
Her breath right on her lips does freeze,
No sound she hears, no sight she sees...
The night has come, the moon goes strolling,
Inspecting all of heaven's arc.
The nightingale in forest dark
Melodious refrains is tolling.
Yet Tanya in the dark can't sleep,
Must with her nanny softly speak:

*She was a girl; she was in love. (Fr.)

XVII "I can't sleep, Nanny: it's so stuffy!
Open the window, sit by me."
"What's wrong, Tanya?" "I'm bored... it's nothing.
Let's talk of how things used to be."
"Of what things, Tanya? When I was younger
I once had memorized a number
Of old-wives' yarns and fairy tales
Of evil spirits and fair maids,
But all grows dark in me, has vanished;
Yes, I've forgot all I once knew,
Yes, time's brought me a real to-do!
I've gone all blank..." "But tell me, Nanny,
About the days when you were young:
Back then were you ever in love?"

XVIII "What nonsense, Tanya! Don't be silly!
Back then we'd never heard of love;
My mother-in-law really
Would have had a fit and chased me off!"
"How then did you get married, Nanny?"
"It was God's will, I guess. My Vanya
Was younger e'en than me, my dear,
And I'd just reached my thirteenth year.
Two weeks the matchmaker kept seeking
To close the deal with all my kin.
My Dad agreed, and blessed me then,
And scared, I started bitter weeping.
My braids they loosened with a dirge,
And sang, and led me off to church.

XIX To a strange family they brought me...
– But you aren't listening to me –"
"Oh, Nanny, Nanny. I'm distraught. See
How I'm sick, my sweet, can't breathe,
I'm going to weep and sob – I will!"
"Oh my dear child, I see you're ill;
Oh, Lord have mercy! Save us all!
Whatever, dear, you need, just call!
Here, let me sprinkle holy water –
You have a fever." "I'm well enough:
You know what, Nanny?... I'm in love."
"Lord bless you, sweetie, what's the matter?"
Making the cross-sign, Nanny prayed,
Above her girl with her hand frayed.

XX "Oh, I'm in love!" again she whispered,
To Nanny in a grieving voice.
"My dearest heart, you're sick. Now listen!"
"Leave me alone! I am in love!"
And all the while the moon was gleaming,
Its murky, dreamy light was beaming
Upon Tatyana's beauty pale,
Her loose hair tossing in a gale
Of teardrops, as her Nanny sat
With our young heroine did fret,
Her bonnet wrapped round her grey head,
A long wool warmer round her back.
As all in peaceful sleep did seem
The moon inspired all to dream.

XXI And as her heart raced, pounding tighter,
Tatyana gazed up at the moon...
And then a thought arose inside her...
"Go now, and leave me, please, alone.
And, Nanny, give me pen and paper,
I'll lie down soon, but move this table.
Goodbye." She's left alone. Deep night.
Now all is still. The moon shines bright,
On elbows perched, Tatyana, seething,
Writes, just Eugene on her mind,
With thoughtless words her soul unwinds
A letter chaste, with pure love breathing.
The letter's written, folded, sealed...
Tatyana! Who's it for, my dear?

XXV A flirt judges cold-bloodedly,
Tatyana's love is artless, wild,
Gives all her heart entirely
To love, like an enchanting child.
She doesn't reason: "let's delay,
Let's raise love's price, and catch our prey
By teasing mixed with flattery,
At first, let's prick his vanity,
And then allow some hope to soar,
Then shock his heart with scorn and ire,
Wake it again, with jealous fire,
Or else, by pleasure growing bored,
A clever captive ever strains
And strives to break free from his chains."

XXVI Another problem I see coming:
To save the honour of our state
I'll be obliged from French to Russian
Tatyana's letter to translate.
For she knew Russian rather badly.
She read no modish journals, sadly,
And words with ease could never come
To her in her own native tongue...
And so – in French, her heart's address...
Alas! I can't complain enough!
Till now, alas, a woman's love
In Russian never was expressed.
Our language proud still nothing knows
Of writing notes in postal prose.

XXXI Tatyana's letter lies before me:
I treasure it with all my heart,
And read with secret melancholy
And cannot read its words enough.
Who first instilled in her such sweetness?
Such tender words, dear indiscreetness,
Such deeply moving foolishness,
Such mad and heartfelt openness,
Such dangerous, yet charming rapture?
I cannot comprehend. Yet here's
A partial, feeble, rendering,
A pallid print of a live picture,
A *Freischütz** sight-read, halting, poor,
By schoolgirl fingers, shy, unsure:

* Carl Maria von Weber's romantic opera *Der Freischütz* and various arrangements of it for piano (particularly of its celebrated overture) were all the rage in Russia.

Tatyana's Letter to Onegin

I write to you – can I do further?
Is there a thing more need be said?
And now, I know, it's in your power
To punish me with your contempt.
But you, in seeing how I suffer,
Will keep a jot of sympathy,
And you will not abandon me.
At first I wanted to keep silent.
Believe me, of the shame that burned
Inside me you'd have never learned
Had I had hope – even most slightly,
If only even once a week,
In this poor place to take a peek
At you, to listen to you speaking,
But say one word to you, and then
To think, both day and night, of when
Oh when at last we'll next be meeting.
But people say that you are shy,
That in these boondocks you're bored silly.
And we...in nothing do we shine,
Though glad to see you, rather simply.

Oh why did you come visit us?
Here in this god-forsaken village
I never would have suffered thus.
I never would have seen your visage.
In time, perhaps, I'd tame the heaving
Of my naive heart (who can tell?),
I'd find a friend fit to my nature
And would have been a good spouse, faithful,
And mother kind – for someone else

Than you! No! I'd have never rendered
My heart to anyone but you!
That's in the highest court intended;
It's Heaven's will! I'm yours, I'm true!
My whole life was but preparation
For our first meeting which Fate gave.
I know that you're God's visitation,
That you will keep me till my grave.
You came to me when I was dreaming:
Unseen, you were already dear.
Your wondrous look my heart did sear,
And in my soul your voice was pealing
Long since!...No, that was not a dream!
You first walked in, and flash! I knew you!
I froze and blazed inside – all through,
And in my thoughts murmured: "It's him!"
I heard you! Isn't it the truth?
In stillness did you speak to me
When I would work to help the poor
Or with a prayer try to soothe
The grief my soul felt secretly?
And, in that flash of recognition,
Was it not you, oh dearest vision,
That slipped in through the darkness clear,
Caressed my pillow, softly moving?
Wasn't it you, with joy and loving
That whispered hope into my ear?
Who are you? Say! My guardian angel?
Or a seducing devil hateful?
I beg of you: my doubts relieve!
Perhaps this all is empty ravings
That inexperienced souls deceive,
And something different is what's fated.
No matter what, from this day forth
I hand my fate into your keeping.

Before you all my tears I pour:
For your protection I am pleading;
I'm all alone – can you not see?
In this place no one understands me.
My reason fails, I weaken badly,
And I must perish silently.
I wait for you: one look would serve:
Restore the hope that's in my heart,
Or tear my heavy dream apart,
Alas, with a rebuke deserved!

I'm finished! To re-read I dread.
Both shame and fear my spirit rivet.
Your honour, though, stands in my stead,
And boldly I entrust you with it.*

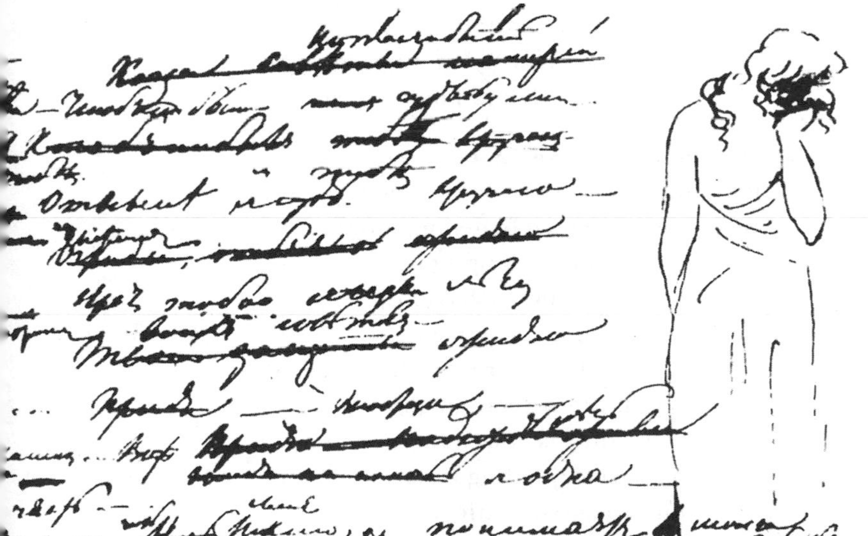

Tatyana Weeping

*In the letter Tatyana switches back and forth between the formal and the familiar second person pronoun (you and thou), but for simplicity's sake 'you' is used throughout.

CHAPTER IV

La morale est dans la nature des choses.*

Necker

VII The less it is we love a woman,
With more ease we appeal to her,
The more unerringly she's ruined,
In our seductive nets held firm.
Before, debauchery cold-hearted,
As amatory art was touted;
Its "artists" could not boast enough
Of taking pleasure without love.
But that amusement, puffed and storied,
Is worthy only of old apes,
From Grandpa's vaunted times, in capes.
Dilapidated now's the glory
Of those Lovelaces stuffed and rigged,
With bright red heels and pompous wigs.

VIII For whom's hypocrisy not boring?
Repeating the same game and show,
With fervour feigned belief imploring
In what we're certain long ago!
To hear the very same objections,
Demolish the same preconceptions,
Which can't be found around the world
In the least thirteen year old girl!
Who of false threats does not grow weary?
Of prayers, quickly fading fears, and oaths?
And – on six pages – "little notes"
Lies, gossip, rings, and moments teary,
Mums, Aunties, watching carefully,
And husbands' heavy amity!

* Morality is in the nature of things. (*Fr.*)

IX

Just such was my Eugene's thinking,
He too, in the first bloom of youth,
Once fell to stormy errors victim,
Felt untamed passions, wild, uncouth.
A little spoiled by life-long habit,
For one thing for a while enchanted,
Soon disillusioned by what's new,
With slow desire wearied through,
Yet of flippant success grown weary,
Hearing in silence and through noise
His soul's ever-complaining voice,
Stifled by laughter, his yawns bleary:
He killed off eight whole years this way,
Wasting his life's best bloom away.

X

He fell no more in love with beauties,
But chased them anyhow, he guessed,
Took comfort fast on their refusing,
When cheated on, was glad to rest.
He'd seek them out without elation,
Leave them, and feel no hesitation,
No twinge of their last love and spite.
Just so, a guest indifferent might
Drive up, for evening whist appearing,
Sit down, then, when the game was done,
Ride homewards, horses at a run,
To calm sleep drifting, disappearing,
Himself not sure, when daylight came,
Where next he'd ride when daylight waned.

XI

But Tanya's missive then receiving,
Onegin was quite moved within.
Her words of tender girlish dreaming
A swarm of thoughts provoked in him.
Remembering Tanya's face endearing,
Her skin so pale, her air so grieving,
In blameless dream delightedly,
He let his soul sink blissfully.
Perhaps he felt old feelings' panging
Deep for a minute in him heave...
But he did not wish to deceive
Or leave an innocent soul hanging.
Now to that garden let's fly fleet
Where with Tatyana he did meet.

XII

They silent stayed about two minutes.
Then up to her Onegin went.
And softly said: "To me you've written.
Do not deny it. I have read
Your over-trusting soul's confession
Of love, its innocent profession.
Your heartfelt truth to me is dear,
You've made old feelings in me rear
Which long ago I chose to stifle.
But I don't want to praise you though.
Instead, I in exchange do owe
You just as artlcss an avowal.
So listen now; I give myself
For you to judge as I confess."

XIII "If, wrapped in a domestic garland,
I'd limit my life's liberty,
If being father, being husband,
By pleasant Fate were granted me,
Were I by family portraits tempted
Just for a moment, brief and splendid,
I doubt that I would ever choose
Another bride on earth but you.
I'll spare you pompous singsong sparkly:
If I my old ideal did seek,
T'is you alone I'd choose to keep
As helpmeet of my melancholy,
My gage of all that's virtuous, good,
And would be happy... as I could."

XIV "But not for bliss was my creation.
No, bliss is foreign to my soul.
In vain is your complete perfection;
I'm quite unworthy of it all.
Trust me (my conscience pledged in honour)
Our marriage would become a torture.
However much I loved you true.
Accustomed, I'd cease loving soon.
Then you'd start weeping; your tears, pouring,
Would touch me no more in my heart,
Instead would make it mad and hard.
So think what roses Hymen's storing
In wait for us – a prospect glum –
Perhaps for many days to come."

XV

"For what on earth is sadder, really,
Than a poor wife trapped in her home,
For her unworthy husband grieving,
And night and day left all alone.
Where her dull husband knows she's worthy,
But still, his fate regretting, cursing,
Forever silently does brood,
Enraged, by jealousy made cool?
That's me. Was that whom you were seeking
With such a pure and fiery soul,
With such simplicity, so bold,
When you wrote me with such deep meaning?
How could it be you were so picked,
Appointed to a fate so strict?"

XVI

"The months and years are not returning.
My soul won't be renewed and freed.
I love you with a brother's yearning,
Perhaps more tenderly, indeed.
So listen to me without raging,
Not merely once will a young maiden
Replace light dreams but with light dreams.
Just so, each greening tree its leaves
Replaces at each springtime's coming.
It seems that must be Heaven's will.
You'll love again one day. But still...
Learn self-control, act more becoming.
Not all, like I, will understand.
In grief the inexperienced land."

XVII Such was the lecture of Eugene.
Completely blinded by her tears,
Tatyana, who could scarcely breathe,
His every word did meekly hear.
He gave his hand. Despondently,
Or, as they say, *mechanically,*
Tatyana grasped it silently,
Leaned, and she quivered violently.
Back through the orchard they did stride,
Came home together. No one thought
To stigmatize our pair a jot.
The freedom of the countryside
Has happy rights in innocence,
Like Moscow in its arrogance.

XVIII Dear reader, I hope you'll agree,
That to poor Tanya so aggrieved
Our friend behaved most admirably.
Not for the first time we perceive
His soul's good, true nobility,
Though other people's enmity
Towards him was bitter to the end.
His enemies as well as friends
(One and the same, perhaps, that horde!)
A bunch of names at him all hurled.
We all have rivals in this world,
But spare us from our friends, oh Lord!
Oh, all of these "dear friends," dear friends,
Deserve some comments on them spent.

XIX What's that? Oh, nothing, never mind!
I lull to sleep dark, empty dreams,
But parenthetically remind
You: worse no slander seems,
Thought up by garret-scribblers vicious,
Passed on by beau monde meretricious,
And there is no absurdity,
No epigram's indignity,
Which your dear friend won't blurt out smiling,
While visiting the club or Palace,
Without the slightest hint of malice
A hundred times keep lying blithely!
And, by the way, a true friend's he!
He loves you so, like family!

XX Hmm! Hmm! Pray tell now, gentle reader.
How do they do, your clan so dear?
Allow me, if it's quite convenient,
To make a little lesson clear.
What does that mean, *our near and dear ones?*
Our near and dear ones are just these ones:
The ones we are obliged to kiss,
Caress and love, and warmly miss,
Also, by custom, in good cheer,
On Christmas we must pay them calls,
If not, at least must mail them cards,
So all the rest of all the year
They'll never even think of us...
And so, God grant them health, I trust!

XXI And yet the love of tender beauties
Than friends' or family's love's more firm.
To love, amidst life's worst storms furious
Your right forever is confirmed.
Of course... Yet...Trust in fashion's whirlwinds?
And nature's whims, ever indifferent?...
Care what the *beau monde* terms not right?...
When the fair sex is feather-light...
Besides, good husbands' judgments always
For all good wives should always be
Considered most respectfully;
Just so your mistress ever-faithful
Sometimes – like that – is torn away:
For Satan loves with love to play.

XXII Whom shall we love? And whom believe?
Who never will betray our trust?
Who measures all our words and deeds
As our own yardstick measures us?
Who never – ever – slanders us?
Who always takes good care of us?
Who doesn't think our flaws a sin?
Who never bores, day out, day in?
There's no point spectres vainly seeking,
Do not waste time in futile stress.
Instead, just always love yourself,
My most respected, noble reader!
A worthwhile object, verily,
There's none more pleasant, probably.

CHAPTER V

Never know such frightful dreams,
Oh, my dear Svetlana!

Zhukovsky

XXV But stretching out with purple hands,
With sunshine gaily in its train,
The light from morning valleys spans
On Tanya's nameday holiday.
All morning to the Larin house
Guests kept arriving; family crowds,
Neighbours that came in wagon trains,
Carriages, coaches, sleds, and wains,
In the hall, they push and jostle,
The parlor with new faces fills,
The bark of lapdogs, kiss of girls,
Noise, laughter, crush and crowded bustle
The bows and scraping of guests' feet,
The nursemaids' yells as children weep.

XXVIII But from his quarters not too far off
The older girls' joy, idol, pride,
The joy of all the district's mamas,
The troop commander has arrived.
Great news! How grand! For our amusement
The regiment will give us music!
The colonel sent the band himself.
Oh what a joy! A ball is set!
With joy the girls bounce, quiver, rowdy,
But dinner's served, and all in pairs
Go hand in hand, sit in their chairs,
Around Tatyana girlfriends crowding,
Across from them, the men. Then crossing
Themselves, the crowd sits, buzzing.

XXIX All conversation's ceased one instant,
As mouths do chew. And all around
The plates and cutlery are whirring
We hear the glasses clink, resound,
But bit by bit the guests bestir,
Begin to make themselves be heard,
Yet no one listens, all just shout,
And laugh and argue, squeak and pout.
The doors swing open suddenly;
Onegin follows Lensky in.
The hostess cries: "Lord! Where've you been?"
The guests crowd in more, hurriedly,
The plates and chairs are moved aside
To seat the two friends side by side.

XXX They're seated right across from Tanya,
Who, paler than the morning moon,
More shaky than a hunted fawn,
With darkened eyes as if to swoon,
Cast down, in stormy passion seething,
Sits feverishly, has trouble breathing,
And cannot hear her two friends' greeting;
Out of her eyes tears could come streaming,
And now she seems about to faint,
But by sheer will she holds back tears,
And forces herself to stay here,
Her feelings checked by mind's constraint,
She murmured two words through her teeth,
And somehow kept still in her seat.

XXXI All types of tragic nervous scenes
Or maidens' fainting spells, and tears,
Had long been shunned by our Eugene –
He'd seen enough, over the years!
A misfit, dragged to this great party,
In cranky mood, and yet remarking
This young maid's pining, trembling state,
Annoyed, he tried to look away,
And fumed at awkward circumstance,
Vowed he'd embarrass Lensky back,
And really be avenged at last.
And now, victorious in advance,
He started drawing in his head
Caricatures of all the guests.

XXXII Eugene was not the sole one there
That for poor Tanya's plight had eyes,
Yet all attention, thoughts, and stares
Just then were fixed on a fat pie
(Unfortunately, over-salted),
But then the bottle got uncorked
Between the roast and blanc-mangé,
Then they brought in the cheap champagne,
And row on row of long thin glasses
Whose waists were delicate as yours,
Zizi, you crystal of my soul,
Sweet object of slight verse in passing,
Of purest love you tempting vial,
Your sweetness made me drunk awhile!

XXXIV Congratulations, nameday greetings...
Tatyana thanked all one by one,
When it was Eugene's turn for speaking
He saw her langourous and wan,
Worn out, embarassed looks of grieving,
And in his heart they stirred up pity:
He only bowed as she went by,
And yet the soft look in his eyes
Was wondrous-tender...Was it because
Indeed his heart was truly touched,
Or did he just flirt over-much?
Unconsciously, or with good heart?
Still, tenderness his eyes implied:
To see them Tanya's heart revived.

XLI Unvarying, yet wild and crazy,
Like to the whirlwind of young life,
The waltzes' noisy whirl keeps racing,
And pairs keep flitting, flashing by.
His moment of revenge approaching,
Onegin, hiding inner gloating,
Goes up to Olga in a whir,
Spins round the other guests with her,
Then sits her down in manner charming,
Begins to talk of this and that,
And after two minutes of chat,
Again begins more frenzied waltzing.
All are amazed; though Lensky tries,
He can't believe his very eyes.

XLIV Buyanov, my too-playful brother,
Presented to our hero then
Both sisters, Olga and Tatyana:
Onegin nimbly grasped the hand
Of Olga, led her, gliding, easy,
Bending, cooing, whispering teasing
Tenderness or sentiment,
And pressed her hand – and then she went
Red in the face from boastful blushing,
As her cheeks reddened, Lensky watched,
And saw it all, and raged in shock;
In jealous indignation, rushing,
The poet frets till dance's end,
Calls her for the cotillion then.

XLV But no, she can't. She can't? Why not?
Olga already gave her word
To our Eugene. Oh God! Oh God!
Could it be true what he's just heard?
From baby clothes but barely slipping,
She's now a flirting, fickle vixen!
Already she is cunning, sly,
Already she can cheat and lie!
Lensky cannot abide it, bristles,
And curses women's cruel caprice,
Storms out, demands his horse, and leaves,
And rides off. Now a pair of pistols –
Two bullets – no more – he won't wait –
Will suddenly decide his fate.

CHAPTER VI

La, sotto i giorni nubilosi e brevi,
Nasce una gente a cui l'morir non dole.*

Petr.

XIX All evening Lensky was distracted.
At times he'd hush, then joke again.
But one on whom the Muse has acted
Is ever thus. Brows knit in pain,
He sat down to the clavichords,
But kept on playing only chords.
Then whispered stares at Olga, asking:
"In truth, am I not really happy?"
Tis late, though, time to ride off. Aching,
His heart, expanded, full of grief,
Took final leave of his maid sweet.
He seemed to feel it tearing, breaking.
Her eyes straight into his eyes bored:
"What's wrong?" – "Nothing." And out the door.

XX Once home, he got his pistols ready,
And looked them over, placed them back
Into their box, finished undressing,
Read Schiller's verse by candlelight,
And yet one thought alone consumed him.
No slumber came to his heart gloomy.
With beauty words could not explain
The face of Olga did not wane
From shining full before him. Closing
His book, he grasped his pen. His verse,
Full of love's nonsense, silly words,
Poured forth, sang out, while he was glowing,
Read them aloud, in lyric trance,
Like Delvig, drunken at a dance.

The poet Schiller

*There, where the days are short and ever-cloudy,
A race is born who feel no pain in dying.
Petrarch (Ital.)

XXI By chance his poem's in my keeping
Right here. I've kept it – lucky thing:
"Where, where've you gone off, flying, fleeting,
My golden, happy days of spring?
What has the next day fixed to send me?
I look in vain for answers ready.
The secret lurks in night's deep pall.
No matter – may just Fate's law fall.
Whether I fall, shot by a bullet,
Or whistling past the shot will sweep,
God bless: of wakefulness and sleep
That hour always comes appointed.
Blessed be both cares of sunny day
And night that takes the light away!

XXII Soon dawn's sweet rays will come up sparkling,
And bright the light of day will play.
Soon I perhaps within the coffin's
Mysterious vestibule will lay.
And a young poet's memory
Will sink to Lethe gradually.
The world will quite forget my shade.
But will you come here, lovely maiden,
To shed a tear o'er my urn early,
And think: he loved me once, kept faith,
To me alone did dedicate
His life's brief dawn, wild, melancholy,
Oh my heart's friend, oh dreamed-of friend!
Come here, come! I'm yours till the end!"

XXIII And on he scribbled: "*darkly*", "*fading,*"
(Romanticism that is called –
Though what's romantic in this vaguely? –
Not that we care too much at all).
And finally just at the dawning,
He let his tired head slip, and yawning,
Over "*ideal,*" word à *la mode,*
Quietly Lensky, nodded, dozed,
But just as sleep's delight embraced him,
Immediately his neighbour entered
His room, saw him in slumber rendered,
And woke up Lensky with words bracing:
"Seven o'clock! Get up! Enough!
No doubt Onegin waits for us!"

XXIV But he was wrong. Just then, Onegin
Slept like a dead man, without qualm,
With shades of night already thinning,
The cock roused morning star from calm.
Onegin slept on, by and by,
The sun's already climbed up high,
Snow flurries having swirled and swept,
Snow sparkling, winding round, and yet
Eugene is still in bed, a-slumbering,
Fast sleep still hovers over him.
And finally he stirred within
His room, opened his curtains broadly,
Looks out, and sees he's rather late.
It's time to race out from his gate.

XXV He quickly rings. Rushing in briskly,
Monsieur Guillot, his servant comes,
Gives him his bathrobe, socks, and slippers,
And also brings his pants and trunks.
Onegin hurries up in dressing,
Orders his servant to get ready
To ride as well and also bring
His duelling-box along with him.
The racing-sleighs by now are ready.
He gets on, to the mill raced off.
Arrived. Tells his valet, straight off,
To bear *Lepage's** barrels deadly
And follow him, then towards two oaks
Through fields to lead the horses, yoked.

XXVI Upon the dam's rim, losing patience,
Lensky just waited, stamped his foot.
The while, discussing mills and grainage,
Zaretsky, the mechanic, stood.
Onegin comes and gives excuses.
"But where" – Zaretsky almost loses
His temper – "is your second?"
In duels, for classic rules a pedant,
He loved method with all his heart.
And wouldn't let someone get killed
Just any sort of way you will,
But by the strictest rules of art
As practiced once in olden days
(For which we ought to give him praise).

* Jean Lepage was a famous Parisian gunsmith. Pushkin used a Lepage in his own fatal duel with Georges D'Anthès.

XXVII Eugene then answered him: "My second?
He's here. My friend, Monsieur Guillot.
I can't imagine much objection
To this idea of mine, you know.
Though he's unknown, I'll say in earnest.
At least, of course, he's somewhat honest."
Zaretsky bit his lip and gasped.
Onegin turned to Lensky, asked:
"Well, should we start?" "Perhaps, why not?"
Vladimir said, and they were gone
Beyond the mill, while further on
Zaretsky and the "honest, somewhat"
Engaged in pacts upon the snows.
With lowered eyes, there stood the foes.

Lensky

XXVIII Foes! How long since from each other
This thirst for blood drove them apart?
Has it been long since they like brothers
Shared common meals, thoughts, cares, and hearts?
And now look at them! Cold and crude,
Like rivals from an ancient feud,
In stillness staring, how they seem,
As if in strange and jumbled dream,
In cold blood plan each other's doom...
Could they not smile and show restraint
Before with blood their hands got stained?
Why not part friends, make up for good?
But cruel society's to blame.
It fears admitting to false shame.

Onegin

XXIX The pistols are drawn out, shine glowing,
The mallet clangs against the rod,
Through barrels' facets bullets go in,
The cocked guns click, from powder wad
Into the pan in streamlets greyish,
The powder's poured, and without flourish,
The jagged-edged-flint is fast secured.
Not far away, by a stump moored,
Guillot looks on and waits, and fidgets.
The enemies cast down their cloaks.
Counting thirty-two steps by rote,
Zaretsky marked and measured, rigorous,
Brought over, to each bound, each friend,
And each one raised his pistol then.

XXX "Now take your paces."
Still not aiming,
Cold-bloodedly, with steady walk,
The enemies are hushed, are pacing,
And each one then four steps did stalk,
Four fatal fateful steps – and ready.
Lifting his pistol first, and steady,
Eugene, still relentlessly,
Advanced five steps more silently,
And held his gun up with a glower,
And Lensky, squinting his left eye,
Began to aim – just at the time
Onegin fired... Struck has the hour!
The time appointed him has run:
The poet, silenced, drops his gun.

XXXI His arm placed gently on his breast,
He falls down. And his misty look
Expresses no more pain, but death.
So, from a snowy, hilly nook,
Down slopes where sunshine, sparkling shines,
A lump of snow falls, slow, sometimes.
As if flooded by sudden cold,
Onegin runs to his friend old,
Looks, calls the youngster, but in vain.
He's gone. His youthful poet friend
Has met with an untimely end.
The storm's blown out, sweet colour's waned,
Snuffed is the altar at its dawn;
The flame that burned there once is gone!

XXXII He moved not anymore, and strange
The languid look on his brow seemed.
His breast shot through at point-blank range,
As from his wound blood poured and steamed.
Past just one moment's expiration,
Where once this heart held inspiration,
Where hate, and hope, and love did grow,
And life did play, and hot blood flow,
Now, as if in a house abandoned,
What was in there's now stilled and dark.
Forever vanished is the spark,
The windows chalked, the shutters fastened.
The mistress of the house has left.
For where, God knows. No clue. Bereft.

XXXIII With biting epigrams it's pleasant
To dare and tempt a downcast foe;
It's nice to see, how he, face reddened,
Horns bent down, stubborn, full of woe,
Looks in his mirror by constraint,
And by his own face is ashamed.
Better yet, friends, if then he'll cry
And howl with folly: "Oh! T'is I!"
It's even better still, in silence,
Preparing him an honest grave,
Gun calmly at his forehead aimed,
While keeping a respectful distance.
But once he's lying in a pall
You'll hardly find it fun at all.

XXXIV What if, by virtue of your pistol,
Your young acquaintance gets cut down
For glance immodest, answer silly,
Repeating nonsense, anyhow,
Offending you over a bottle,
Even if he, quarrelsome and idle,
Himself sends you a glove and bow,
Say, in your soul, at this point now,
What feeling would begin to quicken,
When motionless, and on the ground
Before you, death stamped on his brow,
He'd gradually start to stiffen,
When he'd go deaf, and no more stirred,
And when your desperate cry's not heard?

XXXV Regretful, his heart full of grief,
His hand still clutching at his gun,
Looking at Lensky stood Eugene.
His neighbour said: "Well? Killed. That's done."
Killed! To hear this dread word uttered,
Onegin, shocked, inwardly shuddered,
Stepped back and called the others there.
Upon the sled then, full of care,
Zaretsky lays the corpse, now frozen,
Brings home the frightful load to rest.
Somehow it seems the horses sense
A dead man, and they snort, mouths foaming,
And dribbling on their bits of steel,
Like arrows shot, they fly and reel.

XXXVI My friends, you're for the poet grieving:
His flowering and happy hopes
For this world still so uncompleted,
Still barely out of baby clothes,
Are gone! Where now, hot agitation?
Where now's his noble aspiration,
Feelings and thoughts of youth sublime,
Lofty and tender, brave and kind?
Where vanished, love's desire tempestuous,
And lust for knowledge and for work,
And fear of vice, shame, sin, and murk?
Where now, dear dreams impetuous,
Where, ghost from earthly life set free?
Where, dreams of holy poetry?

XXXVII Perhaps he had been born for glory,
To bring great blessings to the world.
Perhaps a grand, resounding story,
His lyre, now silent, wrapped up, furled,
Would have passed down. Perhaps the poet,
Though he himself would never know it,
Would climb high this world's ladder great.
Perhaps his martyred, suffering shade
Removed from us, by disappearing,
A sacred secret, full of joys,
A lively and life-giving voice,
And he's beyond the grave, not hearing
The reach of hymns of later days,
Of peoples' blessings, tears, and praise.

XXXVIII. XXXIX
Or else our bard awaited, likely,
A fate more ordinary still.
The years of youth would pass by lightly,
The passion in his soul would chill.
He would be changed in much that mattered,
Abandoning the Muse, get married,
A cuckold, happy, out of town,
Wearing a quilted dressing gown,
Would learn what real life's made of yet:
Have gout at forty, bored, would dither,
Would drink, eat, get too fat, then wither,
And finally, in his own bed,
He'd die, amidst his kids in ranks,
And weepy women's wails, and quacks.

XL Whatever might have been, dear reader,
This young lover, alas, t'is sad,
This poet, thoughtful, pensive dreamer,
Was killed, and by his friend's own hand!
Left of his village, there's a spot,
Where this inspired son's not forgot.
Two pines right there their roots entwine.
Beneath them rushing waters wind,
Weaving the brooks of neighbouring valleys.
There plowmen often like to rest
And reaping-maids to white waves' crest
Come, dip their clinking pitchers, dally.
There, by the brook, beneath thick shade,
A simple monument's been made.

CHAPTER VII

You've toured the world – so Moscow earns your scorn!
What place is better?
There from whence we've gone.
Griboyedov

XXXIII When to enlightenment our nation
Begins its mighty bounds to pass,
In time (by my own calculation
Of *philosophic tabulae*,
Five hundred years from now), then roadways
Will likely be transformed for always:
Broad highways will cross Russia's space:
United, to and fro, we'll race.
We'll bridge great spans with steel and copper,
Casting a broad and mighty arc.
And we'll move mountains, tunnels dark
We'll dig with daring underwater.
And Christendom will then set up
At every station-house a pub.

XXXIV But still – for now – our roads are awful:
Forgotten bridges rot for years.
At station-houses bedbugs woeful
And fleas deny one minute's sleep.
There are no pubs. In cold huts tawdry,
With snobby airs, though very hungry,
A menu's put up just for show,
To tease one's vainly happy hope,
As all the while some peasant Cyclop,
Above a fire's sullen glimmer,
Is fixing with a Russian hammer
The light and graceful wheel of Europe,
Blessing the potholes, muck, ruts, sand,
And ditches of our Fatherland.

XXXV But still, at least, in winter chilly,
Then travelling is smooth and light.
Thoughtless as verse in hit song silly,
You glide on winter roads in flight.
Our happy charioteers heroic
Race indefatigable troiki,
The milestones, idly gazed at, charm,
Flash by our eyes like fence's bars.
But Mrs. Larin was employing
– Fearing the bills that speed incurs –
Alas! – not post-horses, but hers!
And so our maiden's stuck enjoying
The endless long dull road's delights:
They rode for seven days and nights.

XXXVI But now they're near. Before them, glistening,
Already white-stoned Moscow runs,
Like fire, with golden crosses quivering,
Its ancient domes gleam in the sun.
Oh brothers! How my heart was happy
To see the churches, bell-towers clanging,
The gardens', courtyards', crescents' sweep,
Before me opened suddenly!
How often in my exile, grieving,
Throughout my errant odyssey,
Have I thought, Moscow, but of thee!
Moscow! How Russian hearts are heaving
At all that merges in that sound!
How much in us it makes resound!

XXXVII Here, by a wooded grove surrounded,
Petrovsky Castle glory claims.
With gloom its proud captor confounded,
Napoleon here did wait in vain,
With last success drunk to the lees,
For Moscow grovelling on her knees,
For Kremlin keys wrapped in a bow,
But no, my Moscow wouldn't go
To him, head bent submissively.
No feasts, no welcome gifts arrived.
Instead, it set a blaze sky-high;
The hero watched impatiently.
From here, wrapped in ambition dread.
He watched the terrible flame spread.

XXXVIII Farewell, witness of fallen glory,
Petrovsky Castle! Well? Don't stop!
Let's go! Look how the gateposts storied
Gleam white! On down Tverskaya they trot,
Their sleigh-coach through the potholes drags,
Flashes past sentry-boxes, hags,
Street urchins, shops, street-lamps with sparks,
And monasteries, grand halls, parks,
Bukharans, sleds, neat garden plots,
Merchants, sad hovels, peasants cassocked,
Great boulevards and towers – and Cossacks,
And pharmacies, and fashion shops,
Porched gates, which lions guard with claws,
And crosses crowned with flocks of daws.*

*This line was deemed impious by the censor, and forbidden for decades.

LI

They bring her into the Assembly.
The crushed, excited buzz, the heat,
The music's crash, candle-gleams trembling,
The flashing pairs in whirlwind fleet,
The beauties' graceful, light attire,
The gallery's bright-colored choir,
The débutantes' half-moon so thick,
All strike the senses to the quick.
The foppish dandies here are flaunting
Their brazenness with waistcoats new,
And lorgnettes they're not looking through.
Hussars on leave are prancing, vaunting,
They rush to show up, seize the day,
To sparkle, shine, then fly away.

LII

The night has many stars delightful,
And many beauties Moscow boasts,
But, brighter than all *belles* at nightfall,
The moon, in heaven's blue, soft glows.
Yet she alone, whom I'm not daring
To stir up through my lyre-playing,
Majestic as the moon does roam,
Amidst the wives and maids alone.
With what unmatched celestial pride
Upon mere Earth her footsteps stride!
And with what bliss her bosom teems!
Her languid look's the stuff of dreams!
Enough, enough, now, stop and rest!
To madness you have paid your debt.

LIII

Noise, laughter, footsteps, bowing, bustling,
The galope, the mazurka, waltz.
Between two Aunties by the columns,
As no one looks at her at all,
Tatyana looks on, nothing seeing,
She loathes this social whirl, is seething,
She can't breathe here, and in a dream,
She flies again to field and stream,
To her own country, its poor farmers,
To her secluded little nook,
Right by the light, clear rushing brook,
To her old flowers, her old novels,
Back to the linden alleys' gloom,
Where once before her *he* did loom.

LIV

And so her thoughts roam way off, distant,
Forget the loud, dull social whirl,
Yet someone eyes her every instant:
It's some important general.
The aunts wink at each other, knowing,
Both then at Tanya start elbowing,
Both whisper then right in her ear:
"Look to the left. Look quick, my dear."
"Look left? Where? Why there? What's the matter?"
"Never mind, just look with care...
See? In that mob, in front, right there?...
Where those two uniforms sit chattering?"...
Now he's turned sideways towards his pal..."
"Who? Not that portly general?"

LV

Here let's congratulate my darling
Tatyana on her victory....

CHAPTER VIII

Fare thee well, and if for ever
Still for ever fare thee well.
Byron

X

Blest he who in his youth was youthful,
Blest who matured when it was time,
Blest he who, gradually rueful,
Grew used to this life's chilly clime,
Who never by strange dreams was troubled,
Who never shunned smart stylish rabble,
At twenty, was a fop or blade,
At thirty, married, had it made,
Who, reaching fifty, lived in freedom
From personal and other debts,
Had fame, rank, funds with interest,
Which he was always calm in seeking,
Whom all did praise – his whole life's span:
"N.N.'s a perfectly nice man."

XI

And yet it's sad to think how vainly
Our joyous youth was given us,
How hour by hour was spent betraying
It – till it in turn betrayed our trust.
That all our noblest aspirations,
Our freshest dreams and expectations,
Did wither one by one and pall,
Like rotting leaves by end of fall,
What dread to see our future bound
By naught but meals in endless rows,
In life to see but ritual's shows,
To mingle with the proper crowd
And ape them, while with them you share
Nor thoughts, nor passions – and don't care.

XII

If you're the butt of noisy gossip,
It's awful (surely you'll agree)
When people you respect as honest
Call all your quirks fake flippancy,
Call you a melancholy madman,
Satanic ogre, ugly phantom,
The very *Demon* of my poem.
Onegin (I'll return to him),
In a duel having killed his friend,
Attaining without work or goals
To naught, though twenty six years old,
Stewing in leisure without end,
Having no cares, career, or wife,
Could not do anything in life.

XIII

And restlessness soon quite bestirred him,
He yearned for someplace new, fresh air,
(A quality most disconcerting,
Which some of us must choose to bear).
And so he left his village rural,
His woods and wheatfields so secluded,
Where every day a bloody shade
Before his vision ever stayed,
And he began an aimless voyage,
Which really only had one feeling,
And travels soon enough were seeming,
Like all in life, boring and cloying,
So back he came to some fine hall,
Like Chatsky* – straight from boat to ball.

* Chatsky, the hero of Alexander Griboedov's verse play *Woe from Wit,* came back to Moscow suddenly after three years abroad — and felt like a foreigner at home.

XIV But soon the crowd began to waver
Through the salon a whisper ran...
Up to the hostess came a lady,
By her, a well-known general.
She walked unhurriedly and grandly,
And was not cold, yet was not chatty,
Cast no rude looks at everyone,
Claimed not her place beneath the sun,
Cared not for posing, phony frillage,
For little imitative tics...
Just calm and stillness in her mixed.
She seemed the very perfect image
Du comme il faut...(Shishkov, my mate,
I just don't know how to translate)*.

XVII Eugene wonders, "Could it be?
It can't be her! It is! No! ...Yet
How? From those barren plains and fields..."
And he an ever-fixed lorgnette
Keeps focused on her every second,
On she, whose traits did vaguely beckon
With memories from long ago.
"Please tell me, Prince, do you** not know:
Who in that raspberry beret
Chats with the ambassador of Spain?"
The Prince looks at Onegin then
"Aha! You've not been out of late.
"I'll introduce you, if you like."
"But who is she, though?" "She's my wife."

*Admiral Alexander Shishkov, 1754—1841, President of the Academy of Sciences, railed nationalistically against the overuse of French and German words in Russian.
**The prince is addressed by the familiar pronoun *ты*, used for family or friends.

XVIII “I didn’t know that you were married!
How long?” “About two years.”
“To whom?” “Miss Larin.” “To Tatyana!”
“You know her then?” “I lived quite near.”
“Well then, come on!” The prince approaches
His wife, and brings along in bunches
His kith and kin and his old friend.
The princess looks at him again...
Whatever in her heart was raging,
No matter how her soul was wracked,
How she was shocked, taken aback,
No sign of it she was betraying:
She acted as if nothing’s wrong,
Her curtsey kept its tranquil calm.

XIX Indeed! No trace of flutter, shiver,
She didn’t start, pale, blush, or slip,
Even her eyebrow didn’t quiver,
She didn’t even bite her lip.
Though he looked at her through and through,
Of the Tatyana he once knew
No traces could Onegin find.
To speak to her once more he tried
But... but... could not. She just kept asking:
How long’s he here, from whence come back?
Not from our parts by any chance?
Then to her husband she was casting
A weary look, slipped from the room...
Onegin froze and could not move.

XXVII Onegin spent all evening yearning,
Just by Tatyana occupied,
Not by that country maid uncertain,
Who loved unhappy without pride,
But by that proud indifferent princess,
By that impregnable grand goddess
Of the Nevá, of regal fame.
Oh people! You are all the same!
You're like our first ancestress Eve:
What you've been given you prize not,
The snake tempts with what others got,
The snake calls to that fateful tree:
Forbidden food you crave and miss –
Or Heaven no more heaven is.

XXVIII But oh, how changed Tatyana seems!
How fixed she seems in her new role!
How her restricting rank that gleams
Has silenced all her habits old!
Who'd dare to seek that sweet girl tender
In this so unconcerned majestic
Lawgiver of the drawing room?
And once he used to make her swoon!
She used to dream of him all night!
Till Morpheus came, bringing sleep,
She'd sit alone in girlish grief,
Lift to the moon her languid eyes,
"Just let me be with him!" she'd pray
To walk with him life's humble way.

XXIX To love all ages are submissive,
And yet to young and virgin hearts
Its sudden gusts are beneficial,
As to the fields spring tempests are.
They freshen in the rain of passion,
They are renewed, matured, refashioned,
Then life gives powerfully, in truth,
Both splendid colour and sweet fruit.
But in late years love's misbegotten,
Fruitless, past turning point of age,
Sad then is deadened passion's trace:
Just so the chilly storms of autumn
A swamp make of a meadow green,
And strip a forest of its gleam.

XXX But there's no doubt! Alas! Eugene
Loves Tanya like a lovelorn child.
In love's fit melancholy keen
He whiles away both day and night,
Hears not his mind scold remonstrance,
Up to her doors, her mirrored entrance,
He drives up desperate every day,
And haunts her like a ghostly shade.
He's happy if by chance he's wrapping
Her boa's fur round her shoulder-blades,
Or if with warmth he does but graze
Her hand, or if he aids her passing,
Parting bright seas of liveries,
Or picks up her dropped handkerchief.

XXXI But she ignores him, doesn't notice.
Though he might die – she still won't see.
Receives him freely as a hostess,
Politely says a word – or three –
Sometimes just curtseys are her greeting,
Sometimes completely isn't seeing,
There's not a drop in her that flirts –
Society this fault forbids.
Onegin soon becomes quite pale;
She can't see – or else pities not:
Onegin drops, has almost got
Consumption, now is truly ill.
To doctors our Onegin's sent,
Who all a *spa* do recommend.

XXXII But he's not going. He's quite ready
To meet his forefathers today.
And yet Tatyana's calm and steady,
Cares not (the fair sex is that way);
But he is stubborn, not desisting,
But hoping still, ever persisting,
Bolder than healthy men, though ill,
He writes now to the princess still,
His hand that's weak writes passionately.
Although most times in letters he
Saw little reason, sense, or need,
Yet his heart's suffering, indeed,
Was just no more to be endured:
Here is his letter word for word.

Onegin's Letter to Tatyana

I foresee all: you'll* take offence
At secret sorrow's revelation.
What scorn, what bitter condemnation
Are in your look so proud and tense!
What do I want? And for what reason
Do I pour forth my soul to you?
What gaiety and gloating teasing
From my appeal, perhaps, ensue!

By chance, somehow, at our first meeting
The spark of warmth within you seeing,
I dared not trust that it could be.
I didn't keep my own dear custom,
I didn't want to lose my freedom,
My stale and loathsome liberty.
Another thing drove us apart:
Lensky, unhappy victim, fell,
From all things dearest to my heart
I ripped away my heart back then.
Stranger to all, and friend to nothing,
I thought remaining free and calm
Was joy's replacement! Oh my God!
How wrong I was! How I've been punished!

No, every moment seeing you,
Just watching everywhere you go,
Your lips that smile, your eyes that move,
Seeing with eyes in love, aglow.
To hear and hear you, understand,
With all my soul, your sweet perfection,
In agonies before you stand,
Turn pale and swoon! What bliss! What blessing!

* Unlike Tatyana, Onegin uses the formal 'you' throughout his letter.

But everywhere, deprived of these,
Hoping to see you, I roam, listless,
Each day is dear, each hour's dear
To me, but I in boredom useless
Do waste the days Fate's counted me.
They're burdensome enough, indeed.
Short spans, I know, life's measured distance,
Yet, to keep going and endure,
Each morning I need reassurance
I'll see you in the afternoon.

I fear how my entreaty humble
Must seem to your regard severe.
You'll see but tricks of clever cunning –
Alas, your vexed rebuke I hear!
If you but knew what t'is to suffer
The awful ache and thirst of love,
To blaze – yet stifle every hour
With logic – passion in my blood,
To want to grasp your knees, and weeping,
Break down and bawl, cast at your feet,
Pour forth confessions, prayers, pleading,
Express all, all, both sad and sweet,
Yet coolness all the while to feign,
With caution speech and glance to arm,
To keep up conversation calm,
Mere cheerful glance at you maintain!

Let it be so. I'm in no state
To fight this further. For good or ill
The die is cast. I'm in your will,
And give myself up to my fate.

XXXIII No answer came.... Another letter...
A second, then a third – in vain.
No answer came. Then to some dinner
He went, had scarce walked in – again
She walks straight by, severely,
Says not one word and doesn't see him.
Oh! Wrapped in cold! She looks so cross,
As harsh as the Baptismal Frost!*
Just barely holding indignation
In check, her stiffs lips stubborn seem!
Onegin fixes a look keen...
Where's sympathy? Where's consternation?
No hint of tears? No, none at all!
Just rage on that face casts a pall.

XXXIV Or maybe she just fears in secret,
Lest husband – or the world – find out
Her escapade, or sudden weakness...
Onegin knows this game throughout...
No! There's no hope! He drove off, hurried,
Was moping, his own madness cursing,
And deeper in it he did sink,
Again abjured society.
Now, in his little study quiet,
The feeling rose again within
Of cruel depression seizing him,
As earlier, 'midst modish riot,
It grabbed his collar, took firm hold,
And locked him up in a dark hole.

* The Orthodox holiday of Christ's Baptism or Epiphany takes place on January 6th (Old Style, or January 19th in the modern calendar). So-called Baptismal Frosts are notoriously bitter. And in these bitter frosts Russians traditionally carve cross-shaped holes out from the thick ice of frozen ponds or lakes, then ritually immerse themselves in the frigid waters. I have done this myself once. The cold seems so extreme that when you warm up afterwards you feel incredibly light and free. J.H.L

XXXV And so he read again at random,
And leafed through Gibbon and Rousseau,
Manzoni, Herder, and Chamfort,
Madame de Staël, Bichat, Tissot,
And read the skeptic works of Bayle,
The works also of Fontenelle,
He even read some of our stuff –
And didn't care, and made no fuss:
Thick journals, almanacs, he read,
Where everyone so loves to preach,
Where now at me they sometimes screech,
Or madrigals sing, au contraire,
I've seen their paeans there now and then.
*E sempre bene**, gentlemen.

XXXVI And yet? Although his eyes were reading,
His thoughts were ever far away.
And dreams, desires, inner grieving,
Deep furrows in his heart did lay.
Between the lines in his books printed
He read – with eyes now of the spirit –
Far different lines, and in these he
Submerged himself in reverie.
Sometimes he'd see old tales, collections,
Of heartfelt, ancient history.
At times confused dreams he did see,
Threats, meanings, plots, and dire predictions,
An endless fable's lively whirl,
The letter of a tender girl.

* And that's just dandy. *(Ital.)*

XXXVII With gradual, fading, soft sensation
His thoughts and feelings lulled to sleep.
For him, then, his imagination
Began its coloured cards to deal.
And so he sees on snowfall melted,
As though but sleeping in a shelter,
A youth just lying very still,
And then he hears a voice: "Well? Killed."
And then he sees old foes forgotten,
Both slanderers and cowards cruel,
Of *femmes fatales* a swarming pool,
And old companions, hated, rotten...
Then country home, then window where
She sits and sits... still waiting there!

XXXVIII He got so used to such discomfort
He very nearly lost his mind,
Or else nearly became a poet.
(Now that would be a welcome sign!)
In truth, as though by magnetism
Russian verse-writing mechanisms
Almost saw him who could not learn
From hopeless case to poet turned.
How he a poet then resembled,
Alone in his dark corner there,
Watching the hearth blaze up and blare
And purring, murmuring "*Benedetta*,"*
Or "*Idol mio*,"** then to flames threw
His paper – or sometimes his shoe!

* My blessèd one. *(Ital.)*
** My idol. *(Ital.)*

XXXIX Time raced, and soon the air was thawing
And melting sullen wintertime.
Yet he did not become a poet,
Or die, and didn't lose his mind.
The spring brought him to life; one day
He stirred from his locked hideaway,
From hibernating marmot-like,
By double-windows' fireside,
And one clear morning went off riding
His sleigh along the Nevá's banks.
On ice floes' blue blocks, cut-out flanks,
The sun is sparkling, sun is shining,
On dirty slush of melting snows,
On shoveled streets where his sled goes.

XL But where's he going? Right! Amazing!
Of course you've guessed it long before,
To her, to his Tatyana racing,
Flies my eccentric unreformed.
Walks in, half-dead, with corpse's pallor,
No living soul is in her parlor;
Into her hall... there's no one there.
Opens a door: the whole place – bare...
Then what a sight his senses shatter!
The princess, pale, before him sits
Alone; her hair disheveled is...
She's reading, reading, someone's letter,
And softly tears flow down her cheek,
Supported softly by hands weak.

XLI Oh, who to her mute grief so hardened
Could not all in a flash perceive?
Who my old Tanya, my poor Tanya,
Could now in this princess not see?
In crazy heartache wistful, saddened,
Eugene falls at her feet, abandoned...
She shudders, sees, and cannot speak,
Looks at Onegin, looks that shriek,
Without a trace of shock or rage...
She sees his sick, drawn, vanquished look,
Imploring, haggard, mute reproof...
She understands. My simple maid,
With dreams and heart of former days
Lives, resurrected in her gaze.

XLII She lets him lie by her, not moving;
She doesn't tear away her eyes.
His hungry lips she's not removing
From her limp arm, which lifeless lies.
Of what is it now that she's dreaming?
A silence goes by, endless seeming,
Then softly she speaks up at last:
"Enough. Please rise. For now I must
Explain myself to you completely.
Onegin, you remember when
We in my garden walkway spent
An hour entwined by Fate? Meekly
I heard the lesson you did teach...
Today it is my turn to preach:

XLIII "Onegin, back then I was younger,
A better person too, it seems,
And I did love you. What resulted?
What from your heart did I then reap?
What answer? Just severity.
Right? You found nothing new indeed
In a submissive young girl's love.
And even now – Lord! – still my blood
Runs cold, recalling your look glacial,
And then your sermon!.. But I
Don't blame you. In that hour dire
You acted fairly, decent, graceful,
Correctly towards me, I avow.
With all my soul I'm grateful now."

XLIV "Back then – right? – in our barren desert,
Far from this noise and vanity,
You didn't like me. Now what's different?
What makes you now chase after me?
Why now am I your goal, your prize?
Is it you know that I'm obliged
To be in high society,
That now I'm rich nobility,
That from the wars my husband's crippled,
For which the Court caresses us.
Is it that you'd be famous thus,
My shame through everywhere would ripple,
And bring you in society
More rakish notoriety?"

XLV “I’m weeping...if you still are holding
Your Tanya in your memory,
Then know: the sharp bite of your scolding,
Your cold, severe, strict homily,
If I had power to command it,
I’d choose over offensive passion,
And all your letters and your tears...
Back then for girlish dreams at least
You had a bit of pity, slightly,
At least respect for tender years.
But now? What’s brought you to my feet?
How could it be? A merest trifle?
How could you with your heart and mind
Be slave to shallow feelings? Why?”

XLVI “For all this pomp to me, Onegin,
This tinsel of a hated life,
My triumphs in the *beau monde’s* whirlwind,
My fancy home and evenings’ style –
Who needs them? Would I could exchange them,
These rags in which I’m masquerading,
And all this glitter, noise, and smoke,
For my old books, my yard o’ergrown,
For our poor dwelling solitary,
For those same places dear where I,
Onegin, first saw you walk by,
And for the humble cemetery,
Where o’er her cross, ’neath branches’ shade,
My Nanny to her rest was laid.”

XLVII "Yet happiness had been so close by,
So possible. But my fate's now
Decided. Rashly incautious I,
Did act, perhaps, accepting vows:
My Mum with tears begged me, imploring...
For me, poor Tanya, all ignoring,
All choices seemed about the same...
So I got married in this way.
You must, I beg you, leave entirely,
I know your heart has dignity,
And pride, and straight integrity.
I love you (what's the point in lying?)...
But now I'm someone else's wife,
And I'll be faithful all my life."

XLVIII She leaves. Eugene's stands all alone
As if by lightning he'd been struck.
What feelings in a seething storm
His heart is plunged into with shock!
But sudden spurs sound sharply, clonking,
In comes Tatyana's husband walking...
Yet from our hero now we go,
Now – in this minute full of woe –
Yes, reader, now – our leave we take,
For long... forever. We have passed
Together with him a long path,
Long voyage. Let's congratulate
Each other on landfall! Hooray!
Long overdue! (Wouldn't you say?)

XLIX Whoever, reader, you might be,
Both friend or foe, my leave I take,
Today, at least, with amity.
Farewell. Whatever in my wake
You once did seek in stanzas careless,
Whether remembrances rebellious,
Or rest from labours unperturbed,
Or lively pictures, witty words,
Or else, perhaps, mistakes in grammar,
God grant, in this brief book you gleaned
Food for amusement, for your dream,
Your heart, or journalistic scandal,
A grain, let's hope, you here could find,
And so, I wave farewell, goodbye!

L Goodbye to you too, strange companion,
And you as well, ideal so true,
And you, my lively, dear and constant,
Though little, work. I've known with you
All that a poet ought to envy,
Oblivion from this world's frenzy,
Sweet conversation with a friend.
It has been many days on end
Since first my virginal Tatyana –
Onegin too, in blurried dream –
Began at first to come to me,
And my free novel's free expansion,
As through a magic crystal's gleam,
Was still not clearly to be seen.

LI But those for whom, in friendly trysting,
My early stanzas once I read...
"They are no more, and some are distant,"
As once the poet Saadi said.
Onegin's been sketched in without them.
And she, that one in whom I found, in
Truth, Tatyana's perfect grace?
Oh how much Fate did take away!
Blest he who early left life's revel
Before he could drink up in time
His goblet, brimming full of wine,
Who did not read all of life's novel,
Who how to part at once well knew,
As I from my Onegin do.

THE END

Alexander Pushkin 1836
Engraving by Thomas Wright

ABOUT JULIAN HENRY LOWENFELD

Poet, playwright, trial lawyer, composer, and translator from 8 languages Julian Henry Lowenfeld – a student of famed Pushkin scholar Nadyezhda Braginskaya – has deep roots in Russian literature. His great-grandfather Raphael Löwenfeld was the first translator of Tolstoy into German, and Tolstoy's play *The Power of Darkness* world premièred in Berlin's Schiller Theatre, which Löwenfeld founded. After the Russian Revolution, the Nabokov family lived in the Löwenfeld home in Berlin.

In 2009, the world premiere in English of Alexander Pushkin's play *Little Tragedies* in Julian Henry Lowenfeld's translation took place in the Mikhail Baryshnikov Arts Centre in New York. In 2010 Julian was awarded the literary artistic Petropol Prize (awarded for the first time ever to a foreigner). In 2012 he translated Archimandrite Tikhon Shevkunov's bestseller *Everyday Saints and Other Stories* into English; the book won first prize at New York's Read Russia 2012 Festival. In 2013 Julian was awarded the Friendship and Cooperation Medal "for his outstanding literary translations and dedicated efforts to popularize Russian culture in the English language."

Among his other translations: the video collection *Animated Soviet Propaganda* (4 DVDs), winner of the New York Times' "Critics' Choice" Award, Eldar Ryazanov's film *Andersen. A Life without Love*, Soyuzmultfim Studios' *The Snow Queen* (based on the Hans Christian Andersen fairy tale), as well as translations from Spanish of two plays by Julio Cortázar: *Nothing to Pehaujó*, and *Bye, Robinson* (staged off-Broadway in 2004).

INDEX OF TITLES AND FIRST LINES

www.ALEXANDERPUSHKIN.com

ISBN 978-1-9110722-5-6